Marie Antoinette's Watch
Adultery, Larceny, and Perpetual Motion

John Biggs

RAY BRIDGE PRESS

RAY BRIDGE PRESS
raybridgepress.com

for Joanna

Epigraph

Dost thou love life? Then do not squander time, for that is the
stuff life is made of.
— Benjamin Franklin

She's got Elgin movements / from her head down to her
toes.
— Robert Johnson, "Walkin' Blues"

Chapter 1

Tel Aviv

On hot August days, when the thermostat grazed 94 degrees
Fahrenheit by the Mediterranean shoreline, there was little traffic
in Zion Yakubov's little shop on Ben Yehuda Street in Tel Aviv.
The jumbled store – a small room, really, filled with brass and
stonework along with jewelry and other knickknacks popular with
the grazing tourist antique hunters – had played host to many
treasure seekers over the years. But on this sweltering afternoon in
2006, a woman named Hila Efron-Gabai entered with the promise
of treasure.

Efron-Gabai was a lawyer, she explained, with a very interesting proposition. She was eight months pregnant with twins,
but she was glowing. She had a thin face, an olive complexion, and
a no-nonsense demeanor. Her dark brown hair framed her sharp
features, and she had large brown eyes over an open, unlined face.
She was charming and seemed used to getting her way.

Zion himself was a proper, older man of about sixty with
close-cropped, carefully combed hair, and small oval glasses. When
he visited clients or went to examine antiques elsewhere in the city,
he carried a small leather satchel, under his armpit. He was a trusted confidant to many rare art dealers and had only been in trouble
once, back in 1980, when he was accused of fencing two silver
vessels from a nearby synagogue. Nothing came of the accusation,
although Zion did spend two nights in jail. He had stayed clear of
trouble since, focusing on above-board art sales.

Yakubov was a better breed of the kind of antiques and

antiquities sellers found in places like Tel Aviv's Jaffa flea market, a bustling souk where everything from old jewelry to antique cooking pots were available for sale. Yakubov's taste was more nuanced, and he owned a number of rare items.

Five of these items — clocks and music boxes — he had loaned to the L.A. Mayer Museum when the family gallery reopened in 1989 after a major theft. These items have resided at the museum for almost two decades, making their small contribution to the museum's efforts to recapture some of the magic and majesty of an original collection of fine watches that had been stolen twenty years before. But it was coincidental that this very pregnant lawyer was about to involve him in further business with the museum, in what would be one of the strangest deals of his career.

Earlier that month, Hila Efron-Gabai had taken on a client with an unusual request. The client, a woman from America, wanted to return some objects to the L.A. Mayer Museum for Islamic Art. Her only stipulation was that the return be anonymous. The client explained that her late husband had owned a few boxes of clocks and watches and that, under community property laws (he hadn't left a will), the boxes were now hers. He had only told her about the boxes late into the yearlong cancer that would eventually kill him, revealing some information that took her breath away: The clocks belonged to the Mayer Museum, and he had stolen them twenty years before.

The client said that she had opened the boxes once, to look inside them, and she knew only that these were "beautiful things" and that they didn't belong to her.[1] "Whatever happens, these things have to be returned to the museum," the client said. The client said she had no interest in making money, but she did want to remain hidden. She left the boxes with Efron-Gabai, asking her to take care of them.

After the client departed, Efron-Gabai took one of the boxes to a conference room in her firm's office and placed it on a table. She thought carefully about her next step. She could contact the museum directly, but first she wanted to be sure the clocks and watches were authentic. Her father, Nachum, often visited a well-known art dealer in Tel Aviv, Yakubov, who had sold the family some candlesticks long ago and done repair work on some of the family silver. She called her father, asking for the jeweler's number, and then she rang Zion Yakubov. She asked that he come in for a consultation on what she would only describe as very unusual pieces. Grudgingly, he agreed.

When collectors and dealers are approached with a secretive deal, they mostly prove to be a dead end. Contrary to the myth of *Antiques Roadshow* and other one-of-a-kind find television programs, the vast majority of items found in attics and basements are junk. The heady days of treasure picking are past. With the rise of the Internet and eBay, collectors know almost to the penny what anything is worth. Even the dealers at the Tel Aviv antiques market rarely sold anything without knowing its provenance and going price — and whether or not it was genuine. That this lawyer would be harboring anything of great value was a long bet, but Yakubov took it.

He arrived on the afternoon of August 16, 2006, driving up the coast through Tel Aviv's honking, jammed traffic to Efron-Gabai's office near crowded Milano Square, a part of town popular with ex-pats and higher-end businesses.

After he sat down, the lawyer began to unpack a box. One after the other, on a wooden conference table, Efron-Gabai laid out a number of the most storied and illustrious clocks and watches Yakubov had ever seen.

Some were in medicine boxes marked with cramped, hand-written care instructions in Hebrew. A bottle of watch oil was included with one, along with a note reading: "These watches are very delicate. Use this oil once a month." It was as if someone had packed up a collection of old trinkets in preparation for a move. The objects lay haphazardly on the table — millions of dollars in watches spread out like a child's collection of toy soldiers.

Yakubov knew instantly what he was looking at: This was the missing Salomons collection, nearly complete and surprisingly intact. Efron-Gabai had brought out forty watches to show him, and she now unwrapped one that was in faded, dirty newspaper and covered with a thin patina of grime and oil. It was a piece Yakubov had hardly dared hope he might see. Behind a rock crystal face, a movement that had taken one man and his son forty-four years to create was still awake and alive. It was the 160, Marie-Antoinette's watch, missing twenty years and now bright as the day it was finished almost two hundred years earlier. He held in his hands a masterpiece of horology, the most coveted, most storied, and most tragic watch in the world.

He held in his trembling hands the Queen. She had returned.

Chapter 2

Paris

A walker in eighteenth-century Paris, his boots caked with mud and much worse, would not come upon the Place Dauphine by chance. To find the quiet triangle one has to traverse Pont Neuf, or the New Bridge (this, the oldest bridge in the city, was also the first one not covered in houses and shops) onto the island where Paris began: the Île de la Cité. A jog to the left, between two four-story buildings, brings him to a small park with a few stunted trees and a bench or two where men speak furiously over plans and scraps of polished metal. The walker, however, could do no better than to sit listening to the quiet susurration of the trees and the gentle *ting-ting* of jewelers' hammers. It was in this courtyard, he would quickly discover, where the mechanical heart of Paris ticked. It was, in fact, the home to some of France's most illustrious horologers.

To look at the neighborhood today is to glimpse Paris as it was in the eighteenth century, when the city was "the mother and mistress of all cities."[2] From the far bank of the Seine, standing by the crate-shaped kiosks selling postcards and books and gazing across the river at the northwestern cusp of the Île de la Cité, you see the dark uneven teeth of the housetops and the white stone faces of buildings that have changed little over the centuries. Crossing the bridge you are suddenly in a much older France.

Looming to your left are the once-forbidding walls of the Palais de Justice, the Conciergerie (the palace prison once known

4

as the antechamber to the guillotine), the pepperpot-roofed Bonbec Tower, which served as a torture chamber during the middle ages, and the square, soaring Tour d'Horloge. These fortifications, built in 1215, connect the old part of the Quai de l'Horloge, at the towers, to the more modern fifteenth and sixteenth century homes along the bank. Quai de l'Horloge means Clock Dock.

All of the city's bureaucratic work has been done here for centuries, and the handsome if overly dramatic clock at the tower's base — built in 1370 by German horologist Henri de Vic and decorated with weather-faded fleur-de-lis, figures symbolizing justice and piety, and two cherubic angels — would have marked the time for vassals coming to their king and, later, for revolutionaries coming to unseat that selfsame royalty. Today it is stopped, due to disrepair, at sixteen minutes past twelve. Farther down the island, however, things changed. The stomping of judges through empty halls was replaced by the sound of hammers. Couriers carrying dockets were replaced by boys carrying small paper packages of glass. Visiting potentates let their care fall away as they entered the warren of houses on the western tip of the Quai. For it was here that the clockwork heart of Paris — and the world — ticked.

Paris had its quarters dedicated to specific branches of manufacture and commerce. Just as Le Sentier in the 2nd Arrondissement was dedicated to clothing and Place Pigalle was the city's storied red-light district, so the Clock Dock was home to almost all of Paris's master watchmakers, opticians, and makers of precision instruments, including pedometers and thermometers. From the front, only a few shops were visible, but the open rectangle the buildings backed onto, the Place Dauphine, was a bustle of activity. Inside the buildings enamelists stoked their forges, goldsmiths hammered their precious metal, and casemakers worked alongside artisans who specialized in the smallest movement components, while runners — apprentices to the watchmakers — darted from shop to shop and factory to factory, picking up parts and placing nearly finished pieces in front of various experts.

The workshops were a maze of machinery, with drill presses and mechanical cutters sitting cheek by jowl beside older machines for toothing gears and polishing the tiny parts that made up a fine watch. There were places on the Quai where a clockmaker could have a bit of gold shaped into a fine curlicue and where a goldsmith could get advice on how best to repair a customer's shattered crystal. This was a site of constant, percolating exploration where, unlike the jealous members of warring guilds and most scientific salons, communication and sharing were the norm. If one watchmaker was unable to perform some feat of clockwork daring, a ready team of experts was willing to take up the cause and perhaps throw a commission back to the original workshop. The occupants of the Quai were in such close quarters that they had no other choice.

At the height of the late eighteenth century, Paris's golden era of watchmaking, thousands of craftsmen plied their trade here. They were led by a constellation of masters and among these some of them were considered good enough for the king.

For nearly a century, the French monarchy had been appointing various watchmakers as *horloger du roi* — official watchmaker to the king — and most of these men kept a shop on the Quai or sourced their material there. For most of the century successive watchmakers maintained the clocks at the various royal residences, making the rounds to wind and clean the timepieces that graced countless mantles and salon walls. By the 1780s, however, these royal watchmakers were more than just common clock winders. They were skilled with metal, enamel, glass, and crystal, and were making some of the most complex artifacts of their day. The Quai was also famous for glasswork and lenses, and the watchmakers often consulted with the astronomers who frequented the other shops, discussing methods for calculating various important days and hours using only clockwork. The watchmakers spent hours together, mulling the problems of the era, from how to achieve perpetual motion (many thought it had something to do with friction, although few could pin down the true meaning of entropy) to understanding the nature of time itself. After all, it was impossible to tell time if it could not be codified and defined, and the horologists of the Clock Dock were more interested in advancing science and industry than supplying simple watches to petty nobles – although their royal commissions were always the most lucrative.

The master watchmakers here included members of the Jaquet-Droz family, from which sprang Pierre Jaquet-Droz, creator of miniature and full-sized automata so fine and esoteric that they would one day be credited as the precursors to modern robots. Each was made from some six thousand parts. Jaquet-Droz built a singing bird that worked by using a series of tiny bellows that blew air into small pipes. When the bird was wound, the clever clockwork blew each pipe in a jaunty sequence, creating a random song. The roboticist's collection also included erotic timekeepers showing rapturous parties making love in various positions. The most popular with the young men at court often featured staid, religious animations featuring Moses and other Biblical figures on the front and considerably more bawdy animations hidden on the back. He was so accomplished at mimicking living motion that he was often accused of witchcraft.

In one particularly fanciful tale, it was said that Jaquet-Droz made a unique clock for the king of Spain that featured a shepherd and a dog under an apple tree. When the clock struck "the shepherd played six tunes on his flute, and the dog approached and fawned on him."

Droz said: "The gentleness of my dog is his least merit. If your majesty touches one of the apples which you see in the shepherd's basket, you will admire the fidelity of this animal."

When the king touched one of the apples the dog turned and barked so loud that the king's own — living — dog took to his master's defense.[3]

Another prominent watchmaker was Ferdinand Berthoud. He was a portly businessman who wore his hair in a short powdered bob and his stern eyes hid a mischievous love of horological debate. Like Jaquet-Droz, Berthoud also came from Switzerland but instead of automata he focused on some of the more mundane, yet most important, aspects of watchmaking, including the management of friction, shock, and environmental effects. He penned the watchmaking entries in the great *Encyclopédie* of Diderot and d'Alembert, and had become *horloger du roi* when he began his work on the marine chronometer, an accurate clock that could survive rough treatment on the high seas. Making clocks for sailors was a particularly lucrative and difficult undertaking given the harsh conditions, including salt spray and violent rocking in storms, faced by the navies of the age.

Berthoud invented the compensated balance, a small wheel made of multiple metals that would grow and shrink, at equal, countervailing rates, in the heat. This mixture of materials would keep a watch from running more slowly in the tropics, and Berthoud sold his technology to the French Navy, giving France the upper hand at sea. While many manufacturers tried to build similar clocks, sea captains knew that "a bad chronometer is worse than none"[4] and Berthoud's were some of the best simply by dint of their precision and sturdy construction.

Here, too, on the Quai was Jean-Antoine Lépine, a dour, long-faced man with a prominent Roman nose who began as a prodigy from Geneva and then married into watchmaking royalty when he wed the daughter of an *horloger du roi* named Pierre-Augustin Caron, himself noted for creating a ring-mounted watch for Madame de Pompadour (and, later, for writing *The Marriage of Figaro* under the name Beaumarchais). Lépine devised a series of aesthetic improvements to pocket watches including a thinner case with a hidden hinge, pioneered a keyless winding mechanism, and invented a movement that used considerably less metal for the bridge, the part of the watch that kept everything else in place, thereby reducing the weight and size of the movement. Called the Lépine caliber, it looked like a set of piano keys under which were the power train, escapement, and the rest of the transmission system. One had only to see watches from a few decades before Lépine's reign — lumpen and onion-shaped — to understand the allure of his work.

Together, on this small triangle of land in the middle of the Seine, men like Lépine and Berthoud brought about a golden age of horology in France. The Quai became the country's engineering hub, and its watchmakers trained others in their art, spreading their techniques throughout Europe and the New World. Every major watch company still in existence owes a debt to the small fraternity of men at the quiet end of the Île de la Cité.

Orders for the military, the monarchy, and well-appointed nobles came in daily, and the Quai's watchmakers, renowned for inventing new complications, attracted an international clientele. Lépine, in fact, was tasked with creating a watch for America's first president. In a November, 1788 letter to Gouverneur Morris, the coauthor of the U.S. Constitution who was then in Paris, George Washington would write:[5]

Dear Sir,
I had the pleasure to receive by the last mail your letter dated the 12th of this month. I am much obliged by your offer of executing commissions for me in Europe, and shall take the liberty of charging you with one only. I wish to have a good gold watch procured for my own use; not a small, trifling, nor finically ornamented one, but a watch well executed in point of workmanship,

and of about the size and kind of that which was procured by Mr. Jefferson for Mr. Madison, which was large and flat. I imagine Mr. Jefferson can give you the best advice on the subject, as I am told this species of watches, which I have described, can be found cheaper and better fabricated in Paris than in London. To defray the cost I enclose a bill for twenty-five guineas on London, payable at sight. Should the expense be greater, for I would have a good watch, I will take care to reimburse it to you. I want nothing more with it than a handsome key.

Morris swiftly replied:[6]

Paris 23 Feb 1789
Dear General,
Upon my arrival at this Place I spoke to Mr. Jefferson on the Subject of your Watch. He told me that the man who had made Maddison's [sic] was a Rogue and recommended me to another, Romilly. But as it might happen that this also was a Rogue I enquired at a very honest Man's Shop, not a Watch Maker, and he recommended Gregson. A Gentleman with me assured me that Gregson was a Rogue and both of them agreed that Romilly is of the old School and he and his Watches out of Fashion. And to say *that* of a Man in Paris, is like saying he is an ordinary Man among the Friends of Philadelphia. I found at last that Mr. [Lépine] is at the head of his Profession here, and in Consequence asks more for this Work than any Body else. I therefore waited on Mr. Lépine and agreed with him for two watches exactly alike, one of which be for you and the other for me.

Even with Lépine's momentous commissions, in 1775 a precocious young watchmaker prepared to take his place among the luminaries on the Quai. His name was Abraham-Louis Breguet and he was just twenty-eight years old. He was five feet tall. His hair was curly at the sides, and beneath a high forehead he had a beetled, clinched brow topped with short but bushy eyebrows. His mouth was prim and closed over a prominent chin. His nose was not delicate, looking almost broken, and his eyes had the narrow focus of a man accustomed to looking at the world through a loupe. He was given to wearing a dark frock with a delicately tied cravat, a seashell-like knot at his throat.

Although technically not yet a master, Breguet showed ability far beyond his years, was already a favored watchmaker at court, and had begun to earn a considerable income. After ten years of apprenticeship, including stints under both Berthoud and Lépine, he was intent on starting his own business.

The launch of the Breguet business in Paris was painstakingly well-executed. The young Breguet, while a prodigy, was a relative unknown in Paris, having plied most his trade in Versailles. His stepfather had invested a good deal in the boy, and he expected great things. But before opening his own shop, Breguet had a matter of the heart to attend to. That August 28, he wed Cecile-Marie-Louise, a beautiful counterpoint to her smaller, gnomic husband.

Hunting for a shop in the city proper, Abraham-Louis inevitably ended up on the Clock Dock, where the very men from whom he had learned so much were concentrated. And he eventually decided on Number 51, at the northern tip of the Quai, where boats coming down Seine would stop to leave shipments for the artisans clustered there.

The four-story building, owned by the well-connected Polignac family, was large and imposing, made of brick and gray stone, with finely wrought decoration around the window of alternating brick in a sunburst pattern. Front windows would allow the watchmaker to show his wares to passersby. But the kind of customer Breguet expected at his shop would not spend much time window browsing, so he also made sure it was a space that, as he expanded, would be able to accommodate a comfortable office and showroom where he could discuss potential commissions with the lights of Paris society. When Breguet climbed the stairs to the atelier on the floor above, he was delighted to find broad windows facing both the Seine, in the front, and the triangular Place in the rear. They made the room bright and sunny — perfect for putting together tiny gears and screws. One floor above that, tall windows in the attic would make excellent additional workspaces for the watchmakers. This would be Breguet's new home in Paris, and although at first he was to rent only the attic and ground floor, he would soon own the entire building, along with a smaller apartment next door.

Because Breguet was officially still an apprentice in 1775, he needed to receive a special dispensation to open his own business

10

without the supervision of a master. It was an unusual move. The watchmaking guild was powerful; membership was necessary to begin building movements and cases for sale in France. The guild had only seventy-two French masters in the horological arts, and each could have just one apprentice at a time. The only way to open a shop was to be either the son of a master or to be married to a master's widow. Breguet, who met neither of these requirements, likely received the favor to do so thanks to his close relationship with the French court. Gabrielle de Polastron, Duchesse de Polignac, was his landlord and one of the royal family's closest friends.

It was here, in this beautiful building with a view on Place Dauphine, that the measure of time with true fidelity – and a beguiling love story whose fire would eventually engulf the whole of Europe — began.

Chapter 3

Paris

Past midnight on January 30, 1774, eighteen-year-old Count
Hans Axel von Fersen, the son of a powerful Swedish nobleman,
found himself in the middle of an enchanting conversation. He had
no idea with whom.

In the plush, oval auditorium of the Paris opera, a thousand candles flickered off the faux marble and pastel frescoes and
tall mirrors and gilded bronze reliefs. The opera house was new,
having replaced one that had burned down four years earlier. It
was a magnificent room: Ionic columns along the side walls soared
past curved tiers of loges, and on the elliptical ceiling an elaborate
fresco depicted Apollo and the Muses. Normally it could seat one
thousand, but for this evening's event the orchestra had been raised
to the same level as the stage, creating a seamless ballroom floor.
Couples spun around each other in perfect minuets as lutes and
harpsichords played baroque melodies.

As they did so, Fersen was becoming increasingly intrigued
by the young woman nodding attentively at his words and responding with such charming bon mots. She was eye-catchingly
slender. Beneath a white taffeta dress, her girlish figure seemed still
to be taking shape, but there was nothing awkward about her. Her
blonde hair was terraced in lustrous curls and adorned with feathers. Her skin was striking for both its whiteness and the delicate
flush glowing beneath it. She carried herself with great dignity, yet
exuded a natural kindness, and her walk – "indolent, half-swaying,
one might say caressing"[7] – gave her the air of grace that could only
come with fine breeding.

This was all Fersen could tell, for like all the mysterious and
fashionable people in the room, including him, she held one of the

12

small half-masks known as dominoes up to her face. The opera was the scandalous destination of the season. Open to all comers, provided they could pay the admission, it allowed for mixing of the classes and sexes. Thanks to the masks, it also afforded an air of mystery and, importantly, a veil of secrecy to the dalliances that took place there. For nobles who spent most of their time scrutinizing and being scrutinized these balls offered a welcome respite. Men and women both enjoyed the privilege of going incognito and mingling flirtatiously, if only for a few hours.

Fersen, for the last three years, had been taking his grand tour, an aristocratic rite of passage that had brought him tumbling through the continent like a polite, taciturn Viking raider. He was tall and slim, with blue eyes and light brown hair, and from the moment of his arrival in Paris a few weeks earlier, he had been accepted into the ranks of the French court. His skills at languages, swordsmanship, riding, and music were much in demand as entertainments, and he quickly fell into the swirl of events in the city and at Versailles. The ladies at court dubbed him "le beau Fersen;" one described him as looking like the "hero of a novel."

"No one could have been more correct or distinguished in his bearing," Count Creutz, the Swedish ambassador, reported to his king, Gustav III. "With his good looks and his charm he could not help but be a great success in society here."[8] His name did much to pave his way. So respected was his family that one Swedish wag even said that he knew three types of men: "Frenchmen, Fersens, and rabble."[9]

This day alone, in the hours before Fersen's meeting with the strange and alluring woman at the opera, had been a dazzling blur of engagements. After a late lunch with the Danish ambassador, he had gone to the home of another aristocrat, Madame d'Arville, for a half hour of banter. Then Count Creutz had driven Fersen to the home of the Princesse de Beauvau, and on to a concert by Stroganoff. At nine, it was back to Madame d'Arville's for supper, which went until one in the morning. Finally, the group went to the opera for the masked ball.

Shortly after Fersen's arrival, a distinguished looking trio came into the room and began mixing anonymously with the crowd. One of them, the lady with feathers in her hair, engaged Fersen in conversation, and for nearly half an hour he enjoyed their exchange, never growing bored and becoming ever more eager to see behind her mask. In his short time in Paris, Fersen had found the city's aristocracy to be world-weary and jaded, but this lady's conversation was lively, even slightly risqué, without being frivolous. Although he detected hesitancy in her speech, which he took to be shyness, he felt an easy rapport with her.

When, finally, she removed her mask, he discovered that he had been speaking with Marie-Antoinette, the Dauphine, next in line to be Queen of France. He had seen her from a distance at a ball at Versailles three weeks earlier, but this was his first direct encounter. He could take in her full face now: Her eyes were a sparkling blue (imperial blue, the color was called), alive with intelligence and framed by handsome eyebrows; her nose was prominent but well proportioned; she had full lips. The overall effect was of a beauty at once vivacious and dignified with a touch of imperfection that made her all the more approachable.

So much made sense now. The hesitancy he had taken for shyness was, of course, her relative unfamiliarity with the French tongue. He had heard of her tendency to speak to foreigners when she was masked, lest her Austrian accent give away her identity to a native French speaker, and he imagined that someone had described him to her as an interesting and important young man from Sweden. Now, realizing who she was, he spoke in German to her, and mentioned that during his recent visit to Florence he had met her brother, Leopold, the Grand Duke of Tuscany.

Her two companions, who were speaking to other guests, had also dropped their masks, revealing themselves to be the Dauphin, Louis XVI, baby-faced and already exhibiting a tendency toward overweight, and his brother, the Comte de Provence whose broad chin and pursed lips had been passed on from his mother, Maria Josepha of Saxony. Now that their identities were revealed, a crowd of people quickly gathered around the group. Marie, at nineteen, was already the belle of Paris, and her normally withdrawn husband was unusually outgoing this evening, chatting freely with the revelers. People assumed this was the beneficial influence of his young wife, but jealous courtiers took note of something else — the handsome young foreigner with whom the Dauphine had spent so much time speaking. The Dauphine, perhaps sensing this, retreated with her party to the royal box. Afterward, Fersen, in his habitual laconic fashion, would write in his diary merely that the Dauphine "talked to me for a long time," a fair bit of understatement. When he left the ball, it was three o'clock in the morning, as any of the many watch-carrying guests could have told him.

Before the rise of Marie-Antoinette and a decidedly more youthful turn of fashion, such balls had been visions of a dissipated hell peopled by ghouls in powder and poufs. "The ball was almost over, the candles had shortened, the musicians, drunk or asleep, no longer made use of their instruments," a contemporary wrote about one of Louis XV's balls twenty years before. "The crowd had dispersed, everyone was unmasked, rouge and powder flowed down the painted faces offering the disgusting spectacle of dilapidated stylishness."[10] These spectacles quickly changed as a younger and more flamboyant generation took to the opera and Fersen and Marie-Antoinette were at the vanguard of this transition.

The balls of 1770s Versailles, if more modern in sensibility, were no less serious affairs. Preparations were begun months in advance; guest lists solidified and reordered to ensure respect to every rank and privilege. The dances, glittering dresses, rich food, and heady perfumes could be intoxicating, but Fersen, who wore a waistcoat, ruffled cravat, and stockings to such events, was of more modest taste, although he did enjoy balls and dinners. He did, however, have a teenager's ambivalence about all the frippery and wrote, after one ball, that "[a]s I was leaving, I thought that the French don't know how to enjoy themselves. They have the bad habit of constantly saying 'I'm bored,' and it poisons all their pleasures."

In 1774, when Axel and Marie met, the *ancien regime* was at its fragile apex. France was nearly bankrupt, having incurred calamitous debts in the Seven Years War that would soon be compounded by the expenses of the American War of Independence. Britain was starting to eclipse France as an economic power, wounding national pride. And the Bourbons' self-indulgence had been stoking anti-royalist sentiment for half a century. Louis XIV, the Sun king, had instituted all manner of rules and regulations, regimenting the day into ceremonial sections and bringing on a large number of hangers-on, including pensioners and special appointees who received money simply for displaying the proper obsequiousness to the king. When Louis XV died three years later, some Parisians would travel to Versailles to mourn his passing, but more people in Paris would celebrate his death. Already the seeds of revolution had been planted in a city that was now divided into, on the one hand, a warren of heated and lushly decorated palaces and mansions, and on the other, a dark tangle of streets where hunger was the norm and bread was increasingly hard to come by. By 1777 the expenses of Versailles would consume one sixth of the French budget,[11] much of that spent on gadgetry like watches and automatons for the introverted king and champagne for the queen's admirers.

It was under these precarious circumstances that Fersen arrived in Paris in 1773, traveling with his tutor, the patient and well-connected Jean Bolemany, a Hungarian baron. They had already ranged through Italy and Switzerland, studying the arts of war — horsemanship, history, and tactics — so that Fersen might follow in his field-marshal father's bootsteps.

In many regards, Fersen was born in the wrong century. He defined himself as a tragic and romantic figure and found comfort in order and beauty.[12] While he was not a poet sighing into a bunch of white lilies, his diaries point to a sensitive young man well aware of his status in a world that was swiftly disappearing. His training and upbringing put him on a trajectory toward a lifetime of service and governance, while his situation and society forced a soft decline on him and his contemporaries. Whereas his father and uncles fought in war after war, there were no similar conflicts to define and hone his skills as a military man. This is not to say Fersen could not have gone to war — many were being waged on continental soil — but none had the same European import as the skirmishes that brought glory to his ancestors. He moved in a circle that was slowly losing its center. Fersen and his ilk were "no longer needed as leaders of their race and vassals in the harsh primary struggle against the oppression of a king or the depredations of some rival lord."[13]

Upon his arrival in Paris, Fersen journeyed to Versailles to see the installation of knights into the Order of the Holy Spirit, a chivalric brotherhood for French courtiers consisting of a hundred boys from noble families and led by the king himself. Bolemany, his tutor, wanted to introduce him at the French court, and viewing a royal order of knights meshed well with the boy's military bent.

The setting of this first visit was Versailles' sepulchral white chapel. The tall room was covered in gold-leaf detailing, and statues of cherubs hung from almost every eave. A balcony allowed visitors to view the proceedings; an almost ten-foot-tall "false

16

window" at the end of the aisle, seemingly out of place, had once hid the Madame de Pompadour, late mistress to Louis XV, in her private prayer room. The king himself sat on a throne topped with a canopy of rich green cloth and tufted in gold thread. It was far more ornate than anything Axel had seen, and the novices, arriving in Louis XIII costumes complete with knee breeches, tunics, dashing cloaks, and neck ruffles, looked like something out of a child's fairy tale. It was a heady way for a young man to make an acquaintance with one of the most magnificent courts in Europe.

During that first visit to Versailles, Axel scored a social coup by meeting with Madame du Barry, the powerful mistress of Louis XV, who was angling to maintain her power even as Marie-Antoinette had begun to rise in rank and importance. Du Barry invited the young man out to court again, to the Dauphine's Monday pre-Lenten carnival ball where courtiers came to dance and grovel, hoping to catch the eye of the next queen. These visits were exciting for a young man angling for influence abroad, and they garnered him still more invitations and interest.

He could speak fluent French, German, Italian, and English and was invited to the homes of France's upper crust, who were fascinated by this handsome soldier. Ambassador Creutz and his secretary, Ramel, accompanied him consistently. They were keeping an eye on him for his father and for King Gustav III, both of whom felt young Axel would make an excellent go-between. Axel enjoyed the dinners immensely, often giving impromptu performances – he travelled with a clavichord – when his hosts at Versailles or in the city proper requested a recital.

The Comte de Saint-Priest, a diplomat, described the young Swede as "having a striking face. Tall, slim, perfectly well made, with beautiful eyes, he was made to create in the eyes of a woman who sought his [eyes] deeper impressions than she expected." Contemporary paintings show him with high, arched eyebrows and a long, thin nose with thin nostrils that "are sometimes a sign of shyness, or, at least, of caution and reserve."[14] His lips, usually pursed in thought, were delicately formed. A half-smile sometimes played on his face, but real joy seldom broke through the wall of his breeding and stern military training.

Fersen had long kept a meticulously detailed diary, noting the hours he spent at various activities, and he was a prolific letter-writer, keeping a copy of each missive he sent in his own files so as never to be at a loss in conversation. When he was a boy, Fersen's journal had recorded hours spent riding (two per day), studying languages and music (another two), and the time he went to bed (usually by 10 in the evening, with an expectation of rising again at seven to dress and prepare for his lessons). Now that he was a young man, with considerable amorous experience, his writing increasingly turned to a chronicle of conquests.

He was picky when it came to women, complaining in April 1773, while on the road to Rome, that "the sex at Milan is not at all fair, very ill-dressed, in bad taste, and slovenly, which is common in Italy except in Turin."[15] But in Paris, he reveled in the women, and their husbands knew to be *en garde*. Axel described one ball in January 1775 with a young man's ardor but the aplomb of a senator's son:

I supped with Baron Ahlfeldt, a Dane who is attaché to the embassy, then at midnight went to the opera ball with Bolemany. I met a very pretty masque who said to me in a low voice that she was sorry I wasn't her husband so that she could sleep with me. I told her that shouldn't stop her. I tried to persuade her but she ran away. Another woman that [a friend] was chasing wasn't so difficult. She sat down in a hallway and we had a long conversation with her. She wore only a light veil over her face, which made it easier to kiss her as we liked and she seemed to do it very well.[16]

Axel spent many evenings wooing women. Like the best Casanovas he broke the hearts of many women. He saved his own for just one of them.

Maria Antonia Josepha Johanna – Marie-Antoinette to the French — was born in Vienna on November 2, 1755, a year before start of the Seven Years War. Her childhood was overshadowed by that conflict. The war dragged on for nine years, and the girl's formative years were spent watching her mother live in privation, her brow furrowed in concentration and her beauty sapped by war and worry. While the empress once sold her jewelry to pay for more and better equipment for her army and personally oversaw the tactics used in battle, this fortitude was not passed on to Maria Antonia, and all she knew in the palace was comfort and boredom. The daughter of Emperor Francis and Empress Maria Theresa of Austria and the future queen of France was profoundly unprepared

18

for what awaited her.

She was one of twelve children, all of whom were, if put cynically, political pawns born only to advance royal goals of secession and national growth. Her gravely overstretched mother had to trust the care of her children to men and women who were more afraid to thwart her requests than to teach the children anything beyond good manners and music.

Maria grew into a quiet, demure girl, who despite her beauty had none of the hauteur of her brothers or the rawer aspect of her sister Caroline. The girls were coddled and modest. Her mother forbade make-up or short sleeves and was notoriously puritanical, outlawing love affairs at court and creating a much-ridiculed "chastity commission" to outlaw ribaldry in the capital. She woke daily at five in the morning and worked all day, a practice rarely seen in similar European courts.

Maria's earliest memories, she would say later, were of being brought before her mother by her governesses and commented upon: Was she eating well? Acting foolishly? Even as guns were trained on Vienna, the children were kept cosseted and controlled.

Her marriage to Louis XVI would be purely a geopolitical maneuver. France, weakened by its colonial losses in the Seven Years War, and Austria, still smarting from the loss of Silesia to Prussia in an earlier conflict, were facing a growing threat. Britain, Prussia, and Russia had formed a defensive alliance, and as riches and resources rolled in from the New World, the alliance began to have designs on larger and larger parts of Europe. This left the Austrian and French Empires open and undefended, and although the Hapsburgs and Bourbons had spent most of the past several centuries as enemies, they had been allies in the most recent war and now found common cause. The French decided that war with Austria was wasteful and foolish, because only the British were serious rivals for control of the seas. The Austrians, for their part, believed that a friend with a long shore would be better than years more of enmity, especially with Prussia at their back. In consequence, Austria and France drafted the Treaty of Versailles, linking the two empires in peace and war.

French and Austrian diplomats sought a deeper, more symbolic union to cement the alliance. For five years, these diplomats maintained back-channel negotiations to connect the two empires via an interfamilial marriage. Maria Theresa finally relented and allowed her daughter to marry into the French royal family, and it was agreed that her husband would be Louis XV's grandson, the portly and quiet Louis Auguste. Once the matter had been decided, there was little for the girl to do but wait for her betrothal and leave all she knew and loved. She received tutelage in the ballet from the dancer Jean-Georges Noverre – whom one contemporary called the Shakespeare of dance[17] — and she received elocution lessons from stage comedians Aufrense and Sainville. Sadly, the French court considered these instructors to be sub-par although only a few of the more fashionable Viennese knew why. Noverre, who left Paris in 1750 and rarely returned, had scandalized the French stage with his naturalist costuming and leanings, culminating in a performance that had dancers capering in tiger skins and tree bark shoes.

On the afternoon of May 7, 1770, the young Austrian archduchess Maria Antonia, on her way to meet her husband-to-be at Versailles, was taken to a small, wooden pavilion on an island in the Rhine River where she would begin her *remise* — her handover. Officially becoming the property of France, Maria, henceforth to be known as Marie, was stripped of all of her Hapsburgian finery and belongings. Her little dog, Mops, was left in the care of Austrian handmaidens who were forbidden to follow their lady.

She did, however, sneak one small item past the sharp-eyed court officials who accepted her at the border: a tiny gold watch given to her by her mother, a token of her familial bonds and, in the end, her most prized possession. That she held this watch above all else — even her trousseau valued at 400,000 livres (at least $8 million, in twenty-first-century dollars) — was a testament to the mystery and importance watchmaking and watches held in eighteenth-century court life.

Just fourteen years old, she was torn from her family, thrust into a foreign court whose language she did not speak – she once pleaded with an admirer to refrain from speaking in her mother tongue, saying "Don't speak to me in German, *messieurs*, as from now on I only understand French"[18] — and forcibly married to a husband who had no more say in the union than she did. Her new life was to be one of constant scrutiny, gossip, luxury, and wealth. She was wed in a white dress caked in diamonds and her husband wore a gold suit similarly bedazzled. After the ceremony she spent the evening in Versailles' Hall of Mirrors playing cards with the old king and Louis Auguste in front of over six thousand surging onlookers, while a planned fireworks display sputtered out thanks to an inopportune thunderstorm.

The scrutiny continued as Marie-Antoinette's every move was watched and noted. Dinners were a spectacle as "honest folk who, when they had seen the Dauphine take her soup, went to see the princes eat their *bouilli* and then ran till they were out of breath to behold Mesdames at their dessert."[19] Members of the court fought among themselves to become close to the new royal couple and Marie-Antoinette could do little but react in her own impertinent way by, for example, refusing to speak to the king's mistress at the advice of her sisters-in-law. Early on, sadly, she could not see the value in playing politics and this was to her early detriment.

Four years later, at mid-day on May 10, 1774, king Louis XV died of smallpox. Marie-Antoinette was, like her husband, jarringly elevated to a position of power for which, despite her long incubation, she was hardly ready.

At first, the citizens of France loved their Dauphine. She was beautiful, with small, pursed lips and blonde hair pulled back away from her small face. Her looks were marred only by the Hapsburg overbite, barely noticeable from the front. She had an "air of nobleness and majesty astonishing for her age."[20]

But among the courtiers of Versailles, Marie found herself lost and frustrated. She was naive, and failed to project an image of courtly grace and intelligence. She spoke French with an accent that was mocked, yet could no longer speak accentless German, and so was trapped between two empires.

She received little support from her husband. Louis was intensely shy and preoccupied with his hobbies. He had an obsessive interest in building and engineering, supervising the construction of more and more wings of the palace and generally stomping about like a bull amid the profusion of delicate statuary and palace decorations. He was partial to climbing up on scaffolds to assist the workmen putting crowning touches on finials and coffer ceilings, and he was often seen dressed much like the workmen themselves, his royal finery abandoned to his earthy pursuits. Louis was a quintessential tinkerer at a time when there was only so much with which to tinker. He was obsessed with locks and even apprenticed as a locksmith, going so far as to build his own workshop at Versailles. He spent hours with the master under whom he apprenticed, working on little mechanical devices. Locks, like watches, were going through a period of rich innovation. A new lock called the Bénardes could be opened from either side, and the introduction to lockmaking of bronze, which was lighter and easier to cast than clunky traditional iron, allowed for smaller and more ornate keys. But not everyone approved of the king's fascination with "mechanical works."

"Sire," the king's *valet de chambre*, Intendant Thierry, was said to have commented, "when kings occupy themselves with the works of the common people, the common people will assume the functions of kings."[21]

Louis XVI's teacher in engineering was Francois Gamain, a lockmaker at Versailles whose father, Nicolas, had installed most of the locks at the palace during the rule of the Sun king. Louis XVI "employed a thousand strategies," Gamain later wrote, to hide from the court and work at his tiny workshop with the master lockmaker. His equipment included vises and a guilloché engine, a specialized engraving tool, and he even tried his hand at blacksmithing inside the palace, creating a mini-forge that threatened more than once to set the whole building ablaze. Later, on the advice of his court horologers, he would establish a school for watchmaking near Paris.

With all his tinkering, Louis largely neglected his wife, who called her husband *le pauvre homme* — the poor man — and pitied him more than loved him. Marie's day was full of formalities, and she rarely saw her husband outside of her assigned duties. Even their bedtime was a codified affair, and the young king would leave as soon as he was put to bed with his wife, escaping through secret passages behind the bedroom walls.

Their increasingly rare efforts to conceive a child always ended in disaster. The king seemed to have a physical condition that made the enterprise painful, and year after year, Marie failed to become pregnant. Under intense pressure to give France an heir, she had to endure constant scrutiny. Seen riding her horse once, an old woman warned the girl that she could lose a pregnancy riding about like a hunter. "In God's name," Marie yelled. "Leave me in peace, and be assured I am not compromising any heir." A moment's reaction from a girl barely out of her teens became, under the microscope of court life and popular discontent, an example of her supposed hauteur.

No expense was spared in an effort to keep the wine flowing. Marie held extravagant masked balls, gambling parties, and theater productions — all at a time when the masses were drowning in poverty. She travelled nightly the thirteen miles from Versailles to Paris to spend hours talking, laughing, drinking, and wagering. At balls, she usually discussed only popular music or commentary — or, as Fersen soon discovered, the season's dirty jokes — and in those early years she annually spent over 300,000 livres on diamonds and pearls, not to mention thousands more on watches.

In 1775 Louis XVI gave his wife the Petit Trianon, a Neoclassical white-stone palace which had previously served as a refuge for his grandfather's mistresses. Marie-Antoinette immediately launched an expensive renovation of the palace, in a more elegant and austere style than the rococo of previous regimes.

She treasured the palace as her place of privacy, where she could escape the intrigues of the court. She was the sovereign ruler in this small domain, and even the king needed an invitation to visit. She had mechanical mirrors installed that slid over the windows, ensuring privacy from peeping courtiers, and because the queen herself owned the little palace, she could deny entry to courtiers whose historical prerogatives had for generations given them access.

In the absence of a close relationship with her husband, Marie was left to the mercy of a petty and vindictive court. Not knowing where to turn, she quickly entangled herself in the web of gossip at Versailles. She was free-spirited, and found refuge in a circle of admirers and fun-loving courtiers. In particular, she befriended a coterie of young ladies including the Duchesse de Polignac and the Princess Lamballe, and Maria Teresa Luisa of Savoy. The Duchesse was almost a copy of the young queen with her slim, roughed face and striking grey eyes, while the princess was a blonde, carefree spirit who was most at home playing milkmaid in Marie-Antoinette's charming faux-village, the Hameau.

Her social habits, too, provoked jealousy. As a girl, she had spent much time in the company of other women — her sisters, her governesses — and it was in small, close-knit circles of women, along with her husband and his intimates, that she felt most comfortable. This predilection for small, exclusive groups inadvertently insulted a court that had previously had ready access to, if not

Louis XV, then his power-hungry mistress.

Her husband's neglect made Marie susceptible to the attentions of older men. Intriguing courtiers laid traps for her to cheat on her husband, and rumors spread that she had many love affairs. Almost certainly, the rumors were false. At first, as a young Dauphine, Marie was too naive to even understand these men's intentions, let alone react to them. She was too virginal and intent on fun to have attempted anything so untoward as an affair, and she was almost completely ignorant of passion and lovemaking.

Later, there would be other rumors, about one particular man, which would prove more substantial. She loved escape, and those moments at the masked ball in late January 1774, speaking with Count Axel von Fersen, gave her what she craved. Her strange, closed world grew brighter for a moment.

Two weeks after the opera ball, she saw Fersen again. The occasion was another masked ball, this time at Versailles, to celebrate Mardi Gras. Fersen arrived toward the end of the evening, and watched Marie and Louis, along with their entourage, dancing. The couple was dressed in the Old French style of Henri IV — their masks frilled with feathers and pale lace. Fersen snickered to his diary, that night, that the king and his brother, the Comte de Provence, were poor dancers, but overall he found that "the coup d'oeil was charming."

Perhaps Axel and Marie felt some connection to each other, because both were foreigners and neither was naturally given to the pomp and preening of Versailles. He thought her beautiful, and he had a penchant for befriending the daughters of powerful men; she, in turn, was drawn to his beauty and high-mindedness. But they wouldn't see each other again for another four years.

He spent most of the time back in Sweden, before once more setting out for adventure abroad. He lived a privileged life. His father supplied him with a not insubstantial allowance, and he was also in the guard of Swedish King Gustav III, a young, fun-loving, enlightened despot whose flashing dark eyes and high forehead, with hair puffed into a powdered confection, was even more popular with the ladies than the laconic Swede. During this period, Fersen spent three months in London courting a rich heiress, who ultimately spurned his entreaties to marry him.

While Fersen was away from Paris, Marie and Louis became king and queen and, at last, had a child, a girl named Madame

Royale. But when Fersen returned to the city in 1778, and was presented to the queen at Versailles just two days after his arrival, she exclaimed: "Ah! Here is an old acquaintance." Even in the intervening few years she remembered the handsome Swede in his dashing uniform.

She was already pregnant with another child, but Marie and Fersen developed a growing affection for one another that year. They took to walking around opera balls together, and once were observed alone in a private box, talking at length. He was frequently at Trianon and became well-known in Paris as part of the queen's small, tightly knit entourage of nobles, hangers-on, and foreigners. When Fersen's application to join the Prussian army was rejected, Marie interceded to secure a place for him in the French Expeditionary Force heading to America. At her request, he visited her private apartments wearing military regalia designed by King Gustav. The uniform included a blue doublet with a white, Hungarian-style tunic, tight-fitting chamois breeches, and a black shako topped by an egret feather. Marie was said to be fascinated by Fersen's dress, and she examined each of his buttons, one by one.[22]

Fersen confided to his diary that Marie was "the prettiest and most amiable princess that I know," and she inquired after him often, asking Count Creutz why her young friend hadn't been attending her Sunday card games. Fersen grew increasingly animated in his correspondence, and a duchess at court suggested to Fersen that the queen was his conquest, a suggestion that he quickly and angrily denied. Creutz likewise became convinced that Marie was infatuated with his young fellow countryman but he was careful to broach the subject diplomatically. He, of course, noticed that when Axel and Marie were in the same room, she couldn't take her eyes off him, and as he prepared to leave on the expedition to North America, her eyes filled with tears whenever she looked at him.

Fersen wrote of most of his affairs in code, jotting down "spent the night" in his diary when he succeeded in a romantic interlude. That summer, he wrote in a cryptic letter to his sister Sophie that he "breathed only for her":[23]

I have taken my stand. I don't want to form any conjugal ties. Since I cannot belong to the person to whom I want to belong, to the only woman who really loves me, I don't want to belong to anybody.[24]

Fersen's presence at court offended many – he was not French, for one, and he was a soldier whose good looks and access to the queen scandalized the pious courtiers who had, in the reign of Louis XVI, been ousted from influence. They began to speculate openly about the relationship, and Fersen, mindful of appearances, may have sought to avoid trouble by leaving the city.

In September of 1779, he departed for Le Havre, to await embarkment on a ship bound for America. To keep time in the New World, he was carrying a watch made by a man named Breguet.

Chapter 4

At the end of a long and languorous summer in 1782, horological legend records that a small carriage painted in enamel the color of pitch, with brightly colored red wheels, rattled onto the Quai de l'Horloge. The coachman yanked his reins, a pair of horses pulled up short in front of #51, and a man stepped out of the hack behind them.[25]

Above him, smoke puffed from the buildings' chimneys, bearing away byproducts of the metalwork taking place inside. A deeply canted roof ended in three wide windows along the roofline, and at street level a front casement window was inset under a large sign: Breguet. Behind the glass, the delicate timepieces on display were brilliant in the fading sunlight, a dozen captured stars.

Fersen had decided to commission a gift to the woman he loved. Given her taste for elegant understatement, he knew that a watch by Breguet, with its lack of exterior ornamentation, would perfectly suit her. He sent a letter requesting the piece, and now, with a bit of time to spare in Paris, he had come to place the order.

Fersen walked into the cool of Breguet's shop and heard the sharp ting-ting of hammers and the rasp of files in the attic atelier above. The air down below was clean and clear. The front windows faced the river, and behind the building the Place Dauphine kept the homes open and bright rather than cramped and tubercular. The rich wood of the showroom shone even in the low light, layers of wax and polish reflecting the sun from outside. This was the shop of a successful man, quiet and warm on the bottom floor and hive-ish with activity in the upstairs workshop.

Fersen, like his fellow officers, was well acquainted with Breguet and his ability to make watches that could survive war, water, and even short drops. Over the years, he had commissioned many watches from Breguet and also had several watches repaired by him. One, a silver soldier's watch, had accompanied him to the New World and returned still running as soundly as the day it had left the bench.

He also knew that the understated styling of Breguet's timepieces were exquisite and that the little watchmaker was pushing the state of the art forward with astounding regularity. A few weeks earlier, he had seen a Breguet watch with a large white face and Breguet's trademark blued "moon" or "Poppy" hands— a circle interrupting the long, thin hand at the tip and culminating in a sharp point. While other manufacturers clad their watches in jeweled cases that were more pomp than function, this watch was different. The Roman numerals were thin and precise, and the movement was perpetual – or automatic — meaning it wound with the motion of the wearer's body. It even had a hand showing how much power it had in reserve — a *reserve d' marche* — and, in addition, could chime the time to the nearest minute.

The watch hid its movement and many complications in a case as simple and elegant as the owner herself — Marie-Antoinette, whom Fersen knew to be much more modest in her tastes than her popular reputation would have suggested. Although rumors circulated that she traipsed through private rooms with floors paved in rubies and diamonds, he knew that she loved the understated work of his favorite watchmaker. The tide of fashion was changing, and she appreciated Breguet's subtle elegance, his way with dark and light, his sense of space and proportion.

None of Breguet's watches were particularly ornate. Instead, each gold or silver case was as sensuous as an August peach, but with a certain hard, diamond edge it was rare to find in an era of curlicues, cupids, and insipid rococo design. Fersen knew that here he would not find watches covered in diamonds or enameled in delicate pinks or blues. Not that the proprietor would turn down a commission if it came in the door — he had executed plenty of designs that would have matched any one of the Sun king's bejeweled antiques — but on the whole each one of these watches, signed *Breguet a Paris*, was a self-contained wonder, free of extraneous pomp and fuss. However impressive the watch Fersen had seen on the queen, he had come to Breguet's shop today to place an even

28

more ambitious order.

Inside Breguet's shop, an unassuming Frenchman, tidying himself and hiding away his leather smock as the visitor entered, greeted Fersen and invited him further into the showroom. Their conversation would be private. The Frenchman introduced himself as Michel Weber, a new assistant, and went away to inform the master of his guest.

Shortly, Weber returned and led Fersen up the cramped stairs to the master's workshop, and between two rows of watchmakers. Each man sat at a small bench with a wide surface on which to assemble the tiny pieces, their *mise en place* of precise tools arrayed in front of them and carried with them in leather pouches. The backs of the benches were low enough to maximize daylight on the work surface and to encourage proper posture. Nine drawers, of increasing size, flanked each side of the watchmaker's legs, and there were three smaller drawers and a pigeonhole to keep papers and personal items. Goldsmiths in the shop usually had a wide leather apron over their laps that was connected to the bench itself.

The floor consisted of wooden slats suspended about an inch from another smooth layer of wood. The floor was specially designed for jewelry manufacturing; it made for easy cleaning, and was swept often to ensure that no gold scraps made it out on the soles of the workers' shoes. It also offered a measure of safety when transporting tiny gears or screws from one bench to another. Chainsmiths were the *fabriquers* most likely to receive new benches during the year. They would slowly chip through the front edge of their workspaces while pressing tiny chains together; benches could become so warped and worn that the watchmaker had hardly anywhere to rest his elbows.

The tinging of hammers was louder here – a few men were making chains, the links falling into place like drops of liquid gold — and light from the outside was augmented by oil lamps that left dull smudges on the ceiling. Each worker had arrayed before him a collection of files, punches, and polishing cloths so thin that many looked as if they were spun from metallic silk. These were the standard tools of the horologist's art, the files and scrapers and polishers that turned lifeless metal into ticking, whirring complications.

Someone along the far wall was polishing a set of gears with a delicately carved piece of wood, while another was using a buffer – a wheel attached to a treadle – to spin a piece of brass to a fine sheen. This sort of work was rarely done outside of the Quai, and it was the end of a long and complex process that began in the metal mines of Germany and Switzerland and ended here in a workshop high above the Seine.

Breguet used more than a thousand different tools to finish a single watch, including drills, pantographs, and milling machines to create perfect circles and notch out gears and wheels with absolute precision. One machine was designed specifically for the placement of holes into tiny disks. A drill was connected to a pantograph that traced a large disk. The watchmaker would then press down on the drill, making a hole in exactly the right place based on the larger pattern.

To a layman, the machines were baffling. One, a Rose Engine, also called *Guilloche* after its supposed inventor, was designed to place repeating patterns on a disk of gold or brass. It was used to decorate fine movements and to hide imperfections in lesser, un-polished movements. The device consisted of a large treadle wheel connected to a set of disks. As the disks spun, they moved the en-graving tip onto and off of the metal, nipping off minute shavings and dropping them into a collection container. The machines were quite sought after.

These machines used almost every material imaginable, including hand hewn and joined wood as well as cast steel, brass, and even a bit of rubber in later years. But each of these machines worked in concert to create standard sized watches for almost all of the company's cases. For example, Breguet created a series of guidelines for *ebauche* makers, requiring them to supply watches with parts "exactly proportional to the model"[26] in question. In this way, each Breguet watch would bear the same hallmarks including similar hands, keys, and crystals.

Abraham-Louis Breguet turned toward Fersen and smiled in recognition. When he spoke his welcome, it was with the barest hint of a Swiss accent. He presented a copy of the commission along with some preliminary drawings. They got down to busi-ness.

Fersen explained that he wanted to place a special order but could not pay for it for until he returned to Paris or until it was complete. Although Fersen barely had the money for a regular, plainer watch at Breguet's shop, he felt that his future was secure enough and the commission odd enough to warrant the watch-maker's interest. If all went well in the coming months, he'd return from America with enough money and stature to stay in Paris indefinitely and pay for the watch.

As Fersen and Breguet talked, Weber, the assistant, took notes. Fersen wanted something magnificent and as complicated as it could be without overwhelming the owner. It needed to be simple to operate but internally complex, and it had to be finished over the next few years, while Fersen was away tending to business. It pleased him to know that something he left here would be ticking away, slowly gaining form, until his return when he could hand the watch to the lady herself.

Breguet, just then, was hard at work on a number of improvements to the standard pocket watch, and he was intrigued by Fersen's desire for "magnificence." He had already sketched out a possible solution on a sheet of paper, his scratching and scribbles outlining a fairly staid and standard watch. Because Breguet had already defined, planned, and built many of the complications that made a modern watch magnificent it would not be hard to make a list of complications and build them. But to hide them all within a single woman's watch and have all of the disparate pieces work together in concert was another matter entirely. Working mostly alone, Breguet had created a number of inventions that were now commonplace in watches. He could have simply copied one of his favorite *perpetuelles* and enrobed it in a finer case. But Breguet was a perfectionist and never made the same watch twice. Each bore a unique number and was designed to order — a service that limited his market mainly to aristocrats who often couldn't or wouldn't pay for the finished watches when they received them. This, if anything, was Breguet's failing: the refusal to turn down a fascinating and potentially lucrative commission. Breguet crumpled up his original notes and began anew.

Fersen continued: The watch he now envisioned, he explained to Breguet, would incorporate everything the man had to offer. Fersen knew of watches that could tell the solar time; Breguet nodded. He wanted it to chime the hours and the quarter hours; again, this could be done. He wanted a thermometer — difficult, but not impossible. A perpetual calendar that would never have to be reset? Very difficult, indeed. And this was to be a lady's watch, so it had to be clad in gold and be appropriate for a woman of stature, beauty, and importance. It had to be delicate yet still contain all of the technology known at that time.

It was a tall order, and Breguet paused for a moment to think.

31

He consulted his ledger, in which he kept descriptions of every watch he had ever built. Nothing remotely like this new watch appeared there except for watch number 57, a unique timepiece which he was in the midst of creating for the Duc de Praslin, one of his patrons, and which contained a few of the features Fersen was describing. Breguet could use the base of the 57 and then build on it, fitting new complications in like pieces of an ornate puzzle.

Breguet inquired as to who was to receive the gold watch. Fersen took a deep breath. While the king was seemingly oblivious to his wife's affair, Fersen had some sense of the gossip that was circulating, and knew that anything that connected him to her could put their careers — and lives — in jeopardy. He needed a watchmaker who could keep his secrets safe, and his relationship with Breguet was close and professional. He knew he could trust the small, genial watchmaker with his commission.

Fersen answered in five curt syllables. Marie-Antoinette. Breguet nodded slowly, understanding the significance of this momentous commission. He had heard the rumors about Fersen and the queen, the chitchat about her pregnancy, the calumnies suggesting that her husband, now "very fat and even more unattractive,"[27] could not possibly be the father. Ironically, Louis XVI, as much as anyone, would have appreciated the mechanical artistry of the watch that was being commissioned.

Watches symbolized love. Marie-Antoinette herself had recently commissioned a watch for Fersen with a blue enamel case and the letters A.F. boldly intertwined on the face. She had made a similar watch for herself, described in Breguet's fastidious ledgers. But this commission was something else entirely, a new sort of watch for a secret love.

Carefully, on a faintly lined page in the leather-bound order book, Weber entered the specifications in a handsome French cursive: [One watch] "with the condition that all the complications possible and known be incorporated in it. Everywhere, gold must completely replace brass. No limit on time of manufacture or on price was imposed." The name of the commissioner and the name of the intended was left blank. It would be a testament to Breguet's skill, this watch, and the culmination of centuries of timekeeping, a technological marvel in an age where technology was just becoming a true art. And it would be a symbol, like so many watches before it, of true love.

Chapter 5

Around the end of May the streets of Manhattan come to a standstill. Bike messengers halt on their rounds and the scions of Midtown come out for a smoke break and look, in amazement, at something called Manhattanhendge. It is on this day that New Yorkers, over-scheduled and anxious as they are, have something in common with ancient druids.

On the day of Manhattanhedge, the sun lines up perfectly with the offset grid of east-west streets. The sun, brilliant between the dark caverns of the buildings, sets over New Jersey like a comet coming to rest. Modern minds marvel for a moment and then forget about this once-a-year happenstance but, in prehistoric times, tricks like Manhattanhendge were, in short, the way humans told time.

Timekeeping was always at the forefront of human endeavor. It gave form to our days and helped us traverse great distances. It called the farmers to their fields and the priests to the vespers. It was — and is — the defining trait of humanity. After all, Robert Burns's dear mousie knew not the time when the farmer's scythe cut through his grassy home.

In about 5,000 BC, Celtic tribes built a tomb at Knowth, on the east coast of Ireland, whose position allowed it to act as a calendar and clock. A small beam of light crawled across the cave floor and carvings indicated various solar phenomena including the solstices. Such tombs – used for both astronomy and burial – played an important part in the daily lives of early humans, allowing them to measure times to harvest and to estimate the Metonic Cycle or the cycle of lunar and solar eclipses. A similar trick played an important part in *Indiana Jones and the Raiders of the Lost Ark*, proving that the play of light in darkness is a compelling meme even in modernity.

Because the ancients had little but sunlight and perhaps the imperceptible motion of a distant planet or star to tell the time (after all, astrology is nothing but time-telling mixed with a bit of hocus pocus), they had a much more fluid view of its passing. The day began when the sun rose and ended when the sun set. The end of twilight left a deserted and dangerous world with no real promise that the day would begin anew, and it was faith in the rising and falling of the sun that constituted early religions.

It is hard to say when "time," or the separation of the day into sections, became a measurable thing. According to one fairly visceral legend, the "division of the day into hours was first suggested by the regular exercise of the bodily functions of a consecrated monkey, called the Cynocephalus."[28] More likely, however, watching the sun crawl across the ground in front of a tower was man's first inkling that his days were meted out in tick-tock bursts. Egyptian obelisks, in fact, doubled as sundials and the Book of Isaiah records the use of a sundial in 700 BC.

The earliest time-telling probably came from the notation of the period between sunrise and sunset, which, at first, consisted of four sections – four primitive *hora* or "parts of the day" – that slowly metamorphosed into the twenty four-hour clock we now use. The Babylonians arguably created the first sixty-minute division of time and this was adopted by early Jews. The system used twelve hours of daylight and twelve hours of nighttime, with each hour divided into sixty minutes (sixty being a powerful number in Babylonian culture because of its easy divisibility).

Roman horologists also divided the day into twelve hours from sunrise to sunset, although the hours changed lengths depending on the season. They chose twelve in correspondence to the number of months — or lunar cycles — in the year.

The sundial was accurate and virtually foolproof — after all, its power source rose in the morning — but it was not always portable, and its transmission system (a stick) and register (a shadow) were imprecise. A cloud or an errant breeze could turn a carefully constructed sundial into a patch of empty earth and the sun had a pesky way of often hiding behind clouds. A sundial also required a great deal of trust that the motion of the heavens was regular and that the sun would never wind down — a tall order for early astronomers. And, of course, sundials didn't work at night.

In order to maintain prayer schedules even after the sun had set, priests in ancient Egypt employed another simple system: a water clock. The clock consisted of a bowl with a small hole that released water at a pre-defined rate. Like an hourglass, it would mark the passage of time by draining away, and it had the added benefit of being readable in the dark. A night watchman guarding the Pharaoh's palace could simply dip his finger into the bowl to see how much time had elapsed. As the bowl emptied — or filled, in another bowl of water, and sank — the changing water level caused chimes to sound or made a tapping noise, thus creating the first mechanical register, the horological term for a read-out.

The Greeks called these devices clepsydras, or water thieves, and they began to take more fanciful shapes and offer a number of unique time-telling features – what horologers now call "complications." A clepsydra known as the Horologion, created by a Macedonian astronomer named Andronicus of Cyrrhus in around 50 BC, showed astronomers as well as townsfolk the time during the day, and at night also provided an indicator for the direction of the wind.

Another clock, devised by Hero of Alexandria around 150 BC, was powered by water filling a drum, and marked the hour using a human figure that pointed an arrow at a meter drawn on a cylinder. As the figure moved upwards it pushed a little water into a circular set of troughs that emptied once a year and adjusted the hour slightly to reflect the differing lengths of days (thereby anticipating leap years). This miraculous invention was called the Ctesibius, after the Greek father of pneumatics, and was one of the first clocks to take into consideration the difference between solar time and man-made twenty-four-hour time. The clock predated similar technology by 1600 years and showed an impressive understanding of the sun's motion. This handling of the "equation of time," or the failure of the day to fit neatly into twelve hour increments, was a dauntingly complex problem that took centuries to solve mechanically, yet it was done by an ancient Greek using only water and some plumbing.

The first modern mechanical clock appeared in the eleventh century, when Su Song, a Chinese official, created a clepsydra that looked less like the primitive bowl-and-basin system used for centuries than an early grandfather clock. It still used water, but as a power source, rather than an indicator. As the liquid flowed downward through a series of buckets, the motion of the stream would power the clock. The clock itself consisted of a complex mash of gears, hands, and bells. It could chime the hours and had animated figures that moved and danced at pre-set times.

But even when used as a power source, water, like the sun, had obvious limitations. As the liquid flowed through the machine, friction caused some buckets to refill faster or more slowly than others. To remedy this, a number of solutions were tried to control the rotation of the wheel — or transmission system — and ensure that it "escaped" at exactly the right period. Some escapements used spinning regulators, while others used weights or even pools of mercury that slowly filled portions of the wheel as it turned. Nothing, however, could be done about the power source freezing in the winter or evaporating under the summer sun. You'll notice that many early water clocks first appeared in temperate climates that weren't too hot or too cold. Northerners, while enamored with the idea of the water clock, would have to think of something that wouldn't be affected by the vagaries of weather.

The first true mechanical clocks appeared around 1360[29] and used falling weights to power the registers. The weights, in this case, acted as a power source and transmitted this power to an escapement that swung back and forth in an exact period. Given a consistent push, a pendulum would move approximately equally back and forth in every subsequent tick, and when connected to the escapement, acted as a balance wheel, controlling the time register as it ticked off the seconds.

These early time indicators, with their ability to move and chime unaided by human hands, must have been magical to lay-people. Once the water stealers and clockwork gadgets began chiming out the hours, priests could call their followers to order, kings could call their people to work at certain times, and the people, if they were savvy enough, could be ensured a fair day's work. The chimes of town clocks helped citizens know when they needed to light their lanterns. Nights were fraught with peril, and many countries had laws requiring citizens to stay locked in their homes at certain hours. In Paris, to go outside at night without a light could get you fined ten sous, about the price of sixty loaves of bread.[30] The town clock, then, was vital and the riotous chimes of many cathedral and church clocks helped define entire neighborhoods as those who could hear one set of bells began to differentiate themselves from those who could hear another set. After all, in

London, the bells of St. Clement's always called out "oranges and lemons" and St. Martin's was always in debt, forever owing the Old Bailey "five farthings."

Many early portable clocks, called *clocca* (Latin for bell), didn't have faces. An internal power source slowly wound down, and usually a hammer tapped a bell once a day or on the hour, making them more like modern egg timers than real clocks. The first Western versions, created long after the Egyptian clepsydrae, still used water pitchers that slowly sank and triggered a signal, or candles that burned down to nubs. Most of the candle clocks were abandoned for fear of late-night fires. Later, *horloges* — clocks with hands — were introduced, with and without bells. Often, clocks had elements of both *clocca* and *horloge*, offering some continuity in the transition from faceless timepieces that didn't require reading to ones with complex dials and registers.

If the *clocca* was a precursor to town-hall, house, and carriage clocks, the *horloge* anticipated the pocket- and wristwatch. It was when clocks began sporting full faces in about 1400 that the term "watch" came into use, to designate the part that showed the time, while the "clock" was the mechanical part with the bell. A "clock-watch," then, referred to a watch with a bell. This was soon shortened to clock for anything that told time but was not worn on the person. A timepiece worn on the person and "watched" by other people (nobles often wore theirs on their chest in order to show importance and prestige) then gave "watch" its modern meaning.

Early clock-watchers set their clocks once in the morning and once at night, in time with the tolling of the church clock tower, which, if the church horologer was doing his job, would toll precisely at the rising, and the falling, of the sun. This is what Iago meant in Shakespeare's *Othello* when he said "He'll watch the orologe a double set if drink rock not his cradle," a double set being a full day.

But time was not equal in every town and city. A clock-keeper on the "drink" could miss a call or be late for duty and clocks ran fast or slow depending on who was maintaining them (in many cases a bad watchmaker was worse than none at all when it came to watch repairs). It wasn't until the rise of the railroads that the world would share a single standard time. Until the 1800s, time was a concept without precision, and what Breguet and his peers were really measuring was the "measured duration"[31] between events, natural and unnatural. A dandy on the Île might set his clock to the bells of Notre Dame, which, in turn, were set to the moment of sunrise or high noon. A farmer in his pasture would set his watch, perhaps, to the crowing of the cock at dawn. Your neighbor's noon was not your noon. Solar time was eventually wrested out of popular use and "standard time" introduced. Huge swathes of the planet grew to share the same time and clock towers finally chimed in unison, much to the determent of a good night's sleep.

The religious significance of clocks shaped the words used to describe them. The spring or weight or water wheel — whatever powered a particular timepiece — came to be called the prime mover, after Aristotle's explanation for the creation of the physical world. The word Germans used to describe nature, *zeitgeber* ("time-giver"), came to mean clock, too. Clocks often had mystical powers attributed to them, and kings wishing to impress visiting potentates would produce them for inspection.

Because clocks involved trapping energy and transmitting it, they gave rise to a new understanding of physics and led directly to such inventions as water wheels and steam-powered pumps, which predated the steam engine by fifteen hundred years.

But mechanical clocks were far too imprecise to trust for more important matters, so obelisks and sundials held their place in scientific endeavor long after the invention of the first timepieces. Only four centuries after the creation of the first real mechanical clock was the sundial finally made obsolete.

Clocks and watches took on a new urgency during the age of exploration. Overseas travel, especially to distant colonies, was full of peril. Ships could easily drift off course, and a small, unintended shift in direction could send a ship already overburdened with sugar, tobacco, and pelts into rocks that would send it plunging to the deep without warning. The measure of longitude became a vital necessity.

In theory, the easiest way to compute longitude was to have a clock on board set to the time of the port of origin. One early solution involved something called "sympathetic powder," a knife, and a wounded dog. Every day, an observer on shore would dip the knife in the powder at a certain time, causing, it was thought, the dog to cry out in pain as the knife once again inflicted its cruel sting through the magic of the sympathetic powder. Luckily, because this method never worked (one questions why the inventors didn't try it on their own self-inflicted wounds before stabbing a pooch), sailors realized they really needed a good watch instead, thus saving the lives of many hapless pups.

Using a watch, a navigator could compare the time in a distant city with the time indicated by the position of the sun, and derive how far a ship had travelled. In reality, while most clocks worked wonderfully on land, they quickly broke down in the wet, salty air on the decks of heaving ships.

The Greenwich Society, a scientific brotherhood of thinkers at the Royal Observatory in Greenwich, England, called for a solution to the Longitude Problem, a request that brought many of the greatest English minds of the eighteenth century to bear on the issue. Solving it was the last piece of the puzzle of navigation. The government able to measure longitude would be able to control the seas and, thereby, trade with the New World and do battle with the Old while knowing exactly where it was on the map, a sort of proto-GPS. France, Spain, and Holland were also attempting to solve the problem, but the Greenwich Society, funded by the British crown and interested merchants, went about it the most systematically. The Longitude Act, passed in 1714, offered a prize of up to £20,000 (about $4.5 million in modern dollars) to the person who could measure longitude to within thirty nautical miles (thirty-four statute miles) — half a degree of a great circle in topographic terms.

A twenty-year-old carpenter named John Harrison, obsessed with clocks since he was a child, embarked on an unlikely mission to win it. He recognized that the single biggest challenge was changes in temperature. The slow contraction and expansion of a clock's wood and metal caused it to slow down and speed up. Thus he codified a set of techniques dedicated to the eradication of the clockmakers primary enemy, friction. Harrison set out to reduce friction on all parts and ensure that the most important parts — the springs, the pendulums, and the transmission systems — wouldn't change shape over time. He would spend the next sixty years perfecting his invention.

Eventually, his chronometer would include a bimetallic strip, a piece of metal made of two connected strips of two different metals. When the temperature got too hot or too cool, the strips would bend and expand at different rates, ensuring that a watch's internal spring would never change during long voyages. The chronometer also contained a rolling element bearing, a ring containing multiple balls, or bearings. The bearings would reduce friction considerably, ensuring that the barrel and major gears of Harrison's clock would never slow down due to friction. This ring reduced the need for messy lubricants and made it easy to swap out pieces when repairing the clock. A third innovation was a mechanism to allow the clock to remain running while it was being wound. By separating the mainspring from the movement during winding and keeping a small spring running when the winding key was engaged, the clock could be powered without having to be shut down and risking the loss of accuracy. And by using a wound spring instead of a pendulum, Harrison's device was considerably smaller than any marine chronometer – the name given to seaworthy clocks — previously built.

In 1761, Harrison's son William boarded the HMS *Deptford* with his new clock, the Number 4, and took it on a straight course from England to Jamaica. He kept the clock under four separate locks to prevent tampering. The clock ran only five seconds slow and, when combined with onboard calculations, left the ship less than a mile off course when it made landfall in the Caribbean, a feat that far surpassed all previous attempts.

The longitude problem had finally been solved, but because the board was reluctant to give an unknown and uneducated carpenter the entire prize for his work, it deemed his clock's exceptional precision to be the result of luck and demanded a repeat performance. Harrison died bitter and nearly robbed of his prize but some of Harrison's technical insights would eventually find their way, in miniaturized form, into the fine watches made by Breguet and carried by seamen on the very same routes made safe by the marine chronometer.

The value and importance of watchmaking, during Marie-Antoinette's rule, was at its zenith. Watches were not just baubles — they were weapons and tools that powered the maritime economies of the New and Old World both. Clocks were also important in bureaucratic and logistical matters. In 1760, a very simple striking clock, probably more like a timer, was installed in a nursery for foundling children in the Magdalen Asylum for Protestant Girls in Dublin by Irish philanthropist Lady Arabella Denny that would "mark, that as children reared by the spoon must have but a small quantity of food at a time, it must be offered frequently; for which purpose, this clock strikes every twenty minutes, at which notice all the infants that are not asleep must be discreetly fed."[32] In short, the clock kept these children alive by regimenting their eating and changing schedules. Thirty years later, in about 1788, a factory whistle, run by a precise clock and controlled by the plant foreman, would prod those same infants, now grown, into the Industrial Age. Watches were commoditizing time and turning organic, loafing wool-gatherers into modern clock-watchers.

Watches and clocks also possessed a kind of mystique. While they were of vital importance to sea captains, on land they were marvels in their own right, as triumphs of ingenuity and technology. In the storefronts of Paris and London, nobles spent vast sums on fashionable clocks. Some bought a watch for each of their court outfits, and many kings and emperors spent fortunes on watches for their wedding or ball guests.

The eighteenth-century watch buyer saw a dash of adventure in each new model. The more complex watches and clocks took years to build, and even the less advanced pieces made by lesser manufacturers were considered *de rigueur* among the moneyed classes. No good home was without a chiming mantle clock or larger grandfather model to keep the family and household in order. In an age of exploration, a watch was a constant reminder of distance and mystery. For the most part, people didn't depend on clocks to meet precise appointments – royals were expected to arrive in timely fashion for religious services and some public appearances, but usually an hour hand would suffice for such occasions. There was no "on time" or "late," just a vague notion of when things — prayer, vespers, and appointments — had to take place.

As watchmaking boomed into a golden age of horology, three countries were dominant: England, France, and Switzerland. In Switzerland, watchmaking was most deeply ingrained. The Geneva/Neuchâtel region was sparsely populated, but because of a historical quirk — the austerity preached by John Calvin — it held a high density of some of the greatest watchmakers in the world. Before the rise of Protestantism, Geneva had been a center for jewelry making. Travelers from points east would roll through and request delicately wrought items in gold and silver, inlaid with precious stones. Whimsical shapes — flowers, crosses, and tiny animals — came out of the goldsmiths' shops along the city's boulevards. Starting in 1541, however, Protestant refugees streamed into Switzerland, led by Calvin, who preached that ostentatious jewelry was an affront to God. Jewelers accustomed to melting gold into flowers adapted by making watches instead. Because watches were tools, they passed muster with Calvin. As one historian later observed, if Calvinists, always counting down the seconds toward judgment, "were not interested in time and its measurement, who was?"[33] Watches were a church-sanctioned way for Calvinist burghers who wanted to add a bit of flash to their black-and-white clothes to do so. Jewelers converted en masse to watchmaking.

Switzerland became a powerhouse in the watch economy for other reasons as well. The metals available to watchmakers in the Jura Mountains were plentiful and trade routes brought them what they could not mine themselves. By dint of geography and climate, the roads to the mountains closed near the end of October, leaving the farmers, butchers, and innkeepers trapped, with time on their hands and little to do. For centuries, these Swiss had spent their winters making lace, the men maintaining the fire and keeping the livestock healthy while the women and children produced the stuff for export. Lace was slightly profitable, but not everyone could make it well. Due to the mineral-rich soil and the proximity to mines, however, metalworking was almost in the blood. Every house had a forge. With the rise of watchmaking, a new business began to bloom.

Watchmaking – or at least the manufacture of small parts for watches – could be done by anyone, and an entire family could stamp out hundreds of parts a week, all within a certain threshold of precision. In fact, in terms of focus and entrepreneurial attention, watchmaking "swept all else aside."[34] Some farmers stopped growing crops and rented their land to men from the cities and simply made watch parts. Watchmaking, after all, was less work and considerably more lucrative.

Swiss families in the mountains – women and children included – were allowed to perform tasks like movement assembly reserved for only skilled guild men in France and England and even nearby Geneva. While this practice may not have enhanced quality, it allowed Geneva to corner the market in small, inexpensive watches made for export. It also trained whole generations — men and women both — in the art of watchmaking.

And Geneva proper did produce many beautiful and sophisticated watches. One, a delicately wrought tulip watch encased by thin, curved panes of rock crystal, used an ingenious set of hinges to open like a transparent flower and reveal the watch within. The fad for these so-called form watches – including crucifix-shaped watches for the clergy – was followed by a glut of astronomical calendars created for Muslim customers, their cases and movements delicately engraved with the repeating motifs popular in the Levant and Turkey. (One Genevan group even moved to Constantinople, which for men accustomed to the bridling strictures of Geneva was a playground; these watchmakers, according to a visiting Genevan minister, lived in "complete license without religion or any restraint, so that they are a subject of great scandal.")[35]

Such a delicate marriage of aesthetics and horology was unusual for the time, and Geneva became an international hub for horological commerce. Middle Eastern merchants would visit Switzerland to pick up Genevan watches of the period, and Swiss watches were also exported all over the world, ending in far-flung courts in Turkey, Russia, India, and China. Orders flowed in at a clip from the fashion hub of France, too, forcing the Jurassien farmers to maintain a grueling pace.

The pressing demand for Swiss watches in the seventeenth century led to the establishment of the *etablissage*, a mode of manufacturing named after the workbench, or *etabli*. The master watchmaker, or *etablisseur*, would plan his inventory and pass out raw materials to various shops and workhouses in the area. He would then collect the pieces and assemble, time (that is, check), and case the watches in his own shop, thereby ensuring he didn't run afoul of strict guild laws that limited, for example, the number of journeymen allowed in any one shop. By spreading out the work to rough *ebaucheurs* (makers of the *ebauche*, or core parts of the watch movement), these early industrialists were able to speed the production of a watch from one man month — one man working on the whole watch from stem to stern for a full month — to about a week, although more complex watches still took months, if not years, to complete. The disparity between the high wages of the Geneva master and the low ones of his workers in the mountains began to grate on some French and German businessmen who saw the Genevans as taking unfair advantage of peasant labor. "That's why Geneva is so prodigiously rich," a French official complained to a Swiss diplomat; "that's why 25,000 inhabitants of Geneva have more money than the 450,000 citizens of the duchy of Savoy and the 800,000 citizens of the neighboring departments."[36]

This also brings up a point that still plagues the Swiss watch industry today. If all of the parts are made by farmers, does the master have the right to put his (and it was always a "he") name on the dial? What constitutes Swiss made or French or British if many of the parts came from Switzerland. Even today the moniker "Swiss Watch" is sharply protected by the Swiss guilds and certain rules were set up to ensure that interlopers couldn't slap "Swiss Made" on their watches and live to tell the tale.

Incidentally, these days a Swiss watch — a timepiece that bears the Swiss Made label — must have a movement assembled in Switzerland and is "cased" or completed in Switzerland. This, of late, has been a very strict requirement although, even as late as the early 2000s, watches that were made mostly in Switzerland could hold the coveted label. In short, assembly is the most important factor and the source of parts is often overlooked.

The Swiss tradition created a hereditary group of skilled watchmakers, metal smiths, and grinders high in the mountains who were masters at the hand production of tiny screws and gears. Watchmaking paid better than almost any other trade, and "from the age of eight or nine children [could] earn much more at it than the cost of their keep."[37] By 1760, eight hundred master watch-makers made their homes in Geneva. They had perfected their art to the extent that they were able to produce eighty-five thousand watches a year.

While watchmaking in Switzerland often meant clock mak-ing — the marine chronometers and ornate wall and mantle clocks that graced the houses of nobles and the intelligentsia — the rest of Europe had a growing passion for the new pocket watches, the more expensive and complex the better.

In France, watchmaking intersected directly with the lives of a number of Enlightenment figures. It was an age in which the border between expert and dilettante was permeable. The gen-tlemen farmers and boulevardiers who eventually redefined the concept of science often got their start tinkering with watches and clocks. Almost every major inventor and scientist of the era built a clock when he was a youngster, the process being a test of a future scientist's mettle. Jean-Jacques Rousseau was born the son of a watchmaker. Voltaire owned several watchmaking factories, and he saw, in the inexorable ticking of a watch, nothing less than proof of God's existence: "The world embarrasses me," he wrote, "and I cannot dream that this watch exists and has no watchmaker."

French watchmakers were proud of their work, and rightly so. While the Swiss were masters at mass production, the French were creating new and better complications and perfecting the marine chronometer for their own navy. French watchmakers found Swiss watches to be "only good enough and nothing better,"[38] while demand for fine watches increased steadily thanks to the profligate French court. A steady influx of watchmakers streamed into the royal capital, where they elbowed for room at the king's side.

The first pocket watch appeared in about 1510 in Nuremberg when a German locksmith, Peter Henlein, created the "Egg," a unique globe-shaped clock about four inches in diameter that could hang around the neck into a pocket. The Nuremberg Egg had only one hand, but it was the first watch to use a forty-hour mainspring, meaning a spring that unwound itself over the course of almost two days. Until then, the only mainsprings available lasted for less than a day. Henlein had to deal with a number of issues while building his Egg including the pounding out of the immensely long mainspring – many clocks of this type had springs as long as ninety inches – and finding iron with a high purity so the powerful spring would not shatter. Henlein went on to create perfume-filled "pomander" clocks, which slowly released their scent as they told time.[39]

The egg quickly shrunk and flattened out, evolving over the centuries into something more recognizable and considerably more complex. Dandies in Paris were constantly consulting their sophisticated timepieces, and the sound of a gentleman's chimes — the tiny bells inside each watch that told the hour when activated — was as telling as the cut of his coat.

For centuries, nobles had worn their watches on their belts or around their necks on chains. But an eighteenth century rise in watch thefts had led watch owners to hide the devices in their vest or pants pockets. Because "fashion abhors bulges,"[40] the "old-school, finically ornamented watches" with which Washington was familiar were quickly going out of style.

Not every French watch was a masterpiece. The overwhelming majority of the watches sold in Paris were mere adornments. These simple watches, with parts made in Geneva (and sometimes smuggled illegally in wagons of malodorous fish to prevent customs officials from examining the loads too closely) and cases made in France, were inlaid in colored enamel with faces depicting a pastoral scene. Nobles would trade these cheap watches with each other and give them out as gifts at royal functions. "[T]he marriage corbeille of a noble lady would be filled with them," a historian would later write, "each more lavish than the next, more than she could possibly use; so the custom arose of keeping some and distributing the others among friends."[41]

By 1775, research in France, England, and Switzerland was coming together to create unique new models of timekeeping for landowners and royalty alike. Swiss watchmakers were known for their business skills and their ability to manufacture almost all the parts of complicated watches. England was well-known for military technology, including improvements to the fit and finish of marine chronometers designed to survive long months — even years — at sea. France had a way with engraving, lacquering, and precious metals, and, with watchmakers like Le Roy, Berthoud, and Lepaute inventing a new, more elegant escapements (the part of a watch that regulated its speed), which allowed for a thinner movement, had become the leader in the state of the art.

Everywhere, the industry was being transformed. The old model of piecework was still in force and would be for centuries to come, but watchmakers were experimenting with new methods of manufacturing that revolved around specifically engineered machines and processes such as pantographs, drills, and milling machines, and the faster, more standardized work they enabled.

Watchmaking was a booming business. By 1780, some Swiss factories were putting out forty-thousand watches a year – a ten fold improvement over the production at Voltaire's own factories in Fernay just ten years before.[42] Ownership of a single, simple watch, then, was nothing special – anyone could have one for about a day's wages, and production was so high that there is still, today, a glut of Louis XVI-era timepieces on the market. To truly stand out at court, members of the queen's and king's inner circle had to own the latest, most sophisticated timepieces, and the number of complications was the yardstick by which fine watches were measured.

At that trick, only one man truly excelled.

Chapter 6

Neuchâtel

The man who, more than anyone else, would provide the greatest timepieces of his age might never have discovered his talent were it not for a tragedy that befell the Breguet family when little Abraham-Louis (or Abram-Louis in the local dialect) was eleven years old.

Abraham-Louis had been born, on January 10, 1747, to an extended family in Neuchâtel, a small city north of Geneva that was built primarily of lake sandstone, which gave the buildings a yellow cast that led Alexandre Dumas to describe it as a "an immense toy carved out of butter." The town nestles against the base of Mount Chaumont along the vast Lake Neuchâtel, where most of the low-lying farmland was reclaimed from the water[43] and a stately, palatial collegiate church tower still chimes the hours.

Breguet went to schools in the area but was neither a very precise nor an eager student. In fact, according to contemporary histories, "he appeared hopelessly stupid, and his masters agreed that he was deficient in intellect;" the "young man received his instructions with great repugnance."[44] His father, Jonas-Louis, was a merchant – he sold lace and bobbins and cloth — and the boy lived a life of relative comfort, first in the city and later at his family's inn at Les Verrieres, near Switzerland's border with France. At the inn, purchased by his father in order to gain some financial security and to be closer to his family in the area, young Abraham-Louis spent his evenings listening to travelers and merchants passing through as they described the lights of Paris or the mighty ships of Seville.

47

It would have been an uneventful youth, but in early 1758 his father died of an unknown illness (probably influenza), leaving four children and a pregnant wife, Suzanne-Marguerite. She had already lost two baby boys in recent years, and Jonas-Louis' death pushed the family into despair. It was decided that they would move from the inn back into town, where they would be closer to the extended clan, and the family began looking for a new husband for the widow — someone who could keep the family comfortable while she raised the children.

That summer, Suzanne-Marguerite married her husband's cousin, a handsome twenty-nine-year-old soldier named Jacques Tattet. Abraham-Louis, now twelve, moved with his family to a wide-gabled house in town, and never attended school again. Though struggling with the loss of his father, his new stepfather intrigued the boy. A lieutenant-captain in the militia, Tattet had studied watchmaking and now had a watch export business that sold Genevese watches to customers in Paris. Tattet, however, wished the trade were the other way around. Disappointed with the quality of most mass-produced Swiss watches, he was enamored with the work coming out of France in those years and so, with his siblings' help, pointed his efforts at Versailles where he could both sell his wares and spy on the watchmakers already working in the state of the art.

The Tattet brothers aspired to a higher echelon. Their name was already well known in Paris and Geneva, and their small firm enjoyed the favor of the French court. Now, they sought still more visibility in that burgeoning and lucrative market. They visited Paris often, and in 1762 they decided that young Abraham-Louis would leave home and school to become an apprentice to a watchmaker in Les Verrieres and then in Neuchâtel, with the expectation that eventually he would join his stepfather and uncles on their trips to the French capital. Having shown little interest in formal education, the boy now had to help support the family. He left his small town and took to the bench, beginning his apprenticeship by cleaning the workshop and organizing and polishing the parts that arrived from the various mountain farms.

The apprenticeship would have appealed to any adolescent boy. Watchmakers' lives weren't all hard work. They were lured from shop to shop with promises of riches, long weekends in the country, private clubs in which to relax, and, in one instance, a master who promised a "new hat with a gold border and a new peruke" to his new employees. They were feted, lauded, and considered singularly respectable in the pantheon of eighteenth-century professions.

Adventure, too, awaited them. Watchmakers were held for ransom by Barbary pirates so often that when travelling by ship, they wrote clauses into their contracts stating that their employer would pay for their freedom if and only if that they would not give up their watches to the captors.[45] Jacques Barthelemy, the grandson of the founder of the watch house Vacheron Constantin (then called Vacheron-Chossat), found "banditry" and frontier justice to be another threat to the watchmaker. While travelling to Rome through northern Italy, he found human "arms and legs nailed to posts, as a sign to travelers that brigands had been executed there because they had committed murder." Luckily the watchmakers lost no limbs on the journey.

Dangers aside, a skilled craftsman could make a nice living, even without a full gentleman's education. Breguet's family had been nearly destitute before Tattet stepped in, and if the boy showed even a modicum of talent, he could make good money in the storefronts of London and Paris. Watchmakers typically made 20-25 Swiss francs a day, compared with 3-4 francs for the average craftsman.

The process of entering the guild was arduous, requiring seven years of apprenticeship — five as a water boy, fire tender, and, eventually, beginning watchmaker, and then two travelling from master to master to learn specific techniques including goldsmithing, plate production, and enameling. The more ambitious watchmakers went on to learn the art of complications and often were required to produce a series of complicated watches — watches with multiple features including chimes, moonphase registers, and perpetual calendars — as a final test before being afforded journeyman status. Even as journeymen, however, they were still forced to work under a supervisor who would sign and sell all of the watches in a particular shop.

A watchmaker's training included the creation of parts from whole metal. One test of watchmaking prowess asked the students prepare a miniature rod, adding facets, points, arcs, and holes to a piece of steel the size of a toothpick. This, in turn, led to the carving of hands and fine springs from pure steel, creating thinner and more brittle objects until the student could do it consistently without the aid of machines.

From the moment Abraham-Louis began his apprenticeship under Tattet's tutelage[46] he took to watchmaking with unusual zeal. Even as an apprentice, it was clear that he had a flair for the scientific and talents in astronomy and mathematics as well as drafting. His hurried drawings were primitive but effective – just a few slashes on a sheet of paper often distilled extremely complex concepts – and his formal drawings were wondrously detailed. This talent for design gave him a distinct advantage. Because most watchmakers were not formally trained, an understanding of the rudiments of physics and optics was enough to turn an unschooled bench worker into a skilled craftsman and businessman. With a bit of study, the Tattets decided, young Abraham-Louis would become an excellent watch designer.

Watchmaking could be a frustrating and expensive proposition. Each individual piece came from a sheet of metal — usually brass but sometimes gold or silver — and had to be painstakingly cut out, milled, and polished. Safety systems on machines were primitive at best, and when a drill or grinder overshot the mark, an entire day's work could be ruined. The tips of the tools only barely touched the metal in most cases, nipping off thin slices of brass, silver, or gold in a rapid, repetitive motion that could best be described as a dance – a turn, a slide, a return to the start. Gears, for example, were first cut or stamped out as metal disks and then placed on another cutter that moved the disk an infinitesimally short distance to the next spot for the drill or file to come down and cut away a notch. Only a patient and delicate hand could coax the finest and most ornate of shapes out of otherwise imperfect metal. The tools employed, which are still in use today, removed just enough metal from a surface to allow for the addition of gears or jewels or the creation of beautifully engraved surfaces.

The watchmakers who worked at the *fabrique*, or watch factory, were called *fabriquers*, and unlike, for example, dressmakers or wigmakers to the wealthy who worked tirelessly behind the scenes to bring glamour to the merchant's wife or the baroness, these *fabriquers* enjoyed a quality of life and education shared by few other craftsmen. Because they mingled with the aristocracy, it was expected that they understand philosophy, politics, and science. During the day, many of them would sit working by the large windows of their ateliers while one of them would read aloud from the newspaper or a book, a habit copied later by *lectores* in tobacco factories in the New World who read the news of the day to busy rollers.

Breguet quickly learned that every clock and watch consisted of the same three parts: a power source, a transmission system, and a register. The power source could be anything that kept the timepiece running: a bucket of water, a spring, a tireless squirrel on a wheel. Pendulum clocks, for example, used a wound spring or cable that pulled a gear down and around and actuated the pendulum itself. Clocks could run on water, air, or heat — anything that could deliver energy to the works.

The tiny wheel that spins back and forth in most modern watches – and some made during Breguet's time – was called the balance wheel. The balance wheel was like a round pendulum. The escapement pushed it in one direction, stopped it, and after it had returned to its original position, the process was repeated, *ad infinitum*. A small spring connected to the wheel ensured that the balance moved only so far and returned at a regular interval.

The transmission system, better known as the escapement — literally a device that allowed the energy stored in the spring to "escape" at a preset interval — converted the power source into a set of ticks. It was the speed of the escapement that defined how a clock or watch's seconds hand would move. Slower escapements released their energy once per second, creating the tick-tock of a grandfather clock. Modern escapements "tick" at up to ten times per second, creating the illusion that the seconds hand is sweeping slowly across the face of the dial. While today watchmakers pride themselves on building high frequency movements, in Breguet's time a *mort* hand, or dead-beat seconds hand, was a complication that forced the hand to tick once a second and was highly sought after because it reminded the wearer of the reassuring tick-tock of an old chamber clock.

Many early watches used gut or chains to transfer the power of the mainspring to the escapement. This system, called the *fusee* or "cone," ensured that the watch remained accurate throughout its unwinding cycle. It consisted of a mainspring and a cone attached to each other with a thin chain. As the wearer wound the watch, the chain would climb up the cone until it reached the top and then unwind, slowly, releasing steadily more slack. It acted like a governor on an engine, allowing the spring to mete out equal amounts of energy at all times, and appeared in Leonardo Da Vinci's drawings as early as 1405. These tiny chains were the Achilles heel of a good watch. They would break on winding or wear out after a few months of use. They also made watches awkwardly thick because the cones had to be quite tall to take up all of the chain.

The final part of a watch was the register or face. The hands, time, and date readouts, and moon phase information were all registers, and each depended on the hummingbird heartbeat of the power source and the transmission.

Looking closely at an open watch, Breguet could see components arrayed in a pattern inscrutable to anyone but the watch's maker. There could be no wasted space, no misalignment, and no sense that anything could be added or removed without destroying the harmony of the whole. A watch's shapes and curves put one in mind of the natural world of shells and planets. If the object was made by a master, it would work for years, decades, even centuries, given proper care. Watches, then, could be considered true perpetual motion machines in that they would stay constantly in motion if certain conditions were met. But almost none of those conditions were present in the eighteenth century. Damp, cold, mud, grit, and inferior oil usually gummed up the works, and the hand of a bad watchmaker could consign a good watch to an even worse fate.

In less than a year, the precocious boy was chafing at the limits of what the Neuchâtel watchmakers could teach him, and Tattet decided to send his stepson to Versailles for further training. This decision was partially financial. The long road between Neuchâtel and Versailles took a week to travel by stagecoach, and Tattet deemed it necessary to have someone he could trust at Versailles who could take orders and make repairs inside the heart of the French court. Ever since Louis XIV had made Versailles his home in the early eighteenth century, French kings rarely travelled outside the palace's plush and luxurious confines. Within Versailles, Louis XV and his retinue were safe from the constant scrutiny of Parisian court life. Paris merchants vying for a royal commission had to travel there to ply their trade.

At Versailles, Breguet's apprenticeship continued under a prominent Swiss watchmaker whom the Tattets knew, but within two years, Abraham-Louis had exhausted this teacher's knowledge as well. He had grown considerably in intellect and discipline. While many watchmakers focused on one aspect of the watch — the *ebauche*, the complications, the hands or face — Breguet showed an overall understanding of each interfacing part, ensuring he could build a watch from start to finish. The boy had a singular aptitude for taking and using everything he learned, and he had the unusual ability to express every aspect of the watch in both written form and through drafting. His notebooks were full of designs for watches, along with detailed descriptions of various complications – the self-winding feature known as the *perpetuelle*, for example – as well as discussions of historical examples of previous versions of his work. He did not like to boast. Many of his creations "were kept secret for a long time, not for the sake of secrecy as many thought at the time, but merely out of modesty."[47]

This formerly poor student was now hungry for knowledge. When his first apprenticeship ended, he asked to stay on. "Master, I have a favor to ask of you," he said. "I am sensible that I have not employed all my time to the best of my ability, in your service, and I wish to be allowed to work three months more, under you, without salary."[48] He stayed the three months.

He still hungered to study under one of the truly great horologists of the age, men he sometimes glimpsed, from a distance, arriving by gilded fiacre at Versailles to perform their duties as *horlogers du roi*. In particular, he wanted to learn about pocket watches.

Seeing an opportunity, Breguet's stepfather moved the boy from Versailles to Paris, where he arranged for Abraham-Louis to continue his training on the Quai de l'Horloge, as apprentice to a series of master pocket watchmakers. The intention was to build the Breguet brand in Paris, where the rich were notoriously desperate in their attempts to impress at court. The uncountable dukes, earls, and courtiers often wore a different outfit each day with accessories to match, and to fail to appear with a beautiful pocket watch was akin to arriving at court without pants.

Watchmakers like Berthoud were attempting to simplify and reduce the movements that they were churning out in their shops. For example, bridges, the pieces that held the wheels and gears in place and acted as a structural support for the entire mechanism, were often superfluous and added weight and thickness to the watch movement. A clock movement — all large plates and minuscule gears — was quite elegant in its simplicity, but the same could not be said of a watch movement. Because of the more confined space, watch movements were much denser and had little room to breathe, as it were. So, to reduce overall size, the trick was to either skeletonize the movement — to remove superfluous metal from around the pinions and leave only the essential parts intact — or to create an entirely new form of bridge with only a few essential parts.

This tendency to simplify often ran counter to the prevailing conception of mechanical beauty. Some watches were decorated throughout, with even certain hidden parts covered in fine carvings of leaves, flowers, and birds. Such ostentation, while impressive to the viewer, weakened the metal if taken to zealous extremes. Some watches were so delicately carved that their cases looked like rotten lace when rust and rough treatment took their toll.

Under the masters in Versailles, Breguet learned important lessons about tool making. Whereas previously every watch was unique and almost completely hand-made, the state of the art now was based on tools and reproducible parts. The use of tools to grind gears and watch screws made it possible for Abraham-Louis to dream, subversively, of one day creating a "popular" watch — for everyone, not just the upper classes.

His apprenticeships meant long hours at a watch-smith's bench. The day started early. He tended the fires and prepared the workspace for the rest of the crew, young men who, like him, were usually untrained and uneducated, giving Breguet a slight advantage due to his natural talent. As they carved the gears and gear plates, Breguet fetched metal or did menial tasks like polishing fasteners or watching the enameling kiln and preparing pieces of metal for refining. He would not repair or even begin his own watch for another few years, even though it was clear that he had a unique eye for the complex and miniature machinery that his masters dealt in.

Because light meant everything in a workshop, he quickly learned how to follow the sun as it moved through the atelier, helping the watchmakers turn to receive direct rays as they worked. Watchmaking by candlelight was possible, but not preferable. The flickering flame could trick even the steadiest hand into dropping a screw into the wrong hole or snapping a gear as it was being polished, forcing the watchmaker to start over again from scratch. A single slip could result in a movement being completely destroyed, and watchmakers had to extensively practice creating their own tools and replacement parts, preparing rods, wheels, and gears over and over again until they got them absolutely right.

Even benches were strictly codified, and most were made

of mahogany or birch. Cedar was forbidden as, one watchmaker noted, "it exudes a sort of gum which forms a sticky deposit on work and tools, and rapidly spoils any lubricating oil that may be exposed to it."[49] Instead harder woods were used and even these became worn and broken with age and use.

Few tradesmen had enough patience to complete these seemingly menial and repetitive tasks, and it was rare to find someone who could accept constant criticism while still maintaining accuracy and thinking about the creative use of limited space. But the best watchmakers knew that their work was unique in every way; they viewed each new watch as a challenge to be engineered rather than as a commodity to be stamped out. This mindset encouraged ceaseless tinkering and improvement of the movements and led to the inclusion, in some watches, of tiny automata such as twittering birds and harp-plucking maidens. If a watchmaker could create a calendar that would stay accurate for centuries without having to be reset, it was fairly trivial to create a watch that displayed a small dog wagging its tail or an erotic scene involving a vicar and one of his more fulsome congregants.

While the average watch took perhaps a week to build, the more complex and expensive pieces took considerably longer. In many cases, complex watches were passed from watchmaker to watchmaker, and each piece, starting with the internal mechanism or movement, was added on in a sort of slow accretion. When a particularly thorny problem arose like the addition of a complication to an already complicated watch, watchmakers spent weeks staring through a loupe each day until the sky darkened and the workers could no longer see, weeks requiring absolute and unflagging concentration and, if the watchmaker was creating a timepiece from scratch without the aid of the master's pre-drawn plans, a flair for invention.

To the untrained eye, these eighteenth-century movements looked less like mechanical things than ornate manuscripts, full of curlicues and dashes, odd shapes and runes etched into the metal, identifying the maker and his employees in miniscule graffito. After repairs watchmakers would inscribe the date and type of maintenance performed on a watch on the inside of the case — small notes from the past to the future, enabling watchmakers to follow each other's work even when they were separated by time and space. The notes could be coded dates or a watchmaker's initials or an invoice number, for when the watch was separated from its case for repair.

From Versailles Breguet moved to the Clock Dock where he studied under both Berthoud and Lépine. His most auspicious tutelage, however, came from Abbot Joseph-François Marie, a professor of mathematics and physics at College Mazarin. Officially named *Collège des Quatre-Nations*, the college was part of the University of Paris and consisted of sixty students from all over the French empire. Designed as a collecting school for citizens from countries without a university system, it taught its scholars French deportment, math, and science.

The Abbot also taught the young Breguet how to comport himself around royalty, an essential skill.[50] While the average watchmaker needed little outside training — rarely being called upon to create anything more than the standard two-handed clock that perhaps chimed the hours and showed the minutes in the day — a watchmaker like Breguet would be expected to create watches with multiple complications, requiring unique skills and education to understand how to re-create these mathematical formulas mechanically and how miniature calendars and astronomical charts found in larger clocks could be shrunk into watches more efficiently.

One such complication was solar mean time — the time indicated by the sun, as opposed to the time on a standard twenty-four-hour clock. Because of intrinsic problems with the Gregorian calendar in the acceptance of the twenty-four-hour day, the measured length of a day often differed by up to sixteen minutes in either direction from the solar length of the day (meaning the time from when the sun was at high noon to when the moon was at its apex). All Breguet had to do was look at a sundial to be reminded of the problem. When the shadow of the sundial's style was gone, meaning the sun was directly overhead, there was a slight and measurable difference between solar mean time and normally indicated twenty-four-hour time. This discrepancy, which was important in measuring the actual time at a given location, was solved, in watches, by adding a bean-shaped cog traced by an indicator hand. The indicator showed the mean solar time — plus or minus up to fifteen minutes — as the date wheel spun. This ingenious solution — essentially creating a miniature representation of the ovoid rotation of the earth around the sun — made possible a number of improvements in timekeeping during Breguet's lifetime.

Years passed and Breguet progressed from apprentice to journeyman quickly. By his twenty-seventh year he was an intellectual juggernaut on the Clock Dock, taking up commissions that frightened other watchmakers. Breguet now had the technical acumen to try to address many of the problems that horology faced including the reduction of friction, the measurement of the heavens, and the general stability of clockwork in rough conditions. He needed the kinds of commissions that could fund such exploration.

Luckily, the Breguet's tutor, the Abbot, was close to the French court and brought young Breguet's watches on visits with the king and queen. With obvious pride he would pull a Breguet from his folds and consult it during the day, mentioning that the maker of his favorite timepieces was a young Swiss artisan named Abraham-Louis. Soon, Breguet was called before the court himself, and a lucrative business bloomed.

Breguet in his prime was handsome in an elfin sort of way and his quiet company and reliable discretion were highly sought after in many circles. It was at court that he met the Polignac family and it was also here that he would meet Axel von Fersen, whose respect and admiration were intertwined with his company's eventual success. It was during the waning years of Louis XV and the ascension to power of Louis XVI that Breguet ingratiated himself with the court, a move that eventually led to his royal commission, which freed the young watchmaker from the toil and drudgery of more retail-minded work. Complicated watches of the sort Breguet was making were expensive, and only in the rarefied air of the French court could he find willing and eager buyers.

Breguet was soon leading a team of watchmakers who were creating some of the most complex clocks and watches of their day. He dressed less like a purveyor of royal watches than a shopkeeper, going about Paris with a high collar pulled up on his dark coat and his hair, and increasingly bald pate, hidden by a cap.

Under Louis XIV, the Sun king, Versailles had been not only the heart of fashion and interior design but also the nexus of watchmaking in France. The first Renaissance clocks had disappeared from the royal possessions before the 1700s — most were made of precious metals and melted down during dips in cash flow. But other clocks survived, including turret clocks based on a German design with attractive but not overly delicate frieze patterns applied to the corners and faces of the hexagonal body. One clock, built in 1696, featured a "rich throne" on which sat a miniature

Louis XIV, surrounded by a procession of "Electors of the German States, and the princes and dukes of Italy," while the kings of Europe appeared out of a small window and chimed a bell, then retiring after paying homage to the Sun king with a curt bow. Because of the unyielding will of William III of England, the clockmaker designed that king's mannequin to bow much lower than the others, thereby pleasing the French monarch. However, this extra dip put a strain on the mechanism and one afternoon, during a public exhibition with the king present, the clock broke. Instead of bowing, the French king fell prostrate before the English king while the clock ground and springs clanged inside. The clockmaker was locked up in the Bastille.

Another clock played an hourly chime and featured a small statue of Louis XIV that, on the hour, received a miniature crown from a winged figure of Victory while a cock at the top of the clock flapped its wings and two sentinels appeared to protect the newly crowned king.

From the ridiculous came the sublime. Under the rule of Louis XVI, a distinctive style of French clock evolved. The movements might be sourced elsewhere (most came from Switzerland, although German movements were also popular), but French case makers saw the clock as a part of a whole, something to be connected, stylistically, with the tables, chairs, and commodes in a room. A clock was not a separate device, toiling away in obscurity. It was a room's lighthouse and center of attention and so played an important role in the French household. It tolled the hours, kept the master's appointments, and kept order in the social whirl that was Versailles and Paris.

Louis XVI and Marie-Antoinette owned hundreds of timepieces in their lifetime, mostly standard pocket watches and table clocks. Because Louis XVI, in particular, was enamored with technology, during his reign almost every room in the palace had a clock or watch running steadily throughout the day. In an era when a family might own one chamber clock — usually a repeater (a clock which chimed the hours when activated by a button) with a handle on top for easy transport — to fill a palace with clocks was unusual, even for a wealthy king.

Marie-Antoinette, strolling with her ladies-in-waiting from room to room, was exposed to a riot of styles, colors, and inspirations. One clock, complete with Medusas, reclining sphinxes, and a winged Apollo, looked more like a reliquary for spent time than a mere timepiece. The face of the clock itself was staid and out-of-place, for its dark case was covered in curlicues and engraved flowers; golden accents, so finely wrought as to appear vibrantly life-like, popped from the case's face; spiral feet shaped like narwhal horns completed the decadent picture.

Another clock looked like something from an astronomer's fever dream. Over two meters high, it featured a glass globe on the top containing a miniature representation of the solar system and the constellations of the zodiac. The face was chased with gold, and the gold hands looked like sprigs of herbs, while the seconds hand ticked around solidly. Marie-Antoinette was delighted by one feature especially: four tiny windows showing the year, date, month, and day above a unique moon-phase register with a jolly, if wan, moon peeking over two hills of gold.

In the Petit Trianon, the small palace that served as Marie-Antoinette's private redoubt, the clocks were smaller models, featuring a large white face and only a minimum of ornate gilding. Her taste was much more subdued than the Bourbon family's, and amid the oppressive complexity of her life, a clock ticking on a mantle offered quiet reassurance.

Even her dressing room was no safe harbor from time. One piece, a small jewelry box displaying a pair of courtiers at leisure, was topped by a small watch guarded by cherubs and crowned with a small bust of a young girl with flowing hair.

In an era of relative imprecision, all these clocks were kept in perfect synchronization. The king's day was regimented into an hourly plan with special times dedicated to church, affairs of state, and appearances before the people. The royal day was so codified, particularly during the rule of Louis XIV, that members of the citizenry were given leave to watch the king go to bed in a special ceremonial chamber.

And so, among the army of assistants and handymen at Versailles, were the *horlogers du roi*. The *horloger* on duty made rounds daily, winding each clock and setting it according to the Regulator — a large-faced watch with the hour hand on one register and the minute hand on another smaller one — that he would carry with him. These portable Regulators were a copy of the larger Regulator clocks that most watchmakers kept on their walls, some of them so well-made that they lasted an entire year without winding.[51] Most of the watches that Versailles' many courtiers carried had to be set in the same way whenever they stopped, which was often.

The draftiness of Versailles posed another challenge: While not as difficult as maintaining a clock onboard a ship or in a carriage clattering over rough European roads, ensuring precision in areas of varying temperature and humidity was a struggle. Royal watchmakers also had to deal with broken crystals, snagged gears, and shattered enamel from watches that revelers dropped on the palace's cold marble floors.

At Versailles, the *horlogers du roi* were considered *valets de chambre* and, as such, were given access to the king's quarters at eight o'clock each morning, a time when the king was expected to at least feign a deep sleep before being officially awoken by courtiers. There were usually only three *horlogers* appointed at any one time, and each received two-hundred livres for four months of service a year, splitting the year into thirds. While for the most part they were glorified clock inspectors, their position of power and access to the king's intimate spaces made them an important part of the king's day. In addition, they received from their guild permission to cast bronze – a unique privilege in a guild system that compartmentalized the trades. Watchmakers could not, for instance, cast gold, because that would impinge on the goldsmith's guild, while lockmakers were eventually forbidden from doing clockwork. The king's watchmakers also received a workspace at the Louvre and could hire as many assistants as they wanted. Thus, securing this official appointment ensured a brisk trade.

The ascension of Louis and Marie to the throne took place just when watches were approaching almost a public mania in France. If clocks symbolized success and comfort, then the new pocket watches signified the ultimate version of those attainments. To own a watch was to be connected with the adventure in the New World and to take part in the burgeoning interest in science and technology. Watches weren't just talismans of power. They were now icons of a new, forward-looking era marked by exploration and intellectual inquiry.

As such, they were a staple of literate conversation and naturally on the mind of a well-bred young man making his Grand tour. In Basel, Axel Fersen had been amused to learn that the town clock always ran an hour fast, supposedly ever since the magistrate had learned of plans to murder him and fooled the conspirators by changing the time. At Fernay, on the French border, a wrinkled, scarlet-waistcoated Voltaire had shown Fersen the part of his house where, as Fersen noted in his diary, the satirist put up "all the watchmakers of Geneva." A love of watches was by now trickling down even to the lower classes, and Fersen saw boys of school age running around with tin pocket watches of dubious quality.

Watches frequently served as gifts, and because one looked at them many times a day, they were often painted or inscribed with terms of endearment. Marie-Antoinette passed out fifty-two snuff boxes and fifty-one watches to the guests at her wedding in May 1770.

The Abbé Marie was responsible for introducing Breguet not only to Versailles but also to his future wife, Cécile-Marie-Louise L'huillier, a twenty-three-year-old beauty with whose family he was close. Their courtship was brief and the marriage itself on August 28, 1775, brought further advantages. The girl's older brother was an agent to the Comte d'Artois, Louis XVI's brother. Without such inter-family ties, Breguet would never have been able to move in the rarefied circles in which he now found himself. Tracing back the skein of happenstance that had brought him to this point must have been baffling and thrilling. If Breguet's father had not died, the boy would probably have stayed in Neuchâtel, perhaps becoming a merchant, or, if family tradition held, a pastor. Now, he was a watchmaker to the French court.

As his wife helped prepare the rooms of No. 51, on the Quai, as a home for their coming family, for the first time in years Breguet settled into a life of domestic happiness. His stepfather saw to it that he was kept in parts and *ebauche*, with regular shipments from Switzerland, and his family there kept up regular communications.

The French court would supply a ready stream of revenue for the company as it grew. The rise of Louis XVI to the throne made the economy "favorable to both the arts and commerce."[52] Even as dark clouds began to mass on the horizon, in the years leading up to the death of the old king, France enjoyed an economic boom. Joseph Marie Terray, Louis XV's finance minister, had increased government revenue – through a series of taxes and reforms – to about eighty million *livres* and reduced deficits to twenty-five million.[53] While his actions angered many French and led to the "flour war," a precursor to the Revolution caused by a rise of bread prices due to government control of reserve flour, the nobles had enough confidence to invest in a young man with a talent for watchmaking.

Breguet's goal was to reduce the size of his watches, at least partly by reducing the number of moving parts and their complexity. While the prevailing baroque style required a great deal of ornate millwork and engraving, Breguet was satisfied with the simplest movement possible. One of his watches contained a large mainspring, connected to a small, square key fitting for winding, and a strikingly simple movement — essentially a few gears connected to a large and finely wrought balance wheel, with a large regulating pin designed to improve the accuracy of the watch. Even in its simplicity, the watch also had a quarter repeater, which chimed the time to the nearest quarter hour. Everything superfluous had been removed — it was a machine designed for one purpose, with little, if any, ostentation, and was so different from the watches his colleagues were making that even masters on the Quai couldn't fathom or re-create the timepieces coming out of Breguet's shop.

Breguet's showroom filled up quickly with customers and employees. It was cramped, but for the time being, the attic atelier was sufficient for his needs. Breguet liked to keep his watchmakers busy making new and ever more impressive complications and often outsourced the assembly of his simpler watches, allowing him to dedicate his time to design and finishing.

Some of his watches made their way into the pockets of courtiers, but many ended up in harsher climates. The war in America was coming to a head, and soldiers of higher breeding needed watches to carry overseas. Breguet's timepieces, stripped of ornamentation and almost impervious to shock and damage, began riding in the coat pockets of allied soldiers bound from France to Boston and parts west.

The business grew steadily. Breguet started receiving regular commissions from royal courtiers, and dukes, ladies, and representatives of the king himself (to judge from the limited records that remain) frequented his shop.

Breguet's young family, too, seemed blessed. His first son, Antoine-Louis, was born in 1776, and two years later his wife gave birth again, to Francois-Louis. The boys were baptized in the church of Saint-Barthelemy, the small parish church of the Île de la Cité.[54] Like young Abraham-Louis, sitting in rapt attention at the feet of travelers at his father's Inn in Les Verrieres, the boys spent their days listening to watchmakers describe their discoveries and chat about politics and history. It was seemingly a charmed existence – a young watchmaker with a beautiful family, all living on the most magnificent street in the history of horological science. Breguet was soon selling *perpetuelles* to nearly everyone at court including the king and queen. He spent long hours at his bench, reveling in the opportunity to think carefully though the thorny problems of horology.

Then calamity struck. Francois-Louis died when he was two. Cecile-Marie-Louise was pregnant again, and gave birth to a girl, Charlotte, but the baby died only hours later. And then Cecile-Marie-Louise herself died on May 11, 1780, perhaps of fever. She was just twenty-eight.

Breguet's world snapped shut like a watchcase. He called for his young sister-in-law Suzanne-Elisabeth to come and raise his child. He would never remarry. The loss changed him, reducing his world to a few primary things – his watches, the business, and his long-term projects. Until then, he essentially ignored little Antoine-Louis. Breguet's wife had been his only love outside of the workshop. Now, he dedicated himself obsessively to the business and his clients, ensuring the shop's continued growth even after three shattering deaths in his small family.

The work was difficult. Fashion changed almost daily at court, and men and women both would clamor for one design one day and another completely different design the next. Breguet boldly removed all fashion-chasing from his watchmaking process, creating one of the first brands that stood on its own merit rather than reacting to national whimsy. No Breguet piece was alike – they did not mass-produce – and so every Breguet piece had its own unique construction but a definite and recognizable style.

As a young widower, he often received invitations to Versailles as well as to major salons in the city. He was also expected to attend balls at the behest of the queen. In this rarefied environment, Breguet found himself countless times proposing diamond-studded watches for the ladies (not for the queen, who loved pearls) — and gold or silver hunting watches for the men. The always business-like Breguet disliked, but tolerated, the extravagant frivolity of the balls.

His deference and understanding smile, even in the face of notoriously dissolute royal appointees, made him popular at court. He was close to a number of the most important men and women in the country, and his wide-ranging network of Swiss expatriates gave him entrée almost everywhere else. When he crossed the channel, a close friend and admirer, the delightfully named Mr. Disney-Flytche,[55] often gave Breguet a pocketbook full of banknotes "in order that he should be spared want when he came to England."[56]

The watchmakers at his shop usually cared for his young son and they treated the boy as one of their own even as his stern, taciturn father groomed him to become the next owner of the firm. He had large shoes to fill, as Breguet's shop was now a landmark for Paris' upper classes. From the beginning, Breguet kept a logbook of watch sales, and his notations ("*pour la reine*" — "for the queen" was a popular one) were a who's who of pre-revolutionary France, as well as a schematic history of timekeeping. He had risen far and fast and the watches he was making were as distant from the earliest clocks as the wooden club was from the flintlock rifle.

He was known on the Quai as a kind employer and a trustworthy shopkeeper, quick to laugh and to offer a young apprentice the chance to learn in a major house. He had a propensity to generosity. When a workman brought in a piece for inspection and then presented a bill, Breguet was said to have added a small tail to any final zeros, turning them into 9s. Young men in Breguet's factory were always encouraged with the words "Do not be discouraged, or allow failure to dishearten you."[57]

In the pantheon of stars on the Quai, Breguet would shine brightest. For that matter, by the estimation of his peers and customers at Versailles and beyond, he was the finest watchmaker anywhere. Known for his *perpetuelles*, for never making the same watch twice, for a fresh, modern style that combined technical and aesthetic innovation, he rose to fashion at a pivotal moment. The very concentration of wealth that was subtly beginning to tear France apart was fuelling a golden age of watches, and the very people for whom he was making those watches were running out of time.

Chapter 7

Meanwhile, in Versailles, the elite played by candlelight. It was a glorious night. Marie's closest friends, Fersen included, all dressed in white and retired to Petit Trianon. There, on the lush green lawn, they danced, drank, and wandered in a haze around the grounds. All through the night, the guests took a small ferryboat to and from the Temple de l'Amour in the heart of Marie-Antoinette's private garden. Lights burned at the foot of every bush, casting puckish shadows on the participants. Workers had dug a trench around the temple and lit a bonfire, making the whole structure look like it was floating in a sea of flame. King Gustav of Sweden, whom Fersen was accompanying in Europe, wrote to his brother that it was "a spectacle worthy of the Elysian fields."[58]

That evening, as the revelers unwound and the dark fell over the palace, Marie-Antoinette gave Fersen a datebook, embroidered by her own hand. In neat stitching, in perfect French, the queen of this fairy kingdom wrote her secret love a short poem:

"Faith, Love, and Hope
Three united forever."[59]

The page was dated June 21, 1784. That evening, a magical one to say the least, occurred at the apex of Fersen and Marie-Antoinette's close friendship. The intervening years had been hard on both the soldier and the queen. Fresh from the fields of Philadelphia, Fersen cast about Europe looking for work and love in

Paris. The queen faced increased scrutiny and she now retired to the Trianon with her children. She had changed much from the coquettish child bride Fersen met at the ball years before.

Fersen, too, was no longer the noble horsemen and icy lover. He was beset economically and emotionally. Marie-Antoinette's favor had cemented Fersen's position in her coterie of friends and, in many ways, made him hers forever. He searched heedlessly for something to light upon, and so on his return he petitioned his father to send him 100,000 livres to buy the Royal Suédois, a Swedish proprietary regiment stationed in France. In the 1700s, proprietary regiments were usually made up of mercenary fighters stationed in a foreign country and led by a non-French commander. While these regiments were military in nature – the Swiss Guards are a well-known proprietary regiment – they offered prestige and entrée to the owners. They brought some income, but as one historian points out, the current analog would be to a rich man owning a baseball team,[60] complete with the associated costs.

Only July 15, 1793, a year before the fete at Petit Trianon, many historians believe that Fersen and Marie-Antoinette became lovers. In his correspondence log, Fersen referred to her as "Josephine." In his diaries, he referred to her simply as "Elle": She. His diary notes he stayed "chez Elle." He used the word *chez* when he meant a sexual dalliance and *Elle*, as we know, was always and forever Marie-Antoinette. Did he and the queen make love in the octagonal *meridienne* bedroom that warm summer?[61] While all signs point to a consummated passion that year, least of all the commission left with Breguet, and, though much of Fersen's diary was destroyed from those romantic years, we know he yearned for her all his life and that their relationship was closer than most assumed. Further proof appeared in another letter Fersen wrote to his sister describing buying "Josephine" a puppy. In the same month Marie herself describes her new puppy in detail in another letter, thus confirming the Josephine connection. With evidence as obviously circumstantial as this it is difficult to assess the truth. However, all historians agree on one thing: the two were, in the end, as close as blood.

That summer Fersen could not stay in France. His father called him back to Sweden and it was torture. During Fersen's next five weeks in Paris, the soldier was able to see the queen often, spending many evenings at Petit Trianon. Their relationship intensified, and when he left Paris in August, headed back to Stockholm with Gustav, he wrote six letters to Marie in the first nine days. Thus they continued to speak, even as miles and situation separated them. They were lovers crossed by more than one dark star.

Fersen visited Versailles again in May of 1785, and over the next several years would spend extended periods in Paris; rumors spread that he and Marie would meet secretly at the Petit Trianon, arriving separately on horseback. In 1787 the queen gave Fersen a Breguet *perpetuelle* with a guilloché-engraved dial and the intertwined letters A and F engraved on the case.

When Fersen couldn't be with her, as during one eight month period when he toured Italy and during extended stays in Sweden, he still wrote frequently to her, and she to him. He numbered every letter to her, so she could be certain that every one had reached her. To ensure privacy, they used couriers and intermediaries. Later he wrote using invisible ink or in a fairly simple keyed cipher. They hid their correspondence by forwarding letters within letters. Fersen might mail a friend in Paris who would then open the letter and forward another envelope inside to the queen. In 1789, she gave him her portrait and a small pocketbook with a flyleaf inscription by her.

In the intervening years Marie-Antoinette was taking care of two sons, the sickly Dauphin Louis Joseph, the hearty and robust Louis Charles, and a daughter, Marie-Therese. She was also mourning another daughter, Sophie Helene, who died at one year. Unlike her mother, Marie-Antoinette was reasonably protected from violence and unpleasantness in her youth. Now, as if fulfilling her mother's portents of "worry and sorrow" that had she felt when her daughters first married, she had since faced miscarriages, false accusations of theft and sexual depravity, and now entered the maw of the people's anger.

In 1789, revolution began in earnest. In July, the Paris mob ransacked aristocrats' homes, and the Bastille fell. August brought the abolition of privileges and the "declaration of the rights of man and the citizen." In October, the mob stormed Versailles, and the royal family fled for the Palais des Tuileries. Fersen was in the procession of carriages that choked the road, ever by his queen's side.

The events soon took their toll on the king and queen. Louis

XVI suffered a nervous collapse, and Marie's hair began to turn white. Fersen would spend the next year and a half in Paris, continuing to meet secretly with the queen in her chambers as various plans to save the monarchy were proposed and abandoned. In October, the royal family finally decided they needed to leave Paris, and Fersen began to plot Marie's escape.

With France's economic crisis deepening, Breguet was increasingly casting his sights abroad to foreign markets. But he remained very much in the royals' orbit, selling Louis XVI a watch in 1784, and the one Marie would give Fersen in 1787.

As that love affair developed, Breguet found himself focusing more and more on Fersen's order, now called the 160 because it was the 160th commission entered in his firm's ledgers. As the watch took shadowy form, Breguet studied its increasingly complex movement, penetrating the three-dimensional structure with his mind and playing a kind of spatial chess: If he put this complication here, then he would have to put that complication there, which would then mean that yet another complication would need to change position, and on and on. Moments when Breguet could meditate, at length, on the unique challenges of a singular timepiece were the times when he felt most alive. While he found mass production an alluring concept — he dreamed of a day when all men could own a good watch, preferably with the Breguet name on it — the prospect of filling his days stamping out cookie-cutter watches was dispiriting. What he loved was exploration, the creation of new complications and the addition of one complication to the next.

With the 160, the challenge was less in the fabrication of the parts, or even in their assembly, than in the daunting geometries of fitting so many intricate, interlocking parts into such a small space, and having them work properly. By now Breguet had facility with a large and widening range of complications including the perfection of the *perpetuelle* to the extent that it could now be considered a mass-market addition to a common watch. Many of these complications he had himself invented or refined during nearly two decades in which he had both made his name and experienced devastation that might have crippled another man — but seemed only to spur Breguet to greater heights of his art. He was, in these turbulent years, rising to a fame that would later spur jealousy, spite, and, ultimately, inspire a thief.

68

Chapter 8

Jerusalem

Near midnight on April 15, 1983, a small car rolled unnoticed through down HaPalmach Street in Katamon, a leafy suburb west of the Jerusalem's Old City. Katamon, spread over a cluster of hills, had long been home to Israel's elite. They favored the area's expansive gardens and twisting tree-lined streets, and it was far from the tumult of the city. It was Friday night and the streets were empty as families prepared for the sabbath.

By day, residents were accustomed to seeing caravans of long, dark state cars threading their way to the Presidential Palace, located in the heart of the district. But few ventured into these parts at night and foot traffic was scarce. While the days were often broken by the loud clarion calls of the presidential guard welcoming visiting potentates with trumpets, the evenings were quiet and undisturbed.

The car, a tiny French Simca 1000,[62] continued north along HaPalmach Street. It slowed as it neared the back of a pale, three-story building, which housed the L.A. Mayer Museum of Islamic Art. Constructed from coarse, beige Jerusalem stone, the museum resembled a strikingly well-preserved Egyptian temple. A broad set of stairs rose to the entrance, and two wings of galleries extended behind it, forming a courtyard in the rear that was invisible from the street.

For almost a decade the museum had mostly played host to Jerusalem's school children and the odd Islamic scholar. It was too far from the tourist center for most sightseers, and only odd buffs

and collectors who knew its secrets made the trip past the old walls
of the city to this posh district. About fifteen-thousand visitors
trod its halls that year, many of them Muslims who were amazed
by the richness of the Islamic collection. One visitor, a "West Bank
sheikh," found the exhibits to be exhilarating, noting in a newspaper article in 1974 that "The world thinks of us Muslims as being
men of the desert, with no culture of our own. Seeing what I have
today, I now know better."[63]

The museum, however, was hardly a likely target for a thief –
the Korans, textiles, and Ottoman edicts or *firmans*, while histori-
cally priceless, wouldn't interest the traditional burglar as it would
be possible to resell them to only the most reckless of collectors.
They would be identified immediately and the thief would be
caught. But here he was, idling briefly, assessing the scene before
popping the car back into gear.

The driver steered the car right onto a service road flanking
the near side of the museum, then right into a small parking lot
behind it. The car slid into a parking space and the engine cut out
with a cough. The driver switched off the lights, and a moment
later he stepped out onto the pavement. He was whippet-thin and
sandy-haired and he moved with purpose. He blinked rapidly,
letting his eyes adjust to the darkness.

He had chosen this time and place carefully. The east side of
the building abutted a tree-shrouded retirement center, and to the
north was an empty lot. The museum had closed early that day and
the surrounding streets were empty. After assuring himself that no
one was watching, the man moved confidently toward the building
and disappeared into a narrow passage, which led from the parking
lot into the inner courtyard.

A heavy steel gate blocked his passage, but the man was
prepared. He approached the gate and ran his fingers over the
bars, their institutional green paint gleaming dully in the lamp-
light.

Over the previous few months he had filled his home with
equipment and wrote out detailed plans in a set of spiral-bound
notebooks. To stay slim and alert he drank fruit juices and ate a
little vegetarian food most evenings. He trained himself to work
quickly and quietly and with little sleep. He kept strong and lithe,
exercising on a handmade gym cobbled out of pipes and makeshift
weights.

Now he was ready.

He carried with him a collection of odd tools he used for these sorts of jobs and, after listening carefully for a moment, he brought out a metal apparatus he had used many times before to ease his way into tight spots: a hydraulic jack. He inserted the jack between two of the bars and pumped the handle. Slowly, the bars spread apart, the jack releasing a muted hiss, which was quickly swallowed by the evening breeze. The man turned sideways to the gate and squeezed through the opening.

Chapter 9

Paris

One bright summer morning in 1784, a few months after Breguet, now thirty-seven, received the title of master Watchmaker from the notoriously protective Parisian Guild, king Louis XVI called him into his study to place a royal commission. It was unusual for the king to make such a request directly – he placed most orders by post and sent notes to the city requesting tools for himself and baubles for the queen.[64]

The king already owned many Breguet pieces, mostly pocket watches with white faces and the trademark blued Breguet hands shaped like small, closed poppies, a detail much beloved by Breguet's customers. But now he wanted something special — the "perfect watch," he told Breguet.

It was clear that the king didn't expect much of an answer, perhaps an obsequious agreement and a bill, later on, when the "perfect" watch arrived at Versailles. But instead of scraping and bowing, the serious if distracted watchmaker answered truthfully within his capacity as watchmaker to the king. He knew there could be no perfect watch, for nothing he tried in his efforts to remove friction — from adding jewels to the pivots in order to reduce the contact of metal on metal, to polishing every spindle and gear, to shrinking the parts — got rid of it altogether. Instead of a bow and a quick retreat, Breguet contemplated the request for a moment. "Provide me the perfect oil, Sire," he said finally, "and I will provide you the perfect watch."

When Breguet was coming up as an apprentice, he had seen

firsthand the extent to which friction impeded the advance of the watchmaker's art. Friction was the bête noire of watchmakers, an ever-present, entropic force working to shorten the life of a watch and diminish its accuracy. Each gear inside the watch that met with another – and that meant all of them – was affected by friction. Because of friction, the rubbing of metal on metal slowed the clock down and would eventually cause the whole mechanism to seize. Because of friction, gears could slip, and teeth and pivots could be rubbed away. Given enough time, a watch movement could conceivably turn into a pile of metal powder.

Breguet's predecessors had tried to combat the problem using solutions that could themselves be problematic. For centuries, the inner mechanisms of watches and clocks had been made of iron, and in an effort to mitigate friction watchmakers lubricated them with animal or fish oil (which is why some older clocks still stink of mackerel). But the oil itself would seize and bind, creating a gummy glue that kept gears from turning and left timepieces with an unpleasant odor — thus Breguet's plea for the perfect oil.

In an effort to find a new and better way, at a time when watches were becoming both more ornate and more precise, watchmakers began using rubies at pivot points for the gears. Although these polished jewels were considered rarities, they possessed a "hardness and capability of taking a high polish"[65] that metal parts didn't have, often didn't require oil, and were relatively immune to temperature changes. There were a number of types of jewels, including "hole" jewels that kept wheel axles (called arbors) in place, and cap jewels that tipped arbors inside their holes. Jewelers eventually also used pallet jewels on the tiny fork that drives the escape wheel and, in turn, spins the registers. In all cases, the jewels acted as a sort of "glove" or cap to prevent metal from touching metal.

Similarly, watchmakers began polishing almost every surface of their creations both for aesthetic reasons and because smooth surfaces meant less friction. In Switzerland, what came to be called the Geneva style — beveled edges, mirrored surfaces, and minuscule tolerances between parts — was invented, presaging the science of precision instruments by almost a half-century.

Friction was only one of several issues confronting watchmakers. Others included the effects of gravity, the fragility of these increasingly intricate timepieces, and the tendency of watches to expand as their mechanical innards became more complex.

One of Breguet's masters, Jean-Antoine Lépine, made one of the great leaps forward in reducing watch size. He had originally been a master at enamel-work, and as an enamelist, he knew that bulbous watches in rounded cases were almost impossible to cover in colored glass. What he needed was a flat, large watch onto which he might place his designs and drawings.

His great innovation was the Lépine caliber, the piano key caliber that reduced the main plate in a movement to little more than a few crossed pieces of metal. Over the years, watches had become thicker and thicker, with some watches approaching two centimeters from front to back. Lépine, after experimenting with different gearing systems, eventually created his caliber, a flat, disconnected series of small metal plates or bridges that simply held the gears in place. The difference in movements was striking. Prior to Lépine's invention, watch movements looked like thick sandwiches of metal held together with little pillars of brass or iron — in short, they looked like miniaturized mantle clocks. Lépine's first improved bridge looked like that same sandwich stripped of its filling — the gears and the springs — and spread out on a plate. The rearrangement allowed watches to be thinner and offered "economical advantages, and removal of the *fusee* also eliminated an important source of friction."[66]

Gravity, too, continued to bedevil watchmakers. With a clock's pendulum, the arc of motion was constant. However, watches used spring a with a balance wheel, which served the same regulating function by "swinging" quickly back and forth. Gravity, especially when compounded by the haphazard position of a timepiece bouncing around in an aristocrat's pocket, could distort the wheel's equilibrium, causing the watch to run slow or fast.

Gravity in the form of a watch hitting a hard marble floor could also put an end to a nicely ticking Breguet or Lépine caliber. Inadvertent shocks could cause the crystal covering the watch face to break, and parts to become misaligned. Wind and rain could get into non-watertight cases, wreaking havoc on the delicate mechanisms within.

Thanks to wine-soaked evenings, and because the king enjoyed hunting, many elegant Parisians' watches ended up falling to the ground or, more harmfully, onto the hard marble floors of Versailles. Breguet saw the effects first hand. When the Comptesse de Provence, the king's sister-in-law, dropped her watch, breaking both the dial and the crystal face, it was to Breguet that she, like many of her peers, sent the watch to be repaired. To address the problem of fragility, in 1790 Breguet developed an antishock mechanism, a taut spring that held the escapement and balance wheel in place. Because it hung in space, he called it the para-chute. When a watch with a para-chute dropped, the springs took the brunt of the force. Breguet's ability to shockproof watches became so renowned that, on one occasion, Talleyrand, a powerful French diplomat under Louis XVI, asked him to give a demonstration. Breguet threw a watch to the ground and lifted it again, showing that it was still running. Talleyrand was surprised and delighted, commenting that Breguet was really practicing wizardry and not watchmaking.

The strength of his watches was also demonstrated by the straight-laced yet curious British General Sir Thomas Makdougall Brisbane, a governor of New South Wales and science buff, who, "possessing one of these chronometers, subjected it to great trials by constantly wearing it on horseback; and during several long voyages, in sixteen months the greatest variation was only a second and a half."[67]

The extremes of temperature and humidity in the New World posed daunting challenges to the durability and accuracy of the watches worn by soldiers and sailors. Breguet worked to make his parts and screws ever more precise, allowing for a more watertight case, and made the first bimetallic thermometer small enough to incorporate into a watch.

At a time when built-in winding crowns did not yet exist, Breguet invented a clever new key to wind watches. It worked perfectly when used properly, but disengaged if turned in the wrong direction, sparing innumerable courtiers from inadvertently damaging their Breguets while tipsy on Burgundy.

In the ten years after Fersen commissioned the 160, Breguet embarked on a wildly creative period of exploration and innovation that would not only address such problems but also dazzle the world with ingenuity and beauty. Breguet had spent most of his early years learning how a watch was made and, then, unlearning those same techniques. He had made his first major breakthrough a few years before, when he improved on the technique of harnessing a person's kinetic energy to wind his watch. When the owner moved — or, in the queen's case, glided — the miniscule movements of the weight would wind the mainspring.

The *perpetuelle* – or perpetual – movement had been a long time in the making and was only just then coming into vogue. The history of the complication is murky, but Breguet's assistant, Moinet, wrote that it was "a German invention copied in France." A number of contemporary watchmakers claimed the title of inventor of the perpetual movement, including a man named Abraham-Louis Perrelet.

The perpetual watch embodied the multitude of scientific disciplines that went into the manufacture of a new complication. Earlier "perpetual" clocks, described but not built in the seventeenth century, were to have been wound using bands strapped across the owner's chest. As he inhaled or exhaled, a worm gear would wind the clock. Because of the obvious discomfort to the wearer, the patent was abandoned and the dream of an automatic watch unfulfilled until around 1770.

The first concern about a perpetual watch was that the weight would pull free and become the proverbial bull in a china shop. If the weight were to crash into the rest of the gears, it would cause quite a mess. Second, if the wearer swung the watch too excitedly it could overwind the mainspring and seize the movement or, worse, the spring could go off like a bomb and shred the insides.

Perrelet had created a form of automatic watch with a free weight that spun in a full circle when the wearer moved, but the weight could spin too fast and strip the movement to ribbons of brass. Perrelet's watches were "double-action" in that the weight spun freely in both directions. This required a transmission system that was quite complex in that the gears that "accepted" this spinning had to be able to control for energy input in both directions. Such early automatics were massive things, weighing at least six ounces, and one collector complained "old-time horologists feared neither size nor weight for their mechanisms. They then overstepped the mark, as they later recognized, by making the power of winding by the oscillating mass so excessive that it jeopardized the running of the movement itself and inconvenienced the wearer."[68]

Another problem was efficiency. Before Breguet's improvements to the automatic movement, it was "necessary for the wearer to walk far and energetically in order to wind them up, but they went wrong all the time."[69] Perrelet's invention improved on this efficiency slightly, but Breguet's creations brought it to its apex, and Breguet was the first to popularize the automatic movement in common watches.

Breguet, by changing the shape of the oscillator to one similar to the ace of spades and limiting its rotation to a back-and-forth motion within a circumscribed arc, was the first to successfully and sustainably adapt the technology to watches. His weight would wind the watch without causing internal damage, and it wound the mainspring with a gentle force that ensured that the mechanism would not be overwound. David Salomons, a major collector of Breguet watches in the nineteenth century, would write that "some of the watches Breguet made have been worn constantly for eight years without having been opened (for repair) and without showing the slightest trace of damage."[70] This was a tall order in a world where the average watch was minutes fast or slow and often stopped if the owner looked at it funny.

To Fersen and everyone he knew, the perpetual was something akin to magic. In an era of clattering clockwork, "watches that wind themselves" – even the description hints at witchcraft – would have been a marvel.

Many questioned whether such watches weren't a figment of someone's imagination. In a letter written in June 1780, a poet and priest named Abbé Desprades requested information from the *Société typographique*, a publishing house in Neuchâtel that also sold watches:

People [at the French court] are incredulous about the watches that need never be wound. In order persuade the public of their existence, it might be advisable to send one here; I will undertake this task willingly, if so wished; I would buy one of this type if I were sure it really worked and that in case of accident I could be sure of finding someone here to mend it, but in any case I cannot commit myself.

The *perpetuelle*, then, was the first must-have gadget.

These watches took far longer to build and were much more expensive than the standard "mechanical" hand-wound models, but Breguet spared no expense, and at this point in his long career he made *perpetuelles* almost exclusively.

Watchmaker Louis Perrot noted in 1780 that an eight-minute walk would wind the Breguet automatic movement for twenty-four hours and that "not everyone is capable of producing them."[71] In fact, they were so difficult that Breguet eventually began to lose money on every one made due to the time, complexity, and cost of materials involved. However, the perpetual watches made Breguet's name in Paris, making his automatic timepieces the first loss-leader.

He had taken a nascent technology and, using simple tools and potentially impure metals, created a device that could last two hundred or more years of constant jostling, winding, and unwinding. It was no wonder that this, Breguet's first major invention, became so popular.

Now, his ideas kept coming. Breguet knew that the only way to differentiate himself in the crowded French market was to create a signature design. While many watchmakers worked in the "old school" style, dressing up their cases with pavé diamonds and enamel, Breguet focused on legibility and elegance. His first contribution to the art was what came to be known as the Breguet numerals. They were spider-thin at the joints and dark and bold on the up and down strokes. The 1 looked vaguely Middle Eastern, while the 7 and 8 were whimsically drawn, the 7 featuring a little brow on the top stroke, and the 8 a fat tummy and small head. The markings between hours were simple, small lines, and Breguet often marked hours with diamonds or little pips resembling miniature fleur-de-lis. He cleaved to this style even for export models, creating a similar typeface — long before the concept of branding through typography became commonplace — for Chinese, Turkish, and other Eastern markets.

Where watch dials had traditionally been covered with enamel, Breguet popularized the use of guilloche, imparting a suave metallic shimmer to the face of a watch. Marie-Antoinette made a gift of one of Breguet's first guillochéd watches to Axel von Fersen.

Another innovation was the *pomme* hand, later to be known as the Breguet hand, which looked like a small poppy bud at the end of a long thin stalk. On a crowded face, it helped with readability, and it also boosted legibility at night. Many watchmakers had already taken to using white dials to make the most of existing light, but long thin hands still tended to disappear in the dark. By crowning the hands with tiny, hollow circles tipped in sharp points, Breguet allowed his customers to see instantly where the end of each hand was pointing, and, in low light, the tiny outline of a circle differentiated the hand from numerals and other shadows. It was an elegant fix to a thorny problem.

During this time, Breguet also popularized the minute repeater and quarter repeater, functions that allowed a dandy wandering the boulevards at night to tell the time; when he pressed a button, his watch would sound the time using a coded series of dings (for each hour), ding-dongs (for each quarter hour), and dongs (for each minute). *Ding, ding..., ding-dong, ding-dong..., dong...* told him it was 2:31 and time for bed.

Breguet changed the sound of those dings and dongs, too, when he invented the gong spring. Previously, watches chimed using tiny hammers striking tiny bells or metal disks; Breguet's invention used a gong made of wire, which when paired with a delicately calibrated hammer achieved a more precise pitch and volume, with a prettier sound, using less space.

As his watches became more and more complicated — in 1785, Breguet made his first watch with a power-reserve indicator (the needle informing the wearer how much energy remained in the spring) — Breguet evolved new techniques to bridge their mechanical intricacy with the elegance their exteriors required. A watch Breguet made around the time of Fersen's commission was a quarter repeater with a retrograde seconds hand — a seconds hand that moved from zero to sixty and then popped back to zero again. Rather than crowding the dial with ornamentation and curlicues, Breguet simply placed the retrograde hand in the corner — a long, thin stick pointing to a condensed collection of numbers and pips — and the current time front and center. Decisions like these almost hid the complication, allowing courtiers a bit more time to enthuse about the functions to a genuinely interested — or politely nodding — lady and creating a conversation piece of muted understatement.

Breguet's most brilliant achievements took place out of sight, within his watches' movements. Nearly all of these innovations were aimed at reducing friction and further miniaturizing watches. Breguet was religious about polishing every part, and then polishing it some more, as a way to cut down on friction. But polishing wasn't enough and in 1789 he developed a so-called natural escapement. A traditional lever escapement worked by starting and stopping, lending watches their ticking sound but introducing a certain amount of friction. Breguet's new escapement had a few more parts, but they worked together to cause the escapement wheel to roll, rather than stop, and reduced overall friction to such a degree that lubrication was no longer required for that part of the watch. Different movements used different escapements, and Breguet made similar, friction-reducing improvements to other common escapements including the ruby cylinder and the detente. However, his natural escapement was his most famous.

As his jealous competitors often noted, Breguet improved on a great many things rather than outright invented them, but the things he pushed to market were accepted without question and would be incorporated into many watches long after his death. "Breguet's genius," a collector later wrote, was the "power that he had even over kings, [allowing him to] force upon them anything that he pleased."[72]

Slowly, gradually, Breguet gathered the skills necessary to complete Fersen's commission. As each part fell into place, the list of potential complications grew. He learned to build a calendar, and also a dead-beat hand — a hand that ticked once a second like a grandfather clock — and added those to the plan for the watch. In his neat, orderly diaries, he drew a number of his improvements, sketching blue and black circles showing interconnecting gears, the delicate curves of gong springs, the scintillating teeth of escapements. Beside them, he wrote copious notes describing each one in detail.

For some time, Breguet had been working on his 92nd commission, a watch for his loyal benefactor the Duc de Praslin, and he incorporated his expanding number of innovations into the watch as a kind of rough draft for the 160. The 92 was a miracle of compression and engineering. It had a rose engraved case adorned with delicate patterns and repeating motifs of astonishing fineness for work done by hand. On the back of the watch, a sanguine moon peered out from the moon phase, and the name "Breguet" floated amid bulbous clouds. The setting and regulation features, along with a power reserve indicator, were also hidden on the back.

The front was busier. One circle, separated into three sections, featured a perpetual calendar, a central seconds hand, and an equation of time. The central hour and minute hands, in Breguet style, were tipped with hollow bulbs, while the rest of the indicators looked like delicate spines that radiated out from the two, six, and ten o'clock positions on the dial. The watch was a minute repeater, which gave off a loud tap — or "toc" — for the ten minutes, and a gong for minutes and hours. Breguet added a small screw to keep the face in place, allowing it to be removed and replaced. Because the screw looked identical to the other small square sockets that controlled the winding and setting of the watch, Breguet made it slightly larger to prevent an overzealous winder from breaking the face. The 92 was a striking predecessor to the 160.

Even as the wheels and gears in Breguet's watches clicked and whirred, even as the craftsmen in his shop worked quietly and efficiently to assemble his one-of-a-kind creations, Breguet faced mounting business problems, exacerbated by the early tremors of revolution that were beginning to wrack the world beyond the Quai.

For years, the royal classes had been in a fury of spending, mostly on credit. To appear at court required ornate costumes, hairstyles, and jewelry, even as most of France lived in grinding poverty. Breguet, a shrewd businessman, had offered easy credit to these spendthrifts. It was understood that eventually even the wastrel courtiers would repay their debts. To fail at business in this court was a personal thing, and no one, not even the courtiers with the most extravagant debts, would dream of defaulting. Bankruptcy was a stain on one's good name. It was only in the advanced throes of the Revolution that members of the royal court would start to default on their loans — either officially, through lawyers, or unofficially, under the guillotine. In the meantime, they were happy to run up outrageous bills throughout the capital and, if matters became too egregious, ask the king himself to cover their debts.

But now, the nobles he had so graciously supplied with credit and merchandise were on the run, escaping their creditors the way they were escaping the rabble calling for their heads. Breguet himself didn't feel entirely safe in Paris. The school for watchmaking set up by the king had lasted only until the beginning of the Revolution, reducing Breguet's employee base. Breguet's firm was in a dire situation. Jewelers who sold his watches on commission were not paying and even the Prince of Wales – a customer from whom Breguet eventually extracted a payment – refused to answer correspondence.

Faced with a growing list of uncollected receivables, Breguet was forced to sell watches abroad, in countries like England, Spain, and Poland, and to pursue new relationships with foreign courts that still had a modicum of disposable income. And in 1787, Breguet took on an investor, the horologist Xavier Gide, who injected 50,000 livres in cash and another 50,000 livres in stock, including a number of mid-range watches. Gide wanted to move the house in a more popular direction, creating large numbers of watches for the middle class instead of focusing on the fickle royals and their sycophants. Breguet, on the other hand, simply wanted to create beautiful and complex watches; though he had keen commercial instincts, he preferred to give his attention to experimenting with the *perpetuelle* and the other techniques he was slowly adding to the higher-end of the range.

He spent most of the early revolutionary years travelling, trying to extract payment from his severely delinquent customers. In London, he sought payment from the likes of the aforementioned Prince of Wales (whom Gide, his partner, said was "not considered a good payer"). At almost every manor house he stopped at in England he was rebuffed at first, but the same persistence, patience, and friendly disposition that had won him commissions now won him a full purse as he returned to France with most of his accounts in order. While in England, he had also visited James Watt's factory in Birmingham, studying the famed inventor's steam engines and machines. And Breguet had met with John Arnold, a watchmaker who, in 1764, built the smallest repeating watch in the world and set it in a ring worn by king George III. Arnold had a soft spot for the French watchmaker. A few years earlier he had found a Breguet watch in London and marveled at the quality and engineering, amazed that "any thing could be so well executed out of England." The two met in Paris, and Breguet decided "to give a proof of his esteem and affection for Arnold, desired him to take his son with him to England and instruct him in their art." A historian notes, with a bit of saccharine, that this decision was "worthy of the imitation of many men of talent, so often divided by jealousy and a spirit of rivalry."[73]

Gide became angry that Breguet was still paying attention to his more complicated commissions instead of spending hours in fancy drawing rooms trying to broach the subject of his customers' credit accounts. Talleyrand, in January of 1791, brought in a broken watch for repair, but he, too, was often late to pay, and in February 21 Gide entreated Breguet to refuse to return the piece until he paid up and "Try and finish with him!"[74]

Gide chiefly wanted to produce cheaper watches and to sell

inexpensive watches under the Breguet brand; he wanted the master to spend his time convincing customers that even watches his watchmakers hadn't touched were worth the *livres* they were asking. In fact, Breguet was so busy selling watches made by others and branded with the *Breguet a Paris* name that in 1791 only 3 of the 31 *perpetuelles* under way in the factory were completed and sold.

Though Breguet had been away most of the year, he stayed informed about the slow disintegration of France and her monarchy. On June 19, 1790, just as he was preparing to return to Paris, he received a distressing note from his partner Gide: "Here are more new decrees which will dismay the aristocrats: no more counts, marquesses and monseigneurs, no more liveries... And that is not all: the figures representing the nations in chains on the statue in the place des Victories are to go before 15 July. And the inscriptions on the statue of Henri IV are also to be removed. You will find Paris and France recast; little by little the authentic rights of man will appear in their true light... How glorious it is to be alive during such a revolution."[75] Ironically, the very freedom Gide was celebrating was exacting a terrible toll on their business and bringing Breguet's most loyal customers to ruin.

When Breguet was in Paris, many of his biggest supporters were still stopping by the shop to discuss the news of the day and have their watches repaired. One evening, he was sitting quietly at his bench, staring at the watch in his hand. He hadn't had many moments like this during his itinerant last few years. An oil lamp burned nearby, casting shadows around the now empty workshop, and its weak flame flickered in the breeze from the river coming through the open windows. His son Antoine-Louis was safely across the channel in England, but Paris still seemed the best place for Breguet. Excepting the odd cry from below – that afternoon he had heard a crowd yell "Kill the Austrian Bitch" and then a hail of shattering wine bottles crash through the streets below – the Île was quiet. He could easily sit at the bench for hours after his workers had gone home for the night, and he felt he needed to be here.

Records are lost from that period, but we know that work on the 160 progressed apace, and whether it was an act of loyalty or an effort to surmount a challenge, the watch on Breguet's workbench continued to come together just as Paris – and France

– was coming apart. Some days, Fersen dropped into the shop, his handsome face drawn and tired with worry, to inquire about the watch.[76]

A leading Breguet historian, George Daniels, admitted that at best most of Breguet's life during these years was best conjecture and at worst fabrication. Although orders and some letters pertaining to the business exist, their taciturn brevity leave only tantalizing clues as to Breguet's actions during the Revolution.

Breguet had been in Paris on July 14 of the previous year, for the storming of the Bastille, but he only heard secondhand news of the Fête de la Fédération, the celebration of the first anniversary of the fall of the Bastille that the *London Times* described as peaceful "excepting the bursting of a cannon, and the fall of a tree by which one man lost his life."[77] It was also reported that the King, fearing assassination, had begun to wear another piece of technology, an armored chest plate called a plastron "to ward off a poniard thrust. Composed of fifteen thicknesses of Italian taffeta, this [shield] consisted of a vest and a large belt."[78]

Even though Breguet rarely played politics he was perceived as soft on the nobles. A royalist, in those chaotic days, was anyone who did business with the royals. This simple equation threatened to get the focused and quiet watchmaker killed on the streets of Paris. The meetings of the National Convention had become less of a circus, but the rabble still took to the streets at the slightest provocation. Thousands of men and women could swarm a prison or palace and call for blood, and these crowds, more often than not, got their due.

Knowing he was unable to remain merely a spectator, in the winter of 1790 he joined the Club des Jacobins, their meeting hall less than two miles from his home, and began to work with Robespierre in revolutionary politics. Many of his friends and customers were members of the Jacobins, which initially favored a constitutional monarchy, with a separation of powers similar to that in the nascent United States. At the same time, he was no radical, and owed his success, as well as the funding necessary to advance his art, to the wealth of the royal family and the aristocracy. Now he had to negotiate a new breed of noble.

It saddened him to know that his most trusted customers, the king and queen of France, were around the corner at the Tuileries, the old palace that for years had been used as the Parisian halls of justice. It was a space barely fit for bureaucratic work, let alone habitation, yet Marie-Antoinette and her family were there, locked away like kidnapped royals in a fairy story.

The royal family had been moved from Versailles to the Tuileries across from the Île on October 6, 1789, a few hours after a crowd of Parisians stormed the royal palace hunting for royal blood. The fracas was a violent one as "the bands of pikemen, the hideous prostitutes of the galleries of the Palais Royal, the infernal viragoes of the Revolution"[79] all coalesced on the palace of the Sun king. The looting began, then, and the clocks of Versailles were torn down and stolen, their guts spilled on the hard marble floor, mixing with the blood from the "livid heads of the hapless, decapitated bodyguards."[80]

With characteristic naiveté, when Louis XVI entered the run-down former royal palace attached to the Louvre and visible from Breguet's window, he said "It is always with pleasure and with confidence that I find myself amidst the inhabitants of my good city of Paris."

The palace, unused since the reign of Louis XV in 1722, was a hulking wreck at the heart of the city. It was "gloomy, out of repair, unfurnished, and undecorated" and the "locks closed badly,"[81] a poignant affront to the king's locksmith's training. It was, in short, the antithesis of the light and airy Petit Trianon and far down the ladder of comfort from the confection that was Versailles.

By some stroke of luck combined with diplomatic skill, Fersen, who spent most of his time in Paris now, was able to visit Marie often – "I see my love freely in her apartments," he confided to his diary — although no one knew of his midnight rendezvouses.[82] He kept the visits secret.

All the while, he wrote furious letters to those who might be able to help Marie and her family, often receiving only cold silence in reply. He saw Marie that Christmas, then spent January plotting and talking love with his old friend Baron Evert Taube, an aide to Gustave III who had been sent to France to assess the strength and danger of the Revolution.

Determined to do something about the situation, with Marie's approval, Fersen began planning an escape. By this time, their relationship, long suspected, was almost public. The king was thought to know about it and, according to a letter by the Comte de Saint-Priest, a minister close to Fersen, Marie-Antoinette had used all of her charms to keep Louis placated, "repeating to her husband all the public gossip she learnt was circulating about this affair, and offered to stop seeing him."[83] The king, understanding the value of a free, valiant, and well-funded foreigner in this endeavor, looked the other way as Fersen completed the preparations. After all, Marie-Antoinette told her husband, "this foreigner was the only man they could count on."

The plan was simple. The royal family would move from Paris to the fortress town of Montmedy, whose Spanish-built citadel and fortifications in northern Lorraine would keep them safe as Louis XVI negotiated the plans for a peaceful move toward what would amount to a new constitutional monarchy. The days of absolute power would come to an end, but the royal family would be safe and they would not have to go into exile. Fersen, on the other hand, had the naive and heartsick hope that his plan would "re-establish everything as it was before the Revolution."

He kept his visits to the Tuileries secret by dressing as a "person of the household." Since at least October, 1789, according to a letter from Quintin Craufurd, an author and intimate of Fersen's who helped plan the escape, to William Pitt, in the dark of night Fersen would don a "frock, with a round hat" and would see the royal couple in the "king's closet," which, understandably, was a bit bigger than a place to keep shoes and clothing. There he saw the king and queen "once or twice a week," maintaining ties to both throughout the planning process.

Fersen's home on Rue de Matignon, a mere five-minute walk from the Tuileries, became a sort of Bletchley Park for those plotting to save the French monarchy. Encrypted letters came and went from Fersen's desk while secret rendezvouses were planned under his roof. Most letters to Fersen were made out to one Swedish Baron Hamilton while others took the names of other neutral parties including the Russian Baroness von Korff — whom Marie would impersonate during the escape.[84]

By March of 1790, Fersen was tapering his social obligations in order to devote himself to working for the release of his beloved. "I now have so much to do and to write that I can scarcely go out, and still I must show myself in society so as not to arouse suspicions," he wrote to his friend Taube. "I am entirely alone here in the city with this secret, for they have not a single person the king can rely on." He did not expect to "demand anything" of the king and queen – although he did hope to be "amply repaid" – but he wanted to be of use to "them."

Fersen then planned the official route. After transferring from a fiacre to a *berline* at Porte Saint-Martin, the royal family would stop in Meaux, La Ferté-sous-Jouarre, Montmirail, Châlons-sur-Marne, Sainte-Menehould, Varennes, Dun, and Stenay, all towns where the king's safety was comparatively assured. Troops would be stationed in each place, with successive garrisons quietly taking up with the carriage as it passed, relieving the previous troops, who would then return to Paris. Austria was expected to stage fake maneuvers at the border to distract curious eyes from a lone carriage carrying a second-rate Baroness across the wide expanse of France. Fersen, who wanted to follow the family to safety, was told to stay in Paris, so as not to arouse suspicion.

The real Madame de Korff ordered the *berline* on December 22, 1790, for 5,944 livres,[85] from the saddler Monsieur Louis, the most famous carriage maker in Paris, who had built many vehicles for the king and queen. Madame de Korff told the carriage maker that her representative, Fersen, would pay for it and drive it away upon completion. By January, Fersen was becoming impatient and threatened Monsieur Louis with cancellation if the carriage didn't arrive by February 2. The saddler and his staff rushed to complete it, and then it sat, seemingly forgotten, for months as Fersen disappeared, engulfed by the minutiae of the trip. By now – with all the plans in place – it was clear that the carriage would be the least expensive accoutrement of the trip. Bouille, the general given charge of moving troops and handling the postilions as the king and queen travelled to Varennes, expected the trip to cost almost one million livres, and he expected payment up front. In all, it is believed that Fersen laid out 600,000 livres of his own money on the expedition, or about $6 to $10 million in today's dollars.

On February 3, 1791, Marie-Antoinette sent a letter to the envoy Mercy describing the royal family's intention to travel from Paris to the French border, announce amnesty to the revolutionaries, and propose a new constitution based on the declaration of the rights of man. She requested the support of Swiss and Austrian troops. "We shall not act in haste," Marie-Antoinette wrote. "It would be better to spend another year in prison and be sure of getting out than to risk being brought back." The letter accompanied a box, to be hidden in Brussels for safety, containing diamonds, jewelry, and some of Breguet's finest watches.

Chapter 10

Jerusalem

Ephraim Mizrakhi woke Zadok Cohen at 10:00 a.m. on
April 16, 1983, the Sabbath. It had been a long night, with a new
moon, and Ephraim had found it hard to stay awake while making
his rounds. He had just patrolled the entire L.A. Mayer Museum,
strolling past the vases and rugs, the darkened halls and the locked
doors that kept the museum's more valuable pieces safe. Then he
went for a quick walk around the outside of the building, checking
for unwanted visitors, but he saw nothing amiss. Soon it would
be time for Zadok to open the doors, and for both of them finish
their shifts. They would run through one final patrol at 10:30,
twelve hours after their last night patrol, and then unlock the doors
at 11 a.m.

Zadok stretched in his chair and yawned, glancing at the
clock on the wall. The museum had closed at two the previous
afternoon, in time for Shabbat, and they had been free to do as
they pleased. Through the night, on a small television in the guard
station, he and Ephraim had watched the Robert Redford film *Jeremiah Johnson*, about a hermit in the Rocky Mountains who fights
against an onslaught of Crow Indians. The museum was quiet, an
oasis high above the tumult of Jerusalem's Old City; they usually
did one or two rounds and then dozed in the office, confident that
no intruder would disturb their sleep.

Now, Zadok walked past the staircase leading to the lower
level and moved toward the family gallery, the room full of old
clocks. Most mornings, he could hear them ticking, their strong
springs still going after a night's work. He knew that the family

88

gallery held hundreds of horological marvels, and that most were in perfect condition. Sometimes they were a bit off, depending on the weather, but he could usually set his watch by them. The collection, people whispered, was estimated to be worth about $7.5 million.

As Zadok paused outside the gallery, he craned his head to listen. Silence. Maybe they had wound down. He stood there a few more minutes. No ticking. He put his key into the lock and turned. The heavy bolts slid back, and the door swung open. He caught a whiff of fresh air that gusted from the open window above the shattered glass cabinets and broken display tables. He rushed back up the stairs to the guard post, calling for Ephraim to contact Rachel Hasson, the museum curator.

Ephraim, after taking in the scene for himself, described it over the phone to Hasson: locks broken, trash scattered on the floor. The guard couldn't say exactly what was missing, but it was clearly most of the collection. Hasson, "shocked" by what she heard, asked about the queen, the most important watch in the group. Zadok re-created the scene in his head, but he couldn't remember seeing the watch amid the jumble of glass and wood.

Hasson phoned the keeper of the watches, Ohannes Markarian, then drove the few kilometers from her home in Rehavia, north of the museum. The then thirty-nine-year-old Hasson had started working at the museum in 1967, while it was still under construction, but even after all these years, her familiarity with the family gallery was limited. Her background was in Islamic art, and her mission was to bring Arab art to Israel. The watches, to her, had always been an afterthought. When she arrived, Markarian was already in the family gallery, running a tally of the missing pieces. He hid his eyes, for as they swept across the broken expanse of empty exhibits, they began to tear up.

If Breguet had been reincarnated, it might have been as Ohannes Markarian, the portly, bespectacled watchmaker who had maintained the L.A. Mayer collection for a decade before losing it on that morning in April.

In Armenian, Markarian's language of birth, he was called a *hanchar*, a word that translated to "a genius who took great care of the talent that God gave him." In Israel, for at least twenty-five years, he was considered the one man who could fix a timepiece and never have it break, a claim that his many satisfied customers repeated after leaving Jerusalem with their newly cleaned and tightly wound watches.

He was born in Istanbul in 1923. His family had survived the Armenian genocide, and after the dissolution of the Ottoman Empire, the Markarians left Turkey. They settled in Jerusalem when Ohannes was four. At fifteen, he began his training in Old Jaffa, where he learned the prerequisites for watchmaking from a "very old man" who taught him carpentry, goldsmithing, and toolmaking. As he grew older and became more established in the watchmaking world, he realized that all of the ancillary techniques he learned from his master helped in his craft. Carpentry helped him rebuild broken clock cases, while goldsmithing taught him to be scrupulous with his materials. He learned to make very small things and very large things, and also learned to create his own tools when there were none to be found in the impoverished Old City.

He was talented at math and science and maintained high enough marks so that when he graduated he could have studied to become a doctor. But that type of training would have required him to leave the country. His grandfather, however, still bore the mental scars of the Armenian Genocide and said, "I have lost one family in Turkey. I'm not losing this one in Jerusalem." Ohannes stayed put, instead becoming a doctor to old clocks.

At seventeen, he moved to Jerusalem's Old City and apprenticed with a series of watchmakers who still kept stalls there. The winding passages of the ancient neighborhood were, like Breguet's Place Dauphin, chock full of experts in every field. Markarian was able to refine his craft by working on ancient clockwork and modern wristwatches alike. There were two other watchmakers in the Old City at the time and they guarded their business jealously, an attitude still encountered there today. When I wandered into a watch repair shop by the Tower of David one summer afternoon to ask about Markarian's old shop, the proprietor pretended not to know the location and then said "I'm the only Markarian you need," as if the name of the master watchmaker now described a profession in itself.

As a teenager, Markarian turned his love of clockwork into a paid position with the British High Command, where he maintained office clocks and other delicate mechanical instruments used by the British authorities in Palestine. During World War II he worked for the British Army repairing naval and artillery instruments.

At twenty-five, he opened his own store in the Old City, on Christian Quarter Road, in a small, rounded stall with a large front room, a 10-by-20-foot rear storage area, and a small corner containing a restroom. Here he cared for and maintained a number of ancient clocks and watches brought to him by distraught curators. And here he kept his replacement parts – a collection that would soon engulf the entire shop – as well as all of his notes. He was a bookworm and meticulous note-taker, examining each piece of a watch and noting its design and problems in a series of notebooks. This habit helped him rebuild the watch when it was time to put all of the pieces together, and it also gave him an intimate understanding of every gear and cog in some of the greatest watches ever made.

He also helped maintain the bronze artifacts at the Church of the Holy Sepulcher and recorded, in his head, a rich history of Jerusalem that he would expound upon from his small shop or over long lunches with friends and admirers. He amassed a personal collection that ran from thirteenth-century carriage clocks to modern quartz pieces. He began wearing a ring of watch keys on his belt, and as his business – and belly – grew he added more and more keys, resulting in a jingling, heavy collection that he carried with him at all times.

The two rival watchmakers in the Christian Quarter tried to keep up with Ohannes, but "everyone realized he was better than them," said his daughter. Markarian became known as a horological miracle worker. A relative claimed that "when he fixed a watch once, it never needed repairs again,"[86] and he was considered a master of mathematics, engineering and art. Those skills, coupled with his experience in metalwork, enamel and woodwork, encompassed everything he needed to know to be a master watchmaker.

His reputation expanded from his little shop and into the wider world. Slowly, business trickled in from Paris and London, then America and Asia. He was very protective of his watches, treating them like tiny, broken birds requiring a calm, careful hand. When he received a new watch for repair, he would spend hours – if not days – brooding over his bench. He sometimes brought his work home with him, but often left priceless horological masterpieces in his little shop. He trusted his neighbors implicitly, and knew they would deal quickly with anyone attempting to steal his broken treasures. When he finished with a watch, he would say, simply, "I made it tick again." He said this thousands of times over his long career. When nearby shopkeepers came in to swap stories and gossip, if they saw him working at his bench they would quickly scamper off rather than risk his wrath at being disturbed.

In 1970, Vera Salomons hired him to prepare her father's watch collection for viewing at the L.A. Mayer Museum, and from its opening in 1974, Markarian presided over the family gallery, maintaining watches so precious and delicate that he was often loath to wind them. But he visited at least twice weekly to wind, oil, and dust off the specimens. Many of them, Markarian said, kept time as well as a "brand new Seiko."[87]

With the esteemed Breguet expert George Daniels, Markarian created a color catalog of the Salomons Collection. Published in 1980 in West Germany, the 318-page book featured notes and images for every item, from the mechanical "Singing-bird in a cage," a nearly life-sized bird that twittered and tweeted with the turn of a clockwork key, to the crown jewel, the watch they called the Queen.

On the morning of the theft, Markarian arrived at 11:39 — he was characteristically precise in noting when events transpired — as the sun was high over the pale stone of the museum. He ran to the family gallery and was horrified. The room had been ransacked, but he was surprised by how orderly it still was, even amid the chaos. There was little broken glass, just pita-sized circles cut out from the vitrines and placed carefully on the floor. Some empty food wrappers, Coke cans, and cigarette butts lay there, too, along with something that looked like a blanket, but nothing else was amiss. It was as if someone had come in, made very specific choices about what to take, and then calmly departed with the haul of a lifetime and one of the biggest watch heists in world history.

He saw where a line of modeling clay had been placed along the inside edge of the room's door to prevent the guards from seeing light inside. The clay was devoid of fingerprints. A piece of black cardboard lay below a window that was slightly ajar. A seventeenth-century French table had been broken, probably when the thief dropped a bag onto it as he jumped down into the room from the window. The damage was limited but the theft complete.

92

Markarian could hardly believe it; a large portion of the contents of the family museum, which had survived undisturbed for nearly a century, had vanished overnight. He walked wistfully past the holes and stands that once held the watches and clocks he had maintained for over a decade. He brushed his hand over the empty spaces and idly thumbed the curatorial notes that remained.

Moments later, the head of the museum board, Dr. Gavriel Moriah, arrived and surveyed the damage. Right away, he saw that the most magnificent pieces were gone: A singing bird gun (a clockwork novelty by the Roche Brothers, which played a jaunty tune on tiny whistles when wound and fired); a Swiss-made automaton of a walking woman; and almost all of the Breguet timepieces, including the Sympathetique, which used a main clock to wind and set a perfectly matched pocket watch, and, most devastatingly, the Queen. In all, the thief had taken one hundred watches, four oil paintings, and three antique books.

The police had been called, and the first officers on the scene found leftover strips of cloth that had apparently been used to bind the clocks for packing. The officers were amazed that anyone could have gotten the clocks out through the window, let alone that a human being could have slid through the tiny opening undetected. "Only people with a thin build could enter that narrow window," an officer reported later, matter-of-factly.

An air mattress lay unfurled on the floor, probably used to cushion the fall of the equipment pushed through the small window. A can of Coca-Cola and a bag of sandwiches lay unfinished near one of the cases, and a bag nearby contained long-handled pliers and a heavy hammer. A rope ladder, probably a spare, was still in its original packaging.[88]

By the size of the job, it looked to the police as if at least three men had been involved. That they were able to make off with over half of the collection in the course of an evening suggested that they had gathered all of the clocks together first, then quickly moved them out through the window. One man would have been inside, pushing the bags out, another outside, grabbing them, and a third one sitting in the car waiting for the getaway.

Felix Saban, Deputy Commander of the Jerusalem police, soon arrived with a mobile forensics van. His team traced the thieves' steps from the side of the museum, where they must have parked, to the bent bars in the fence, to the climb through the thin window leading into the clock room. They began dusting for fingerprints, but this effort quickly proved fruitless — the room was already full of prints, and the thief had been unusually careful. The police were also surprised to find a listening device: a microphone by the door, attached to a wire running to an amplifier and a pair of headphones that the thief used to listen for the sound of footsteps through the door; there were some prints on the cable, but they were too fragmentary to be useful. Later, as the legend of the theft grew, some police officers would report seeing a half-eaten ham-and-cheese sandwich on the floor, seemingly a taunting gesture given the location and heritage of the museum. In truth, it was quite difficult, if not impossible, to get sliced ham in Jerusalem.

"This theft was more daring than sophisticated," Ezekial Mc-Carthy, the spokesperson for the Jerusalem police, told a Sunday newspaper. "The burglars knew the place well and did not leave themselves open to surprise. It is possible that they visited the exhibit several times and they may have also walked in with a catalog in hand and took only what was ordered by their higher-ups. They chose an amazing collection of watches and left a number of uninteresting ones, which suggests a selective knowledge."

Another clue came from the tags stolen. Most of the watches and clocks had English and Hebrew curatorial notes, but the thieves had taken only a few, leaving behind the notes for paintings they took and some of the clockwork. This led police to believe it was a planned job, probably commissioned by a dealer in Europe. "They stole what was on their list, and would have been expecting payment for those items," said a police officer. "The extra stuff [like the paintings] was, well, extra."

On further investigation, the police discovered that, almost ten years after the museum's opening, its directors were still bickering over what kind of security system to install. As a result, there was almost no security at all. The *Jerusalem Post* reported that "there was a single alarm for the entire building and this had never worked from the day it was installed." Without the alarm active, the museum had security "about equivalent to that of a medium-sized kindergarten in an old neighborhood," as one investigator said.

News of the theft spread quickly through the watch world and beyond. The Swiss watch industry was already suffering a major downturn and consolidation. Japanese quartz watches had decimated the market for low-cost mechanical watches. Smaller houses like Breguet, which had been in continuous business for two centuries, were out of money, and investors were swooping in to buy them in what amounted to a fire sale. Stories about the break-in appeared in the *New York Times* and the *International Herald Tribune*. Watchmakers were put on high alert; Interpol scrambled to monitor all prominent collectors moving in and out of Israel.

Gavriel Moriah, the museum board chairman, was certain that the thieves could not be working for a collector. "There's no such thing as a collector who keeps his most prized possessions in a safe and never shows them to anybody," he said. "A collector collects for gratification, and part of that gratification is to be able to show them off."[89]

An Associated Press story, which appeared the week after the theft, pegged the stolen collection's value at $5 million and mentioned the most famous of the missing watches only in passing, describing it as built of "gold, crystal and glass."

Ohannes returned home on Sunday after almost twenty-four hours of nonstop work. He fell, exhausted, into one of the kitchen chairs. His wife, after hearing the story of the break-in, stood quietly looking at her husband.

"You won't have a job, now," she said, finally. "What will you do?"

He shook his head. "They're accusing me of the theft," he said. The police had taken every staffer's fingerprints, including his, but, for obvious reasons, his were the prints that showed up the most in the family gallery.

His daughter, Araxi, remembers the weekend vividly.

"He was very, very upset. I didn't understand at the time, because I was too young. Nobody spoke to him in the house," she said.

Mrs. Markarian told the children to play quietly. "Keep away from your daddy, he is very upset. The watches and the clocks have been stolen and they think he stole them," she told them. Araxi's sister Silva laughed.

"Why would he ever steal them? He's the one who loves them the most!"

After the theft, Markarian did the best he could with the remaining timepieces, continuing to visit weekly to wind them. The museum loaned two of the clocks, one made by Hinton Brown of England in 1770, to the presidential palace, where they would presumably be safer.

Markarian gave tours of the remaining collection by appointment only, and one visitor remembers him sighing when he pulled open a drawer containing the boxes that once held some of horology's most beloved masterpieces. He ran his hand along the indentations in the soft red silk where the watches once lay and then shut the drawer firmly, as if trying to forget the loss of his beautiful charges.

He missed all of the watches but the watch that pained him the most, the watch that would later be valued at $11 million dollars and hold the world, for a time, in a thrall, was the Queen, the eighteenth century's most complex artifact, a watch of such beauty and precision and freighted with such tragedy that it would later become known simply as the Marie-Antoinette.

Chapter 11

Paris

On the eve of the summer equinox a fiacre rolled through the narrow cobbled streets of Paris. It was a dowdy carriage, unrecognizable and unassuming, with nothing about it that would attract special notice from the city's watchmen and lamplighters. It was big enough to hold seven people, and inside the carriage, according to papers accompanying its occupants, were the Russian Baroness de Korff, her servants — Madame Rocher, a governess; Rosalie, a companion; and Durand, a valet de chambre — and daughters Amelia and Aglae. One of the little girls slept soundly on the carriage floor, under the baroness's petticoats.

But nothing was as it appeared on this summer evening in 1791. The baroness was in fact Madame de Tourzel, the actual governess to the royal children whom Fersen, not trusting any of the queen's courtiers or employees, called that "wretched woman-of-the-bedchamber." The "governess" was the queen herself, Rosalie was her sister Elizabeth, and the butler, Durand, was Louis XVI. Only one of the children was a girl: twelve-year-old Marie Thérèse, daughter of the king and queen. The other, lying on the floor, was her brother, the six-year-old dauphin, Louis-Charles, who had asked, on being told of their late night mission, to be allowed to wear his "sabre and boots" but had been dressed up in girl's clothing instead. The carriage the royal family was travelling in did not belong to them, and none of their servants had been made aware of its existence. The palace prison that J.B. Gouvion, liaison to the Paris National Guard, said was so secure that "not even a mouse could escape from there" had just been breached.[90]

The coachman, who now pushed the horses along, had long before procured the coach and planned the daring journey. Now, weaving through the fetid byways of the darkened city, periodically checking his silver soldier's Breguet, he kept a wary eye on the empty streets. Axel von Fersen, dressed as a footman, with his face obscured by a wide-brimmed hat, snapped his whip to goad the animals onward.

Eventually, the carriage ducked through a gate at the city perimeter and came to a stop. Fersen left the party and returned momentarily with another longer carriage, a *berline* pulled by six horses, large enough to accommodate the entire family comfortably. Its slender iron wheels looked as if they would give them trouble over rough roads, but for passenger comfort the carriage couldn't be better. No expense had been spared in its construction, at least on the inside. The interior included "white taffeta [cushions], double curtains of taffeta and leather on all the windows, two cooking stoves of iron plate, [and] two chamber pots of varnished leather."[91] All of these perks came from the pocket of Fersen, who also provisioned the carriage with "beef a la mode and cold veal together with a bag of small change for use at the posting-houses, a bottle of still champagne, and five bottles of water:"[92] a feast for a king and his retinue, in exile, complete with tolls for the trip.

At Bondy, ten miles outside of Paris, Fersen said good-bye. He had wanted to continue to accompany the royal family, but the king had amiably but firmly refused, and now did so again. Later, some would suggest that the king had not wished to be chaperoned to safety by a man who was sleeping with his wife. Madame de Tourzel, the queen's handmaiden who was impersonating the Russian baroness, would write: "The king, in saying good-bye, expressed his gratitude in the most affectionate manner, saying he hoped to be able to do so other than in words, and that he expected to see him again soon."

Marie Thérèse later wrote of Fersen's leaving with a decided finality, noting "he bade my father goodnight, mounted his horse, and disappeared."[93] Fersen was heading north toward Belgium.

By the time Fersen left, the royal family was already hours behind schedule, and they fell even further behind in their new vehicle. Had the family purchased two or three smaller carriages

— rather than the single, larger berline on which the king insisted — they could have travelled farther faster.

Only after dawn had broken, and they had entered the Marne valley and felt safely away from Paris, were they able to relax for the first time. They ate the food Fersen had supplied, and, ever the explorer, the king unfolded a map of the countryside and began checking off the names of the towns they passed.

Despite the dangers that still faced them — earlier, Fersen had written to Bouille, "One can only shudder at the thought of the horrors that would take place if they were stopped" – the king became almost reckless, periodically getting out to empty his bladder or stretch his legs, and offering hearty farewells to loyal subjects who recognized him immediately, thanks to a wedding trip north in 1775 and a number of drawings passed out as gifts in the preceding years. At one point, he got out of the carriage and leisurely discussed the harvest with some local farmers. "We're out of danger now," he explained to his coachman Moustier, gravely underestimating the power and reach of the Revolution.

Threats to their mission accrued inexorably. At one relay station, the royal family accepted the posting master's invitation to come inside for refreshments. They stayed half an hour. Back on the road, they tried to make up for lost time, and in their haste, a wheel came off the carriage, necessitating another half hour's delay as it was repaired. At Chalons, the king stuck his head out the window, and received many well wishes. After the carriage left the town, even Marie was becoming more confidant, and announced, "We are saved!" But the people of the town had already fallen into argument over how the royals should be treated. An hour later, a lone man on horseback, who has never been identified, approached the coach and said, "Your plans have gone awry. You will be stopped!"

The royal family was approaching the string of towns on the road to Montmedy where General Louis de Bouillé, the loyal military leader, had moved a succession of garrisons under the pretense of protecting a shipment of money to the provinces. But by now the soldiers had been waiting for hours and were growing nervous that the royal family had yet to appear. In the first town, peasants angry at the unexplained presence of the military began to congregate with guns and pitchforks, and the garrison abandoned its post. Half an hour later, the royal carriage rattled in, the royal family expecting to come under the protection of Bouille's troops, only to find no one waiting for them. A similar situation arose in the next town, Sainte Menehould, and by the time the carriage reached the town after that, Varennes, the tragedy of errors was complete. A mob surrounded the *berline*, the family was arrested, and, under guard, they were brought back to Paris and to the end of monarchy.

At that moment, Axel Fersen, after a night of riding, reached Mons, where he slept soundly, expecting the king and queen to contact him when they arrived at the fortress town in the French hinterlands. Word never came. On the 23rd, he saw Bouillé, who told him what had happened. That night, Fersen wrote to his father: "All is lost, dearest father, and I am in despair. Only imagine my grief and pity me."

For six months, Fersen remained abroad. His involvement in the flight to Varennes had been discovered, and he was banned from entering France; a friend with whom he had left his diaries destroyed them, lest they be confiscated by the revolutionaries. Writing to Fersen in cipher and in invisible ink, the queen said, "How worried I've been about you and how I feel all that you must be suffering not to have heard from us!" Through an intermediary, she gave Fersen a gold ring inscribed *Lache qui les abandonne* – "Only the Coward Gives Up." — before sending the ring off, Marie wore it for two days.

Though Marie had begged Fersen not to come back to Paris, lest he be killed, on February 13, 1792, wearing a disguise and carrying fake papers, he returned to France. He saw Marie that same night, sneaking into the Tuileries and afterward noting that he "Went to the queen. Took my regular way. Fear of National Guards. Her lodgings marvelous. Did not see the king. Stayed there." That last "laconic" note[94] suggested that Fersen and the queen still had a physical relationship even under arrest.

It was the first of several visits. Three days later, he was with the royal family from six in the evening until six in the morning. By now, more than half a year after the failed flight to Varennes, Fersen and King Gustav had taken it upon themselves to attempt another escape. Louis XVI, however, rebuffed the proposal, and Fersen retreated to the Paris home of Quintin Craufurd and his wife Eleanor Sullivan, a long time lover of Fersen's. For nearly a week, she kept him hidden in an attic room, secretly meeting with him during the day to sooth his sorrow. Fersen came down out of the attic near the end of the week, when Craufurd was home, and knocking on the door, pretending to have just arrived from Tours.[95] On the 21st, Fersen returned to the Tuileries and stayed until midnight. Then he departed for Brussels.

With Gustav's blessing, Fersen continued his machinations. He travelled Europe much as he had travelled it as a boy, approaching the heads of state for a mission of the heart. However, all was lost. By March 1, 1792 Leopold II was dead of a sudden illness. Fifteen days later, Gustav III was shot and wounded at a masquerade at the Stockholm opera by a group of masked revelers who, it was believed, were fighting for the Jacobin cause. Two weeks later, Gustav was dead, and with him Fersen's last hope that Sweden might intervene on his beloved's behalf. "I am afraid of being persecuted if I should return to Sweden and am entirely decided not to go there," he wrote on April 13 in his diary.

Fersen continued to write to Marie-Antoinette (during the course of the year, he would send her twenty-two letters, and she would send him seventeen), still scheming how the other European powers might be moved to help her cause. But in August, Marie and her family were moved to the chilling Temple prison, and communication was no longer possible.

As Fersen roared through Europe, seeking ever-more-elusive allies in his bid to save Marie, he bore witness to the advance of the French Revolution, as increasing numbers of bedraggled aristocratic refugees passed him on the road. In November, in Brussels, Fersen was urged by the Russian ambassador, Ivan Simolin, and by Lord Elgin (of marbles fame), to burn the portfolio of the queen's papers that he had, lest they fall into the wrong hands, but he couldn't bring himself to do so.

Breguet, for his part, remained loyal to the French royal family. While they were still in the Tuileries, his partner Gide had visited the palace to accept for repair a watch that had stopped because the queen had dropped it. Breguet himself visited the Tuileries many times, usually to assist with some horological service, although his exact catalog of work has been lost. It is, however, a compelling picture to imagine the watchmaker to kings puttering through the drafty Tuileries maintaining his ticking charges as they sliced off the seconds before the death of the monarchy.

On September 4, 1792, now imprisoned in the Temple, Marie-Antoinette sent a request for a simple, steel minute-repeater.

101

Although the 160 was still on the order books, Breguet's workshop began work on the 179, an austere pocket watch with a winding hole to the right of the central pinion, at two o'clock. The long, thin hands and elongated stem gave the watch an air of delicacy his other pieces could not attain, and the bare, white face, the name Breguet in tiny letters along the bottom, would be the only measure of the downcast family's hours that year. Around the same time, another member of court, the Comtesse de Provence (the king's sister-in-law), bought a 3,600 livres watch while living on 400 livres a month. The old ways of the nobles were still prevalent, even in the face of the maelstrom.

But the easy credit afforded the royal family was drying up, and Gide was fuming. "I hope you have found success with those accursed princes," wrote Gide to Breguet, when he was in London trying to collect debts from the British royal family. "They are catastrophic to deal with. Thanks to the energy of the French people, we are rid of them [in Paris]."

Gide saw Breguet as too soft on the English royal family and asked that he "summon up all his courage" in his dealings with them. "If you had received everything due to you, we should now be comfortable," he wrote. Finally, Gide was done with Breguet's trips to London and called him back permanently. "Do not sacrifice any longer your health, your time, or the profits we should be making. Try to get your money or letters of exchange and send England to the devil for ever."

Gide's increasingly business-oriented requests were the antithesis of Breguet's love of experimentation and novelty. On Valentine's Day, 1791, Gide wrote, in what would be one of his last requests, "I hope, my friend, that on your return the firm will be run differently, for I think the main problem for our business is that you never make two watches the same. Novelties are expensive. You have considerable talents; you should put them to good use."

The average Frenchman could now afford to carry a watch, and the novelties Gide so despised were popularly regarded as overly ornate and vastly extravagant, valuable only to decrepit and deposed monarchs or exiled noblemen, relics of a vanishing gilded age of absolute power and endless riches. The sheer act of producing a watch with complications was, in Gide's eyes, folly. In an era when two hands and a spring were enough to get a peasant to and from Mass on Sunday, a moonphase, an equation of time, or a chronograph were wasteful overkill, the sort of trumped-up frippery that had gotten France into its mess in the first place. In a land of that clamored for table wine there was no call for champagne.

It is hard to know how Breguet felt about this endless badgering. He was not very literary, never wrote a personal memoir, and left only letters, notes, and scattered fragments of prose behind. A recent trove of documents found to be written in the master's own hand described little more than his engineering techniques, shedding light on a particularly tricky and unusual method for adding a jeweled arbor to an escapement, but describing little about the man who seated the stone.

In his effort to maintain the business, Breguet found himself further and further from the bench. Work continued in his shop, but he often couldn't touch the finished products. He had become a businessman, something he decidedly did not like.

He did return to Paris to close a few watches made by his workmen, among them the 173, a repeating pocket watch with a jump-hour hand, a hand that "jumped" from hour to hour with each pass of the minutes hand around the dial. Instead of incremental movement, then, the wearer would see the hour hand pointing to the exact hour at all times and the minute hand pointing to the changing minute. The jumping-hours complication would later appear in the 160.

Breguet's watches during this time were inspired by John Arnold and the long discussions they had had in London. The 215 was a repeater with a sub-seconds hand (one that spun on its own pivot, lower on the dial than the main hands) and blued main indicators. It looked plain but used a highly complex and delicate bimetallic spring detent escapement, requiring hours of work simply to carve it out, then file it, and then tap in the minuscule holes that would connect it to the watch plate.

As Breguet prepared to break his partnership with Gide, he knew that he had to instill in his son a sense of pride in the craft. He began organizing an apprenticeship with Arnold for Antoine-Louis, who was now almost fifteen. The boy had his father's small features. But with his mutton-chop sideburns and husky build he was considerably more strapping a man than the diminutive watchmaker. As a teenager, he looked more like a young barkeep than a watchmaker. In May, Breguet called his son to London, where he began his tutelage with the Dumergue family, a clan of well-known scientists and scholars, and would continue on to John Arnold's workshop. Thus was Breguet's only son protected from the riots in France.

For Breguet himself, returning to Paris after each trip wasn't hard. He loved his adopted home and admitted as much in letters defending his business to the National Convention. Even in these difficult times, Breguet was trying desperately to keep working, but he took additional precautions to keep the 160 hidden away. Watches for royals and nobles were political gunpowder.

Unable to find common ground, Breguet and Gide dissolved their partnership on October 1, 1791, just as Gide's revolutionary fervor was reaching a boiling point. Gide was granted the rights to any outstanding debts he could collect — a job the tactless Frenchman relished — while Breguet took control of some of the company's unsold timepieces as well as the rent on 51 Quai de l'Horlage. The company was back in Breguet's name, and in 1792, the firm increased its output, building some sixty-two original watches. But the Revolution was becoming increasingly disruptive.

By the end of 1792, the revolutionary council conscripted Breguet into the National Guard and was forced to patrol the heart of Paris. During these months, he also applied for and gained French citizenship, claiming that he was descended from French Protestants who escaped to Switzerland from Picardy. This small change in status would protect his business from confiscation and, although it was based on a small lie (recent research has confirmed his family was Catholic and had deeper roots in Switzerland than even Breguet knew), it bought him time until he could decide on a next step.

Even the art of telling time was facing revision. In the early days of the Revolution, those who wished to publicly identify themselves with one side or the other would wear a watch depicting their support. An illustrated crown on a watch indicated a royalist, while clasped hands, a Phrygian cap (a red bonnet worn by revolutionaries), or the god Mithras symbolized revolutionary allegiance. Breguet made watches featuring the symbols of both sides, but the Revolution was soon to have a more profound effect on his watches.

In an effort to redefine everything in post-Revolutionary France, the Jacobins commissioned a group of French thinkers to create a calendar that would reflect the forward-thinking nature of the National Convention. The politicians in charge were

Charles-Gilbert Romme, Claude Joseph Ferry, and Charles-François Dupuis. Romme was a small and clumsy man, a doctor and mathematician by training. His goal, as head of the Committee of Public Education, was to create a simpler calendar than the standard twenty-four-hour/365-day Gregorian abomination. He worked closely with Ferry, a military engineer, and Dupuis, a mathematician and astrologer. They then approached the mathematicians and astronomers Joseph-Louis Lagrange, Joseph Jérôme Lefrançois de Lalande, Gaspard Monge, and Alexandre Guy Pingré to help with calculations. Finally, pursuing new names for the days and months, they hired the poet Fabre d'Églantine, who in turn consulted André Thouin, a gardener at the Jardin des Plantes of the Natural History Museum in Paris.

And so came the lowest point, if not the end, of French horology. The new system created twelve months of thirty days each, with year one beginning on September 22, 1792. The extra days at the end of the year were named "festival days" and celebrated the struggle of the *sans-cullotes* or poorer members of the revolution who could not afford the fashionable knee breeches of the time. That an entire calendar system should end with a summer celebration of unfashionable Parisians probably doomed the effort from the start.

These last five days (six, during Leap Years) were set aside as holidays and named the days of Virtue, Genius, Work, Reason, Reward, and Revolution. Each day was segmented into ten hours of one-hundred minutes, and there were ten days in a "week," each named for its place in the order — Primidi, Duodi, Tridi, and so on.

On October 24, 1793, after almost a year of planning, the French Revolutionary Council would officially accept the French Republican Calendar. France's new, decimalized calendar was not well received by those who had been happily using the Gregorian calendar for the past two centuries. The Pope in Rome condemned the move, reducing the Revolution's popularity with the more pious Parisians.

But watchmakers were willing and ready to assist in the adoption of the new calendar. They began making decimal watches complete with dual time registers, one showing the decimal time and the other showing traditional time. One watch displayed revolutionary time on one half of the dial — five hours worth — and regular time on the other. A famous model featured revolutionary time above a twelve-hour clock, together with a thirty-day calendar register. Liberty, seated with an axe and sheaf of rods, held a level to symbolize concordance, and a trio of soldiers danced gaily around a pole with the Phrygian cap on top.

Counter revolutionaries also had their watches. Some of these watches looked as if they supported the Revolution — with scenes of lazy bourgeois trodding on the heads of the workers — but concealed hidden crosses or the risen Christ or even crowns in honor of the royals. With Breguet's influence waning in fashionable circles, watchmakers fell back into their old habit of adding curlicues and adornment to their watches. Breguet's famous complications — retrograde hands, clever calendar complications, and movements that fit into delicate cases of silver and white gold — were forgotten in the rush to stamp out the old. To Breguet it seemed the artistry of horology had been vanquished forever.

On Monday, January 21, 1793, at eight o'clock in the morning, Louis XVI left the Temple for the last time. For the previous five weeks, he had been subject to a trial for treason, in which he was dubbed with the revolutionary name Citoyen Louis Capet and condemned to death by guillotine. In one of the trial's more offensive moments, the locksmith Gamain, who had been happy to serve as the king's mechanical tutor and take his money for decades, revealed the secret chest he had built for Louis to hold his private papers, and leveled far-fetched accusations that the king had given him a poisoned cup of wine that resulted in a long illness. Throughout the trial, Louis had been kept apart from his wife and children, but the night before, he was permitted to see his family once more.

It was a cold and rainy day, and the carriage, guarded by twelve hundred men on horseback, moved slowly through the streets, which were lined with a gantlet of armed citizens. Louis was silent for most of the ride, but after an English priest who was accompanying the carriage lent him the king his breviary, Louis began reciting psalms. Two hours later, the carriage arrived in the Place Louis XV, which had been renamed the Place de la Revolution. The king stepped out and, surrounded by guards, undressed. Then he mounted the scaffold. "I die innocent of all the crimes laid to my charge," he told the crowd; "I pardon those who have occasioned my death; and I pray to God that the blood you are going to shed may never be visited on France."

He was interrupted by a national guardsman who ordered a drum roll. The axe fell at fifteen minutes after ten, the blade slicing the king's head off just as a scattering of quarter-repeaters tinkled in the crowd. A young guard took the head by the hair and paraded around the scaffold, holding it up for the crowd to see. "Vive la Republique!," the crowd chanted, as the mob pressed forward to dab their handkerchiefs in the king's blood. "Vive la Republique!"

Marie now became the "Widow Capet," mourning in simple black dress, sitting for hours in silence, no longer going outdoors for fresh air, dead-eyed except in the presence of her children.

On January 24, Fersen, unaware of the king's execution but fearing for the lives of the entire royal family, wrote to his sister Sophie from Düsseldorf. "My happy days are over and henceforth I am condemned to eternal regrets and must finish my sad days in desolation. Their faces will haunt my memory forever. Why, oh God, did I ever know them and why didn't I die for them?"

When he learned two days later that the king was dead, the report he heard was that the entire royal family had been killed. "She who was once all my happiness, all my life (for I never ceased loving her nor could I have done so for an instant), she for whom I would gladly have given a thousand lives is no more," he wrote in another letter to his sister. When he learned that Marie was still alive, it only became cause for more anxiety about what would befall her.

Over the next nine months, Fersen could think of little else, and his grief tore him to pieces. He grasped at any shred of information about what was happening in France, and consoled himself by ruminating on how to save the queen. By April, he was joyful, having convinced himself that the queen was out of danger. But each day brought news and as the bad surmounted the good, he grew despondent. He fretted about the queen's failing health, interrogated other travelers for wisps of news that might support his sanguine outlook, and persisted in advocating military invasion by the European powers.

Breguet's business continued to suffer, as courtiers chose exile over beheading and disappeared with their jewelry and watches, leaving little else but their baronial estates and debts. His customers and friends in the city's intelligentsia were also bringing him closer to peril.

One day in April of 1793, three months after Louis's death, Breguet went to a house on the rue Greneta, not far from the Les Halles market. He was with his friend Jean-Paul Marat, the journalist and rabble-rouser who, by now, was an enemy of the business-oriented Girondins. Breguet and Marat were an unlikely pair. At first, their friendship had made sense. Marat was a fellow Swiss, whose sister made watch hands for Breguet. As a court physician, he shared with Breguet the ambivalent role of one who was both a member of the elite and a worker subservient to it. And, like Marat, Breguet saw the need for reforms in French society. Breguet himself had joined the Jacobin political club in its early, moderate days. But by the spring of 1793, the men had little in common philosophically. Breguet remained largely apolitical, while Marat, now radicalized, had taken to accusing one-time comrades-in-arms of being "enemies of the Revolution."

Nonetheless, they maintained a tenuous friendship (recently, while in London, Breguet had obliged Marat's request to secretly gather together and sell some jewelry that the revolutionary had left in England), and on this afternoon, they were visiting a mutual acquaintance and talking politics.

By evening, an angry crowd of protesters sympathetic to the crown had gathered outside the home. The Revolution was entering its most violent period of mob rule and factionalism, and the house was rumored to be harboring an anti-government radical. When the crowd outside began calling for Marat's head, chanting "Down with Marat!," Breguet and the home's owner employed subterfuge to save his life, dressing Marat up as an old woman. Marat suffered from a disfiguring skin disease that had left scabs and open sores on his face, so they lavishly powdered his skin and rouged his cheeks. Then, after hooking his arm through the disguised Marat's, Breguet stepped outside into the torch-lit gloom. On Breguet's arm, the crowd saw a woman with slightly exaggerated make-up on her face. Perhaps because Breguet did not dress like the watchmaker to the king more like a common citizen, the crowd held no grudge against him, nor, apparently, against the homely, odd-looking lady who accompanied him. Breguet and his companion discreetly blended in with the shrieking crowd, disappearing into the night.

Breguet's own situation was becoming precarious, and he attempted to appease the authorities by taking his part in the National Guard. As a result, on May 29th, he found himself in the terrible position of having to guard a prisoner who had once been his greatest benefactor.

Through one day and into the next, Breguet worked a twenty-four-hour shift keeping watch at the Temple prison, where Marie-Antoinette, now the Widow Capet, was being kept. It was heartbreaking duty for a man who had once visited the royal family in their private chambers, and who, only months before her husband's death, had received a commission from the Queen for a repeater watch. This watch, delivered to the Temple by a municipal officer named Coutelle, arrived alongside some toys for the Dauphin from a Parisian shop called the Green Monkey. The package included "a cup and ball, a solitaire, and a beautiful checkerboard."[96]

The queen was held apart from the guards, for fear she would try to send messages out to the wider world, so Breguet's duty was limited to patrolling the lower halls of the prison, sparing the her majesty from the knowledge of his betrayal, and sparing Breguet the distress of seeing her in her diminished state.

With his clients all mounting the scaffold and his business in shambles, Breguet decided it was time to leave his adopted city and began preparing his workshop and employees for his departure. He had spent two decades on the Quai, but now he was embattled from left and right: His assistance to Marat was becoming known, and his longstanding relationship with the royal family cast a pall of suspicion on him under the council. Breguet's landlord, the *comtesse de* Polignac, had escaped Paris in 1789, and as a natural citizen of Switzerland, Breguet's property would soon be in question. Patriotism and fraternity were turning into a frenzy of anti-Royalist fervor and violence. It would be only a matter of time before the National Convention acted.

Only two days after he guarded the queen, Breguet was called before the Convention to explain his refusal to summon the rest of the National Guardsmen in his small district to arms in the Pont-Neuf section of Paris after a call for a general uprising. This traitorous refusal to upset the peace only angered the Convention's members and, in the end, as he wrote, "assured him certain death." His son, who was back in Paris now, was also in danger.

In the middle of June, Breguet went to visit Marat. He found him in his bathtub, having a medicinal soak to ameliorate the constant itching brought on by his skin disease. By now, Marat was a leading member of the most radical Revolutionary group, Robespierre's Montagnards, while Breguet was a moderate the group viewed as reactionary. But some flicker of their old friendship survived, and Marat had not forgotten Breguet's life-saving efforts in spiriting him safely through a hostile crowd only months earlier. Marat told Breguet that he would intercede on his behalf with the Convention, but that Breguet must first apply for paperwork through official channels.

Breguet immediately applied for passports for himself, his son, and his sister-in-law to leave Paris and return to his ancestral home. Now, Marat was able to repay the favor of several months before and help his old friend. On June 24, the National Convention Committee for General Security and Surveillance granted Breguet's request, but it would take weeks for the passports themselves to be issued. Marat's intercession had come just in time, for in mid-July, Marat was stabbed to death, while soaking in his tub, by a royalist sympathizer named Charlotte Corday. Finally, on August 10, 1793, the Committee issued the passports.

On August 12, leaving his firm in the hands of an assistant, Boulanger, Breguet found himself in a stagecoach, together with his son and sister-in-law, clattering away from the city center toward the edge of Paris. The road was full of other carriages heading in the same direction, all fleeing the Revolution. Breguet was in a daze. He felt fortunate to have been permitted to leave the country, but his sense of relief was tenuous. He had left his home and workshop behind. He didn't know when or if he would return. And, on the road ahead, he saw carriages slowing. Breguet experienced a rush of anxiety. He had left all of his tools and watches behind on the Quai — it was too risky not to — but he hadn't been able to part with the one object that embodied all of his work and innovation. Secreted in a hidden compartment aboard the carriage, packed in excelsior, was the 160, Axel von Fersen's watch for Marie-Antoinette. Now, as the carriage approached Fontainebleau, Breguet saw with alarm why the other carriages were slowing. Up ahead, there was a security checkpoint. But his worries proved for naught. After a cursory inspection of his papers, he was waved through. Breguet could rest with relief, at least for a moment, and his carriage rolled onward, toward the border with Switzerland.

On the 14th of October, Marie-Antoinette went on trial before the Revolutionary Tribunal. Among the many smears directed at her in her sham trial—from carrying on orgies at Versailles to funneling French treasury funds to her native Austria—by far the most wounding was the accusation that she had sexually abused the dauphin, her son. "If I have not replied," she said in response, "it is because Nature itself refuses to respond to such a charge laid against a mother." After two days, she was declared guilty of treason. Later that morning, her hair was cut short, and she was wheeled through Paris in a cart. Then, at a quarter past twelve, in the same square where her husband had died nine months earlier, she was executed under the guillotine. Her body was thrown into a mass grave and covered with a sprinkling of wet dirt.

Chapter 12

Zürich

Allen Kurzweil, a journalist, author, and enthusiast of the bizarre, was sitting across from famed watch collector Teddy Beyer on Zürich's Bahnhofstrasse. Kurzweil, a messily coiffed reporter with a shock of black hair, who was doing research for his first novel, *A Case of Curiosities*, had come to ask about a mechanical defecating duck, a famous automaton built by Jacques de Vaucanson in 1739 which consisted of four hundred moving parts that could, in theory, grind, digest, and then defecate kernels of grain, recreating the entire digestive system of a water fowl in brass. It had been so exciting in its day that Voltaire exclaimed, upon seeing it, "without [...] the duck of Vaucanson, you have nothing to remind you of the glory of France." Sadly, the duck never really worked, and most exhibitors introduced actual duck droppings into the rude mechanics to simulate the end of the process. Vaucanson, who died in 1782 and probably worked with Breguet on the Quai, had believed that someone would successfully re-create the digestive system of a bird in his lifetime. To his dismay, no one ever did.

Now, in April of 1983, the conversation between Kurzweil and Beyer ranged over the history of automatons and clockwork. The discussion lighted upon the Marie-Antoinette, Breguet's famous watch, and Beyer waxed euphoric on the topic. He described the complications and was even able to pull out a few original renderings by George Daniels of London—some of the only technical drawings of the watch in existence.

Just then, the phone rang. Beyer stood up to answer it and

listened. A moment passed, and the collector blanched, his face turning ghostly white. He sat back down, and after he had hung up Kurzweil asked what the matter was.

"The Queen," said Beyer. "She has vanished."

Kurzweil would later say that when Beyer said vanished he really meant kidnapped. "How could the loss of a half-pound of metal and rock crystal," wrote Kurzweil, "so devastate a sixth-generation watchmaker who himself oversaw a time museum packed with horological treasures?"

Similar calls to multiple collectors confirmed the watch world's worst fears — that one of the most important objects in their field was now missing. Kurzweil, intrigued by the watch and its story, set the defecating duck aside and followed the mystery across the continent and into the United States. Everywhere, when he mentioned the Queen, he encountered the same reaction: sadness intermingled with regret — regret that the watch was probably destroyed, that it hadn't been better taken care of, that the Marie-Antoinette, like its namesake, was likely dead.

He visited the Breguet archives and the Biblioteque Nationale in Paris. He also travelled by boat to the Isle of Man, where he went to the village of Ramsey, to the home of George Daniels. Daniels, born in 1926, had come to his love of watches at the age of five, when he found a wristwatch on the street, opened it, and found that the inner workings were like looking into "the center of the universe."

"I wanted to spend the rest of my time with watches," he said.

While serving in the British Army, in 1944 Daniels became watchmaker for his regiment. At that time, watchmakers were in demand to repair delicate field timers and watches of enlisted men who slammed their timepieces into walls and mud. He continued to work as a general repairer and restorer until the 1960s, when he began to study the oeuvre of Breguet and became enthralled by the watchmaker's miraculous and beguiling work. Daniels, whose pursed lips and precise manner masked his preference for fast cars and the occasional afternoon beer,[97] told Kurzweil almost everything he knew about Breguet. He had studied Breguet with such intensity that he often said he could think with the master's mind. Kurzweil told me, conspiratorially, that many of Daniels' stories may have sprung from this innate understanding and not from the truths of historical research.

Breguet's work ran like a seam of gold through Daniels' life. He married Julie Marrayat, the pretty daughter of respected Breguet collector Robert Marrayat. He then met George Brown, proprietor of Breguet, in about 1962. The company, at this time, was wobbling on the edge of bankruptcy but Brown was still proud of the traditions and techniques of the master. Daniels became the London Agent de Breguet á Paris, essentially taking a non-paid position as Breguet's London distributor. The job had been open since the 1920s when the last distributor retired and it was largely symbolic. However, Daniels did meet a number of collectors in the line of (albeit limited) duty.

For most of the 1970s Daniels travelled with a Leica camera and a tripod to photograph all of Breguet's work, a task that later became the body of his book, *The Art of Breguet*. Daniels' simplistic photography style was much reviled by professional photographers but, as the clear photos in the book attest, it was more than sufficient. Because he could not shine bright lights on the watches for fear of heating and cracking the enamel he instead took forty or more photos of each watch, ensuring that he accounted for all the vagaries of natural light. Around the same time the Salomons collection was in the process of being moved from England to Israel, a decision that enraged Daniels, he wrote "I made the strongest possible noises to stop the watches going, for they were essentially European and had no Middle Eastern content or relevance." He suspected political pressure because "all entreaties fell on deaf ears."[98]

Daniels also dealt with the museum curator Ohannes Markarian firsthand and found the Armenian to be "very amusing."

"He clearly didn't trust me (Armenians are not noted for trusting others)," he noted, sagely, and he would fiddle with the watches, pretending not to understand their functions or cases, just to watch Markarian squirm. In reality, Daniels was probably the foremost expert on the pieces at the time, with Markarian running a close second.

When the watches were stolen, Daniels was furious. The board of trustees wrote him to ask if he could keep an eye on the markets for any of the watches that had appeared in the catalog and Daniels replied that he "would prefer to buy them for my own collection," reminding them that the move was a disastrous idea in the first place.[99] His photographs and detailed drawings were the last known representations of the Marie-Antoinette in the world.

Daniels himself became a celebrated watchmaker in his own right and had created the co-axial escapement, one of the first improvements to the modern escapement in a century. The new escapement allowed for almost friction-free control of the escape wheel with absolutely no lubrication. Breguet would have been proud.

Daniels knew as much about the Queen as any man besides Ohannes Markarian. He was one of the few people to have seen and analyzed the entire watch. While Ohannes understood the Queen with his heart, Daniels grasped it with his mind.

After his day with Daniels, Kurzweil travelled to Israel, where he began to unravel the skein of hearsay and lies that had already accreted around the heist. Kurzweil was one of the first to hear the apocryphal rumor of the "partially eaten ham-and-cheese sandwich" at the scene of the crime. In the offices of the *Jerusalem Post* he cracked open ledgers marked Crime 1983 and Murders 1979-1985 to research the gangs of Jerusalem, and then he went to visit Markarian himself in his little shop in the Old City, and then at the curator's quarters at the L.A. Mayer Museum.

It was there that he saw the Queen's old "shagreen case" and that Markarian asked him to inhale the scent of its empty compartments. In his novel *The Grand Complication*, Kurzweil would enshrine the theft in fiction and re-create this moment verbatim:

"Take a whiff," he said as he unlatched the red leather box. "I want you to smell a fragrance more enchanting than the finest perfume." I sniffed the interior of the case. "What you are smelling," he said, is the odor of sanctity." I pressed him further. "The Queen was one of my children—my favorite child," the curator acknowledged. "And now that child is gone."[100]

Kurzweil wasn't the only detective on the case of the missing watch. Secretly, so as not to draw attention to the investigation and embarrass the Israeli police, the trustees of the museum had hired their own detective to hunt down the lost Queen.

Chapter 13

Brussels

Axel Fersen was visiting his lover Eleanor Sullivan, when he learned of Marie's death on October 20, 1793. In his diary, the next day, he vowed "an eternal hatred which can never end" against the judges who had sentenced *Elle* to death. Soon, his rage was joined by profound sadness. "Every day I think of it," he wrote, "and every day my grief increases. Every day I feel even more all I have lost." As the days wore on, memories of her face haunted him.

"It follows me wherever I go I can think of nothing else."

Breguet was in Geneva, where he had been for two months, when he heard the news. He had sent his son and sister-in-law to his cousins in Le Locle, a small town in the Jura mountains, far from the hustle and bustle of Neuchâtel. Breguet would join them after conducting business in the capital city, where he was meeting with old friends and partners who had been supplying him with parts for more than twenty years, while contemplating his next move. He had considered remaining in Geneva, but found it expensive and, suffering from a blockade by France, a hard place to live and do business. He had also thought about setting up just over the border in France, at Fernay, where Voltaire had run his watchmaking concern, but such a move would clearly be too dangerous. He was mulling these options when word of the queen's execution arrived from Paris. If Breguet had any remaining doubts, the death of the queen made clear to him that a way of life, one that had nurtured his livelihood and given him many friends, was over.

For the next two years, Breguet would do his best to manage his business from afar. Every day brought more distressing news. Boulanger, the assistant he had left in charge, wrote to inform him that the revolutionary calendar had been officially adopted, effectively destroying the value of his current stock of watches in France. Another day, he learned that his former client, Princess Thérèse of Monaco, had been guillotined. In the summer of 1794, the revolutionaries forced Boulanger off the Quai into lesser premises around the corner. His assistant quickly gathered up the stock and papers and locked the doors of the shop, but with little effect. Looters quickly snapped the locks and made off with machinery, records, and tools. They burned many of Breguet's old logs. Today only a few dozen remain, kept in a sealed vault at the Breguet boutique in Paris and protected by Emmanuel Breguet, one of the master's remaining descendants.

As Breguet muddled through the uncertainties of exile, he continued to work on the 160. Occasionally, he would receive a letter from Axel von Fersen, now far away and heartbroken, asking after other watches he had left in Breguet's care, but never mentioning his grand and tragically moot commission. Breguet would always reply quickly and kindly, if cryptically.

Fersen was in a stupor of mourning. As if expecting cosmic recompense for everything he had lost, he went to Vienna seeking reimbursement of the 1.5 million livres he had raised for the flight to Varennes. From Brussels, in March of 1794, he wrote to Breguet, his last living connection to Marie.

Sir,

You remember perhaps Sir that I was one of your regulars. I already have a military watch from you, in silver, similar to the one you made for the Duke of Guiche, and experience has shown me the perfection of your work. I am rather happy to possess as well a gold watch of those which winds itself, that you made I believe in 1784 or 1785 for the late Queen. There are initials on it and in the interior of the cover there is 1100 14 .

As these works which wind themselves are rare and there are few clock makers who know how to fix them and that moreover this watch does not ring the minutes, I would like to have the cover and the dial preserved with its same engraving and I'd like the same done to another work by you which ordinarily winds itself and which rings the minutes with a sound like that of a watch Mr. [Crauford] has from you.

June 20, the anniversary of the flight to Varennes, brought still more unhappy memories. "I can only think of this day in 1791," Fersen confided to his diary, lacerating himself yet again for the failed escape. In September, Fersen received a reply from the Hofburg, in response to his request for reimbursement for himself and two older ladies who had given most of their savings for the Varennes mission, but it merely suggested his petition would have been better timed had it been filed while the king and queen were still alive. Just then, Fersen learned that his father had died. Two days later, he wrote to Breguet once more, now with a touch of desperation. "Do you know what became of the watch that the unfortunate lady used to wear?" he asked.

Sir, it was only at the time of my departure from [...] on June 28th that I received, sir, your letter of May nineteenth responding to mine regarding the watch of the late Queen that I had wanted and my planned travels... I replied to your letter on July 2nd or 3rd but as I fear that my letter may not have reached you. I write again to beg you to tell me where I should send my letter and how I might deliver to you my watch and arrange with you my movements to do this. Please send your reply, sir, to Düsseldorf at the home of J.S. Junge Senior. I am honored to be your humble and admiring servant.
Count Felsen
General Major in the service of Sweden

This was Fersen's last letter to Breguet, and his most despondent. In none of these letters did Fersen mention the Queen, whose original purpose had died with its intended recipient. The secret of the 160's provenance now remained solely in Breguet's own records.

Fersen set out for Sweden to oversee the disposition of his father's property. October sixteenth, the date of his lover's execution, found him crossing the Baltic Sea. "Today is a terrible day for me," he wrote in his diary. "It is when I lost the person who loved me the most in the world and who loved me truly. I shall mourn her loss until the end of my life and all that I feel for Eleonore can never allow me to forget what I have lost." The date became Fersen's "day of devotion," and year after year, he would morbidly note its passing.

Back in Stockholm, Fersen observed that when he entered the opera, everyone turned to look at him. He was thirty-nine now. His hair had begun to whiten, and his brow to furrow. When the dauphin Louis-Charles died in the Temple prison the following year, Fersen was at his country property in Stenige. The boy's death severed Fersen's final connection to the country that had brought him so much happiness and pain. "He was the last and only interest remaining to me in France. The news is too painful to bear and it brings back memories that are heartrending."

Breguet knew that with Marie-Antoinette dead, Fersen would no longer want to proceed with the commission of the 160. But the watchmaker was determined to continue. The watch might have lost its meaning as a token of deep and clandestine love, but now it would serve another end, as a grand canvas for Breguet's artistry.

In France, the revolutionaries had consumed themselves. The Reign of Terror was over, the Jacobins disbanded. In the spring of 1795, Breguet received a letter from Boulanger. It was safe, Boulanger wrote, for the master to return to Paris.

As the century turned, Fersen and Breguet were moving along starkly different paths. They no longer had occasion to see or write to one another. Fersen had seemed to wash his hands of the watch, of France, of anything at all that might remind him of the tragedy of his love.

By the end of 1803, Fersen had settled in Sweden permanently, at peace with his position and his place there. He held large *soupers* for hundreds of people and was happy to find, when the French legation arrived, that many "had forgotten old France," freeing him however briefly from the bonds of his past. His chef recorded preparing almost daily "at least 15 dishes to serve, sometimes 20, other times 30 or 40," an abundant feast for the once almost ascetic Fersen. Traces of his old wit remained, as when he complained that Swedes went to bed far too early and that "this is what makes all the women fat, wrinkled, and old before their time."

He had fewer love affairs than before. One was with a twenty-six-year-old beauty named Emelie Aurora De Geer, but little came of their constant letters back and forth. Fersen, now fifty-one and more rugged than handsome, was a bit too proper for the young woman's taste. Danish King Christian VIII, an old friend of Fersen's from his time on the continent, noted in 1803 that "sorrow and misfortune have aged him so that he looks twenty years older than he is."[101] His niece described him as possessing, by this time, a distant hauteur that "covered his inner emptiness."

The next two years brought a change in continental feeling toward Napoleon Bonaparte and the new French Empire. As Britain, Prussia, and Russia fired up their war machines against burgeoning French expansion, Sweden's Gustav IV began calling for war against the emperor and a restoration of the Bourbon monarchy.

As time went on, Fersen seemed to drift out of favor. He spent little time in Stockholm, visiting Uppsala occasionally on official business but rarely being summoned to meet with the king. One contemporary wrote that Fersen "busied himself with entertaining, seeing how his horses were looked after, sometimes himself driving an excellent team, sometimes riding."[102] He lived the life of a country gentleman possessed of the discipline and propriety on which Fersen prided himself.

Around March of 1808, a new cautiousness seems to have overtaken Fersen. The entries in his diary, once voluminous, start to taper off, and his sister wrote that Fersen burned "a number of papers," deepening the mystery.

On May 28, 1810, while practicing cavalry maneuvers in the beech forests of Skåne, about 340 miles from Stockholm, the new crown prince fell from his saddle and died immediately. The cause was almost certainly a stroke, but back in Stockholm a different narrative began to weave itself into the minds of the populace. The crown prince who had, in a sense, deposed the old king was gone, and the prime suspects were a group of "counterrevolutionaries" supposedly led by Fersen and Sophie. They were suspected of poisoning the Dane. Murder by poison was a fairly common accusation in an era when common ailments could strike a person dead in a few hours.

Was there any truth to the rumors? Almost certainly not. But there had been talk of Fersen displaying "coldness" toward the new "prince of the mob." And Fersen and his circle stood to gain by the reinstatement of Gustav IV as king. These were the dots flimsily connected by an agitated public.

Within two weeks of Christian's death, popular pamphlets were calling for "The People, August's Avenger," to rise up against the counterrevolutionaries. Two days later, a sailor stationed near Stockholm's southern sluicegate reported that the people were prepared to take up arms "against those they believe had poisoned the crown prince, and they have decided to murder Count Fersen just at the time of the prince's funeral" and then attack "many other distinguished persons who it is claimed did not love the prince."[103]

The funeral was scheduled for the twentieth of June, and Fersen returned to the capital on the nineteenth, ignoring the warnings of his friends and family. As the country's grand marshall, he was expected to lead the coffin to the cemetery. Stubbornly, Fersen refused to turn down his position in the cortege, lest his absence imply guilt. While Fersen dined in Stockholm that night, more pamphlets were circulating, calling for a "Fox Hunt" at the funeral.[104]

On the twentieth, as Fersen rolled down a long avenue on the western shore of Stockholm's Old Town, he found his carriage under attack. According to one general in attendance, the grand marshall was riding in a large state coach driven by six white horses with "red morocco harnesses" and "richly ornamented with gilded bronze," notable because the crown prince's hearse was simply covered by a black canopy "dusty after the journey."

"He looked like a triumphant conqueror dragging behind him a defeated foe," the General wrote later.

The long procession moved quietly, until it reached Stora Nygatan, a thin, cobbled avenue lined by sharp-peaked three-story houses that opened onto Riddarhuset Square. There, with the heat of the day rising as Fersen passed, a crowd began to chant "Murderer." Finally, the police asked Fersen and his driver to turn off the processional route to Riddarhustorget, south of the royal palace and close to the local police station. Witnesses would recall Fersen "sitting pale as death in the most frightful fear and distress."

Suddenly, rocks shattered the carriage windows, and the crowd surged forward, nearly toppling Fersen's coach. Fersen managed to take refuge in a tavern called Hultgren's, a small inn on the second floor of a building on Stora Nygatan. But the crowd rushed up the stairs, surrounded Fersen, accused him of causing the French Revolution, and claimed he was trying to duplicate it in Sweden. They began to strip him of his regalia, tearing off his

121

medals, sword, and coat and throwing them in a bundle out into the street below.

Authorities soon arrived and were able to negotiate a safe passage for Fersen out to the street. But there, when he appeared, the crowd called for blood. As Fersen passed out through the doors he was heard to say: "I see that it will soon be my last hour."

The police brought him to a room in Riddarhuset Square, a noble-looking building clad in white plaster and outlined in black. A police garrison was nearby, and the building promised sanctuary. But again the crowd followed, tearing the door down and rushing in.

The hundreds of soldiers who were also in the funeral procession watched the whole spectacle, and the police surely looked down upon it from their barracks, but no one in power lifted a finger. "One is almost tempted to say that the government wanted to give the people a victim to play with," a contemporary of Fersen's later wrote, "just as when one throws something to an irritated wild beast to distract its attention."

The mob dragged Fersen from the room and threw him to the ground outside. A group of more responsible members of the mob tried to lead him out of the square and toward the courtyard of the Royal Palace. But there, his guards were overwhelmed, and he was trampled and kicked by his countrymen. For more than an hour, his body was beaten and savaged. Finally, a Finnish seaman named Otto Tandefelt stomped on Fersen's ribs, crushing his chest and his silver soldier's watch. That evening, sixteen years, eight months, and four days after the death of his beloved, Fersen was pronounced dead.

Even when Breguet heard the news about Fersen, he did not stop working on the 160. Breguet's last living link to the Bourbon monarchy and the great commission of 1783 was gone. But he continued to assemble the watch, slowly.

He was busier than ever. Two days earlier, on June 8, 1810, Breguet had delivered the world's first wristwatch. The recipient was Caroline Murat, Queen of Naples and sister of Napoleon I. The Number 2639 was simply a small pocket watch, but it had two lugs – essentially loops of metal on the top and bottom that could be tied down with a ribbon. This miniscule watch, made as a one-off novelty, would redefine watchmaking in the next century. Because the watch could be worn around the wrist, it was unobtrusive and ensured that the queen would not have to fish in her bustle or bag for her pocketwatch. This wristwatch – a form of horological design that didn't reappear until the early twentieth century – was essentially a precursor to every modern watch made. The size, the shape, and the method of wearing were all far ahead of their time.

With the business running smoothly and his assistants handling matters of finance, he was now free to tinker and create, and he built his watches one after the other, making a few hundred a year. In 1802, competing against firms from across Napoleon's far-flung empire, Breguet had won a gold medal at the French Industrial Exhibit at the Louvre, a show comprised almost entirely of French luxury items that one British visitor described as "not having a single item of ordinary consumption on display."[105] Competing against over five hundred famous French silk-, tapestry-, and porcelain-makers as well as vintners and distillers of fine brandy, Breguet's small firm and famous watches were right at home in the luxurious confines of the show grounds. The Exposition was immensely popular, and it was moved from the Champ de Mars (then "waste" lands outside of the city) and eventually included 1,422 exhibitors in 1806, all flogging France's most luxurious doo-dads.[106]

Breguet and his fellow watchmakers showed off their precision pieces, including astronomical and marine chronometers and Breguet's unique "tact" watch, which could be read by rubbing a finger over the closed case. Afterward, Breguet was invited to a dinner where Napoleon was present, but the watchmaker did not speak to him. Napoleon had turned against the royal-friendly Breguet, boycotting his wares. The fickle emperor wouldn't resume his purchases from Breguet until 1805.

The 1806 Industrial Exhibit was Breguet's watershed. At this event, he competed against old pupils and rivals, including Louis Berthoud, but they weren't prepared for the masterwork up his sleeve. Breguet had patented his tourbillon on June 26, 1801, naming it after the French term Descartes used to describe "whirling planetary systems,"[107] but it had its public coming out at the 1806 trade show. It was the most complex single mechanism (horologists have never called this a complication, per se) ever attempted.

Breguet continued to innovate. Three years after he completed the world's first wristwatch, in 1813 he finished the Sommariva, a watch for Comte Giovanni Battista Sommariva, a onetime barber's assistant who had grown up to become an important barrister in the revolutionary courts. The watch, really a watch and a clock, consisted of a complex watch complete with tourbillon, equation of time, annual calendar, and chronometer, along with a complex clock with a tourbillon. Breguet himself described the piece as his "highest achievement" – the 160 had not been finished yet – and the Sommariva had a peculiar feature. A small, tilted rotating platform on the top of the clock held the watch and turned it in three-minute long revolutions. A small reservoir of oil inside the watch held old lubricants and washed the gears anew in fresh lubricants. This way, the watch never "settled" or stuck. The watch itself was lost in a fire in Sommariva's palace, and only scant descriptions remain.

As the years passed, more and more prestige accrued to Breguet. Even as Napoleon had ignored him at the dinner in 1802, Breguet's presence there placed him in the pantheon of great French scientists and made him a number of connections in the burgeoning science of telegraphy.

The growing recognition of Breguet led to intrigue and backstabbing. In November 1806, his enemies spread a rumor that he had died in a coach accident, resulting in all of his Swiss suppliers refusing to ship watch parts to the company. Breguet had to again invite various important members of the French and Swiss watchmaking industries to his shop to show that he was very much alive.

Breguet received a string of accolades. He was named a member of the Office of Longitudes. In 1815, he was presented with the Legion of Honor medal, available only to French nationals, by king Louis XVIII, which must have evoked striking connotations and memories for the aging Breguet. His long struggle to be recognized as both a watchmaker and a French citizen was complete. That October, he achieved the highest honor for a watchmaker under France's new constitutional monarchy, when he was given the official commission to become Horologer to the Royal Navy. Breguet succeeded Louis Berthoud, the same watchmaker who, it was suspected, had put him out of his workshop during the Revolution. The horologer to kings was now horologer to another king, Louis XVIII, uncle to Marie-Antoinette's son, Louis XVII, the dauphin.

The commission was not lucrative at first. The title was becoming increasingly outdated, as new navigation techniques, including rudimentary ship-to-shore communication systems using semaphore flags, were beginning to develop. And Berthoud's factory would still be completing and delivering already ordered new chronometers for another six years. Finally, Breguet was able to make his first delivery, of twenty-two chronometers, the clocks he fabricated went to private individuals, including sea captains, and he published a small book instructing sailors as to their use and upkeep. His large, white-dialed timepieces became well-known in port cities for their durability and legibility. One striking example, the 2741, was made in 1813 and belonged to Monseigneur Belmas, Bishop of Cambrai, who received it from Breguet as a gift. The clock, encased in a dark wooden box, had a white face with a guilloche dial and even an early stopwatch. It featured two separate mainsprings, along with two *reserves de marche* to show the energy left in the springs.

Like most marine chronometers, this one was connected to brass gimbals, which kept the clock flat even in violent seas. Every chronometer box was inscribed: Breguet et Fils, Horloger de la Marine Royale. This one bore an additional inscription, Pour Mr Belmas ami de l'auteur – for a friend of the creator.[108]

Breguet was also finally inducted into the Academy of Science, replacing Berthoud as representative of the horological sciences, a position that Napoleon had blocked him from in 1796 and 1807 for political reasons. Membership fulfilled one of Breguet's lifelong goals. Here, Breguet was among equals. The members, whose number included mathematicians, engineers, and biologists, would meet regularly to discuss new inventions and discoveries and publish papers on, for instance, the reduction of "overturning accidents by public carriages." (Breguet was a coauthor.) Breguet did joint research with "his old friend the mathematician Prony, the loyal architect of his successive election attempts," a historian would write, "on the regulation and length of oscillations of pendulums, the mathematician providing the theory, formulae, and calculations, while the watchmaker made the pendulums for their experiments."

The academy's ornate building, almost a miniature Versailles in scope, became Breguet's second home, and he visited as often as he could. There were endless things to look at. The academy was a kind of *wunderkammer*, with mirrors and globes and the skeletons of men and beasts hanging from the walls. A taxidermied ermine watched vigilantly from the corner of one room while members debated the finer points of engineering and explored early experiments in electricity, communication, and horology. The old man attended Academy meetings regularly, reveling in his new position, and he was a familiar figure at the museums and symposiums on science and engineering. After decades of assiduous work, he was finally being treated less like a tradesman and more like a scientist.

Breguet was now such a renowned personage that, starting around 1819, a watchmaker named Moinet came to the workshops and spent two years poring over firm records and documenting the history of the house. Moinet's book, a mish-mash of technical data and history, did not do justice to the firm's rich history, but it was a start. Through his work, many theoretical descriptions destroyed in the revolution were restored, and many of the business practices that had made Breguet famous came to light.

The Bishop of Cambrai — for whom Breguet also built the first pocket watch with a crystal back, to better show the movement — wrote in 1821 that the workshop, like Breguet's watches, was like "a crowd of people shut up in a tiny house, living in peace and working efficiently together to create good order." Moinet's book also showed that Breguet was active on the Ile, assisting the needy and playing his part as a community leader during the Revolution and after.

Breguet's influence was felt in other ways, for his ingenuity had extended to inventions beyond the realm of simple timekeeping. His "musical chronometer," which kept perfect time and could be slowed down or sped up by a musician wishing to set the tempo for a piece of music, would enter the standard conductor's repertoire as the metronome. Although the original idea seems to have come from the delightfully named Dr. Crotch in the late 1600s, Breguet exhibited his own version of the device at the Paris Exhibition on the Champs de Mars in 1794, and Ludwig van Beethoven, after learning of it from his friend the inventor Johann Nepomuk Mälzel, quickly created a little ditty based on its repetitive ticking. The resulting song ended up in the second movement of the composer's *8th Symphony*.

Breguet also explored a number of tangential topics including the principle of "voluntary movement" in insects, even writing an

"Essay Upon Animal Strength, and on the Principle of Voluntary Movement." Noting that a butterfly pinned to a card — still alive — would beat its wings interminably for hours, and even days. He wondered if he could somehow harness this organic energy in his clockwork. The resulting experiments presaged the development of organic chemistry.

In his later years, Breguet began moving back toward his overarching obsession: precision. His war on friction, the fight of his youth, was finally won, and now he was able to dedicate himself to the measure of seconds and sub-seconds in a way that was previously unfathomable.

He began supplying laboratories and observatories with striking clocks that could measure the passage of time while astronomers observed the heavens. One model fit right onto the telescope itself, allowing an observer to make highly granular measurements without having to glance at his watch.

Breguet also built some of the first stopwatches, complete with stop and run buttons. A model built in 1820, the number 4000, was a split seconds stopwatch, which allowed for the measurement of two concurrent events. When the stopwatch was engaged, two seconds hands would simultaneously move across the dial. With the press of a button, the first hand would stop, while the other hand continued. Another press, and the other hand would stop. A final press, and the entire movement reset itself, seating the hands back into place. The complexity of such a watch, called a *chronometre a doubles secondes*, dazzled Academy members and was invaluable to its explorers in their attempts to time steam-powered locomotives, and, more ambitiously, measure the speeds of sound and light. Experimenters in the early nineteenth century also worked with various Breguet inventions – including the miniaturized bimetallic ship's thermometer – to show that sound could heat a metal plate and that iron conducted sound better than air.[109]

Always present in the background was the 160, which Breguet worked on in bursts. He seems to have put it aside for a decade or more. The first nineteenth-century record of him working on it appears in 1809. Then, suddenly, it again became an obsession. He worked on it 284 days in 1812, 228 days in 1813, and 212 days in 1814, a considerable outlay of time and talent for his small company. When his most trusted customers visited the shop, he favored them with glimpses of the Marie-Antoinette, its sharp cornered gears and pushers bound against a small disk of brass that was polished to an impeccable shine. By 1820, his workshop was putting out a few hundred watches a year at most. The 160, nearly complete, lay on his assistant Michel Weber's bench, where the final complications were being added. Maybe, when it was finished, Breguet would show it in an exhibition. Maybe it was destined for his pocket alone. The records never stated to whom it was decreed.

The Revolution was already thirty years old, and the 160 was now a dictionary of all that Breguet had learned in the intervening years. Like a great architect sweeping his arm across the face of his defining edifice, Breguet could point to the 160 and explain that everything – everything he knew – was in that single piece.

This watch was the apex of his art. It was his personal masterpiece, a marriage of technology and art that amazed all who saw it. Like the technological gadgets that would follow it — the X-ray machine, the iPod, the Mars Rover — it was at once beautiful and full of utility. It was almost impossible to describe how hard it had been to build — nothing like it had ever been attempted — and the efforts of so many men for so many years had not created a jumble of clashing gears but a symphony that played in perfect harmony.

His sons and business partners had come to view the 160 as a strange obsession for the master. Hadn't he created the finest watches in Paris? Hadn't his timepieces traversed the globe, from France to Turkey, from the horn of Africa to Brazil? They were perplexed that he was still drawn to this massive nest of complications, which was more pomp than substance, a gold watch with a crystal face stuffed with all the tricks of his art.

On September 15, 1823, Breguet set out on his daily constitutional, which traced a course from the Quai de l'Horloge, south over the Pont Neuf, then along the Seine to the Quai de Conti, to the Academy of Science. Most days, Breguet, now 76, would spend a few hours at his bench and then, when his legs would carry him, come here to the domed edifice that housed the Academy.

Physically, Breguet was diminished. His hair had gone gray long ago, and his small face now looked even smaller against his high collar. The summer months, when the Seine ran like a sewer and the fetid city air hung heavily all around, were the worst for the old man.

A year had passed since the first signs of illness, a severe shortness of breath that kept him in bed from August 1822 until January. His friends at the Academy visited him often during his illness, one friend noting: "It would have been far too early to lose you."[110] They spoke loudly at his bedside, because his hearing was going, possibly a side effect of the metal-fabricating din he had been exposed to over the years.

The next year was difficult, but by September he was back behind his bench. His sure hand now strayed, and his lines in the ledger and his notebooks grew thin and unsure. He was limited to sketching now, and no longer drafting. One of these rough drawings, about an inch high, showed a carriage clock shaped like one of the equal leg arch windows of the Academy. In the clock's center, he scrawled three registers. Below the equation of time — which he marked simply "equation," in his cramped script — were small windows for the *jour*, *mois*, and *année*.

It seemed a larger cousin of a watch he had completed in 1819, the 2522, with its main dial, subsidiary hour, minutes, and seconds registers, and central stopwatch. The 2522 was a precursor to the chronograph, with an elegant, tripartite face and three tiny hands that beat the time.

Recently, Breguet had noticed his symptoms resurfacing. His legs were weak and pained him, and his walks were less and less frequent. A few weeks earlier, he had spent an afternoon at the Academy's exhibition at the Louvre, acting as advisor and jurist, and found that by the end of the day he was completely run down. Just four days before, he had returned with his grandson, Louis-Clement, already a renowned watchmaker in his own right, to continue his judging duties, and circled through the exhibition a full four times.

Today, he was still feeling the effects of his exertions. As he walked along the river he had worked beside for half a century, he tried to inhale deeply and found that he could not. The breathlessness was back. He barely had the strength to check his watch, but he knew he needed to rest. His difficulty breathing came and went throughout that night and into the next, as he lay in bed listening to the soothing percussion of all his ticking clocks and watches. On the morning of September 17, 1823, at his home on the now renamed Quai de I'Horloge du Palais, as he lay in bed and his son held him, Abraham-Louis Breguet died.

"Master Breguet is gone," shouted apprentices along the Quai, as they made their delivery rounds. Soon everyone on the Quai knew, and then everyone in the city. Watchmakers walked along the Quai in a long procession, paying their respects as they passed beneath the window where the master had worked for so many years. In their pockets, their own creations ticked, but so much of what they knew had come from him. The shape of a gear, the precision of a transmission, a method to maintain accuracy – they were all Breguet's. His colleagues built watches, but Breguet had built watchmaking.

The day after his death, thirty carriages carrying the crème of the watchmaking world followed the hearse to the Père Lachaise cemetery, where La Fontaine and Molière, among so many other eminent Frenchmen, lay buried. The cemetery was still far from the city in those days, and its narrow avenues were at once close and cluttered. When the peasants heard that Breguet was dead, they began to follow the procession, talking of Breguet's generosity.

The funeral began at 1 p.m. Noblemen spoke, as Breguet was laid to rest. A ship's navigator, Freycinet, who carried Breguet watches twice around the world, said a few words about the man's work, and the Duc de Praslin, for whom Breguet had made a watch to rival the Marie-Antoinette, spoke of his business acumen and rigor. The paeans were brief and marked by sobs. "The grief of all these eminent men crowding around your tomb is your finest eulogy," Charles Dupin, a naval engineer, said in remembrance. "The entire nation will mourn your loss, for you have contributed so greatly to the triumph of her arts. Thus the title 'pupil of Breguet' ensures the holder the justified esteem of the whole of Europe."

Joseph Fourier, the mathematician and fellow member of the Academy, offered a touching panegyric, stating that "to place oneself in the first rank of a difficult and necessary profession, to invent and give perfection, to guide navigators, to give new instruments to science, to create one's own fortune whilst founding it on public usefulness, to enjoy friendship, ignore ingratitude, and be above envy and jealousy—that is a happy and honourable destiny."[111]

And then Breguet was laid in his crypt. As the door closed,

the assembled crowd checked their watches and began the long ride home.

Four years passed. On December 31, 1827, the feast of Saint Sylvestre in Paris, Antoine-Louis Breguet had something else to celebrate besides the dawning of the New Year. Across the city, families sat awaiting the clarions and horns that marked the cusp of another January, and Antoine-Louis raised a coupe of champagne in a toast.

After his father's death, Antoine-Louis had assumed full control of the firm. He was now fifty-five years old, a major figure on the Quai in his own right, and his life had come to resemble his father's in other, more melancholy ways. At the turn of the century he had begun an affair with Jeanne-Francoise Maleszewski, whose husband Pierre was a friend of the master, a tireless supporter of the brand who sold his watches throughout Central and Eastern Europe. He was an envoy and diplomat with many military ties, and it was through these connections that Breguet had been able to sell his nascent telegraphs to General Desolle of the French Imperial army, a financial coup.

Between 1798 and 1804 Maleszewski worked in Warsaw, leaving his wife and children with the Breguet family in Paris. Meanwhile, his wife Jeanne lost her father in 1799 and then two infant children, conceived during the brief periods that Maleszewski was in Paris. The strain was too much, and she became close to the master's son, Antoine-Louis, who was handsome and kind. Jeanne divorced her husband in 1809, and the couple moved to Bourg-la-Reine, south of Paris. But Antoine-Louis' happiness was cut short like his father's. In 1813, Jeanne-Francoise died, leaving a boy and a girl in the younger Breguet's care. The master's son returned to the Quai and lived with his widowed father. The children were sent to Neuchâtel to live with relatives.

Now, four years after laying his father to rest, Antoine-Louis finally closed the 160. It was finished. With him was Michel Weber, his father's trusted old deputy, who had toiled on the 160 for nearly half a century. Antoine-Louis, born in 1776, had grown up watching his father and Weber work side-by-side, had seen the 160 go from a hazy, over-ambitious dream to an increasingly intricate work-in-progress. Someone in the firm, most likely the conscientious Boulanger, wrote in bold letters in the logbook, below the notations recording the final work, an anticlimactic coda to an epic endeavor: *"Mettre les nouveaux frais qui pourraient se presenter au compte the marchandise."* "Put the new fees that may arise in the goods account." Then Antoine-Louis and the others said good night and went their separate ways for the evening.

The greatest watch ever made, born of love and genius and tragedy, which took forty-four years to complete, which outlived its creator, its commissioner, and its intended recipient, was finished at last, and then nothing. There was no special fanfare, beyond this quiet celebration by its makers.

Later that night, as fireworks exploded over the Seine, red, blue, and white bursts of light flashed in the sky and reflected off the big windows of the house on the Quai and the crystal faces and blued hands of the watches displayed behind them on velvet cushions. The New Year had arrived.

Amid the darkness of the workshop, the 160, nestled in a silk-lined box, ticked quietly among its sisters — the big Regulator on the wall used to set each watch, the repeaters, the subscription watches, the carriage clocks, the tourbillons, the case clocks — all of them ticking in a murmuring chorus, their midnight chimes echoing through the empty workshop against the fading peals of the bells of Notre Dame.

Chapter 14

Paris

After Antoine-Louis Breguet and Michel Weber celebrated the completion of the 160 in 1827, the watch remained in the Breguet showroom, a silent testament to its late architect's genius and a marketing beacon for the firm he had left behind. His son, less obsessed with the art of watchmaking, stayed busy expanding the company as a major supplier to European navies.

Some years later — records of the exact date were lost — the firm priced the 160 at around 17,000 gold francs and sold it to an unnamed buyer. By 1838, it was in the possession of the aged Marquis de La Groye, Marie-Antoinette's former page, who had it for a few years before sending it back to the firm for repair. The childless Marquis died soon after, and when no one came to reclaim the watch, ownership reverted to the company.

The watch then sat, untouched, for the next half-century, until, in 1887, an English collector named Sir Spencer Brunton bought it for six hundred pounds. Brunton was a financier whose daughter, Enid, a stage actress in London, would in 1905 take up the role of the mother in J.M. Barrie's popular new play, *Peter Pan* ("the revival has been received with such acclamations that there seems a serious danger of 'Peter Pan' being made not a little ridiculous, as the object of a cult," wrote one reviewer).[112]

By this time, the allure of a watch such as the Marie-Antoinette had only increased from the days when Breguet was alive. In the eyes of industrial Britain, with its electric lights and new modes of thinking, the previous century possessed a sepia charm. Reminders of a more chivalrous age were a welcome distraction from

133

the dirt and grease of industrial London.

The 160 kept changing hands. Brunton sold it to one Murray Mark, another collector who left no trace of his purchase save a note in the Breguet firm's ledger. Eventually, he, in turn, seems to have sold the watch to David Lionel Salomons, an inventor and industrialist who was passionate about Breguet and his work.

Like Axel von Fersen, Salomons, born in 1851, was a man out of time. But if Fersen was trapped in a courtly past, Salomons' thinking penetrated far into the future. He was hindered only by the limits of his age. An early proponent of electricity, traffic control systems, and "horseless carriages," he helped pull England into the twentieth century.

He noted that he "was born a mechanic," and that his favorite toys in childhood were "a clockwork engine, some building bricks, and a box of tools." His great-grandfather had been an astronomer and mathematician, his father an art collector. "Thus," he wrote, "it comes about that I admire the beautiful when combined with mechanics."

He had a decidedly Victorian grumpiness about him, along with the air of a sly professor. His biography described memberships in societies dealing with "astronomy, chemistry, civil engineering, geology, geography, meteorology, commerce, physics, military, inventions, archaeology, law, statistics, zoology, botany, agriculture, electrical engineering, photography, microscopy, and 'self-propelled traffic.'"[113]

He wore impeccably tailored but slightly rumpled suits and kept a beard and mustache in the style of Freud over his sharp eyes and prominent nose. He often carried a watch attached to a long chain. At the other end was a small mechanical gun, a miniature six-shooter with an inch-long barrel. Some of his stolidity, as well as whimsy, comes out in his description of his early years, which he spent banging tools together rather than playing with soft toys:

A mechanic cannot be made any more than a painter, a poet or a musician. When I was young, nurseries were not 'toy shops' like they are today, and children were happier in consequence. I did want one thing more — a Statham's 10s. 6d. "Chemical Cabinet for Youths." For years I looked into the window of a chemist shop where some were displayed in the king's Road at Brighton, but my l0s. 6d. was not to be forthcoming for a long time. Looking back from my age today to that period, it may have been a merciful thing for the household that I did not possess the chemicals then.

Salomons' love of watches came early. At the age of fourteen, he "made friends with a little working watch repairer, and I induced him to let me come into his shop from time to time in the evening, to learn to make pivots and do other work, also to repair jewelry." He began taking repair work home, and he scraped together money for tools, "which were not many."

At twenty-three, Salomons, having heard "Breguet's name spoken of with reverence," hunted down some of his work. On Regents Street, he found a larger Breguet clock, but at 150 pounds, the price was too dear for him. Ever the engineer, he was content to "study it carefully in his mind" and leave it for another, vowing "never to buy on my own judgment until I have had proper experience."

The bug truly bit when he visited another shop on Bond Street. There, he found a Breguet *perpetuelle* that was not running. A quick inspection of the movement found that an "inexperienced watchmaker [had] broken a wheel," a quick fix for a polymath like Salomons, and he discuss the piece with the proprietor of the shop who "pointed out and explained all the complicated details and the beauty of Breguet's workmanship."[114]

Over his lifetime, Salomons would assemble a massive collection of Breguet timepieces — some 140 of them, including a number of contemporary works by the firm that still bore the watchmaker's name. It was the defining assemblage of Breguet's oeuvre, and Salomons kept it at Broomhill, his castle-like estate in Kent County, England, which had an opulent theatre with side parlors bearing the names of various great inventors.

Salomons' crowning achievement as a collector came on the day, when, as he was hurrying along Regents Street to get out of a downpour, he passed a jeweler's where he had only ever seen modern timepieces. There in the window, nestled on felt, lay a "curious-looking watch differing from the usual display." A small card next to it identified it as the "Marie-Antoinette," and there was no price.

"Could I afford this?" he asked himself, and, the rain worsening, he ran the rest of the way home, the watch hanging heavy in his mind. Realizing that such a unique piece wouldn't "stop long in that window if the rain ceased," he put on his Wellingtons and weatherproofing and went back to the shop, the bell jingling as he brushed the rain from his coat and folded his umbrella.

The proprietor was a long-time admirer of Breguet who had taken the watch on commission and only just placed it in the window for sale. After settling on a price with Salomons, something in the hundreds, the proprietor claimed that he would have to consult with the owner; he said that he would send word by ten o'clock the next morning whether the agreed-upon price would be acceptable.

Salomons spent a long night thinking about the watch and at 9:30 the next morning the bell rang at his Grosvenor Street home. It was the red-faced proprietor, carrying a small parcel.

"The price, if advanced £50 pounds, would be accepted," he said, after setting down the parcel.

"I could not quarrel over the extra £50, so I gave a cheque and kept the watch," wrote Salomons. "It turned out to be a good purchase, judging from seducing offers made to me later on to part with it."[115]

Just when Salomons was laying the foundation of his Breguet collection, Baron R.M. de Klinckowstrom, the great-uncle of Axel Fersen, was destroying whatever hope scholars still harbored that they might learn the true nature of the relationship between Fersen and the former Queen of France. In 1878, Klinckowstrom published *Le Comte de Fersen et la cour de France*, a collection of excerpts from his great-nephew's letters and diaries. But Klinckowstrom elided a number of important passages, including almost all of those that detailed the relationship. Later, on his deathbed, Klinckowstrom had a servant build a fire and burn the original letters, one by one. As a historian notes, "for this Baron von Klinckowstrom must be condemned without reprieve."[116]

From the pyre of Fersen's papers rose vaporous plumes of hearsay and speculation. The simplest questions remained open to debate: Was Fersen the queen's lover? Was he the man who ordered the 160 for her?

The story linking her and Fersen to the 160 had spread by word of mouth. There is no clear entry in Breguet's ledgers specifying that the 160 was *"pour la Reine,"* although many similar notations do appear in his ledgers for watches for the king and queen. Because the Breguet workshop was ransacked during the Revolution, little documentation outlived the era. All that is known is that Breguet continued to work on the watch long after commercial prudence dictated that he should have stopped, and long after he had reason to expect any recompense from the original commissioner. The story, as passed down through the Breguet family, and various historians, was simply that an "Officer of the Queen's Guard" had commissioned the piece. But the only known officer who would have had the impetus to commission something so "spectacular" was Fersen. Fersen's family, it should be noted, continued to buy Breguet's watches as the nineteenth century progressed.

Over the years, occasional publications would rekindle public discussion of the relationship. In 1902, the Klinckowstrom book was published in English. In 1928, a previously unknown, revealing letter between Marie and Fersen was discovered. In 1930, a Swedish historian Anna Soderhjelm produced fresh revelations about the relationship, and three years later another letter was discovered in the Swedish Royal Archives, in which Baron von Taube, writing to Gustav III in 1779, described how Fersen and Marie were conspicuously spending time together.

By the time that Salomons started to amass his watch collection, the company that bore Breguet's name had branched out considerably, a testament to the breadth of the man's interest and innovation.

Breguet's contributions to science were difficult to exaggerate. He had brought a new precision first to the lives of royalty and then to the lives of common men. Scientists, astronomers, and sailors were indebted to his quest for accuracy, and his advances — either wholly invented or adopted from others and improved — had become standard in mechanical wristwatches. The same ruby pinions and cylinders, the same polishing techniques and beveling, and the same tricks to reduce shock and ensure even running would remain fixtures in even the most modern mechanical watches.

He had perfected the art of metallurgy and metal engineering, understanding the intrinsic values of various metals set to various purposes. To design he had introduced a neoclassical style that was a striking admixture of the very old and the very new. His watches, their faces white as snow and the blued hands as clear and bright as a distant flare over a calm sea, anticipated the drive toward elegance and legibility by centuries.

With his advances in miniaturization, Breguet had laid the groundwork for precision engineering. Clockwork, of which he was the foremost avatar, would form the basis of robotics, and metamorphose into telegraph machines, bomb timers, and control systems for airplane engines. Breguet's experiments in measuring speed would pave the way for avionics. His mechanical process of "getting" and "putting" data from the movement to the face would make possible such later creations as Babbage's Difference Engine, forerunner of the computer. Breguet's secret signature, in short, would be indelibly stamped on the twentieth century.

His descendants, in particular his grandson Louis-Clement, broadened his legacy in other ways. Even as the firm continued to cater to the likes of the Rothschild family, Napoleon III, and Queen Victoria, and expanded to more distant markets, it extended its technological horizons. Louis-Clement's gifts in science were equal to his grandfather's, and he continued the tradition of watchmaking ingenuity. He invented a number of electric clocks and devised a tuning-fork to replace the spring balance in chronometers, a precursor to quartz technology. He also built a master/slave clock system, which allowed clocks in a building to be set from a central location, and created an inking thermometer for the University of Kazan in Russia that could record the daily changes of temperature in that frigid region. His system of mirrors, designed for Dominique Francois Arago, helped that scientist measure the speed of light.

Like his own father, who had invented an aerial telegraph that used a series of flags to send messages across long distances, Louis Clement, too, pioneered several advances in telegraphy, as well as the first speed and braking control system for trains. Near the end of the nineteenth century, the firm began producing telegraphs, including a unique alphabetical model that could send letters down the wire without relying on specially trained Morse code operators. The Breguet firm also brought Alexander Graham Bell's telephone to France, dedicating new workshops to the company's new passion, electricity and telecommunications.

By the end of the century, the Breguet company had left the hands of the Breguet family completely and been turned over to workshop foreman Edward Brown who maintained the focus on scientific tools and communications systems.

Through all this, David Lionel Salomons did more than anyone to maintain the allure of the Breguet name. In 1921, he published *Breguet 1747-1823*, a book exploring Breguet's entire career and output, establishing the first detailed record of all of the watches Breguet handled, including the 160. Two years later, on the centennial of the watchmaker's death, Salomons exhibited his private collection at the Palais Galliera in Paris, uttering his famous epigram that "to carry a fine Breguet watch is to feel that you have the brains of a genius in your pocket." Another two years after that, on April 19, 1925, Salomons died, and his Breguets began their unlikely peregrination to Palestine.

The field of watchmaking, even before Breguet's death, had begun to move away from him. By 1800, what had once been the province of the wealthy and powerful had been democratized, and the industry's center of gravity had crossed the Atlantic Ocean. There were hundreds of watch companies in the United States, situated mostly along major rail lines in Pennsylvania, Ohio, and Illinois. Watches were integral to keeping trains running on time, and manufacturing centers proliferated around railroads' farm hubs. These watchmakers created multiple styles and versions of each timepiece, from the dollar watch — an unadjusted, untrustworthy hunk of tin for the average buyer — to the highly precise railman's watch.

The move toward mass production, which would eventually overturn the old methods of the Swiss masters, had begun with an American named Eli Terry. Born in 1772 in East Windsor, Connecticut, as a teenager Terry apprenticed with a local maker of grandfather clocks and with a maker of more sophisticated clocks who taught him engraving and passed on some of the engineering knowledge required to fashion complications.

In 1793, Terry moved to Plymouth, Massachusetts, to start his own business, but the expensive, then-standard brass clocks limited the size of his potential market, and Terry spent much of his time engraving, at times repairing spectacles to make ends meet. He had begun experimenting with wooden clocks, however, and their material costs were lower, enabling Terry to charge less for them. Soon he was focused entirely on making wooden watches, and had established himself as a profitable local watchmaker. He had other innovative and cost-saving ideas, such as using unskilled workers to cut out cogs roughly (with a skilled clockmaker doing only the finishing work) and using water, rather than people, to power clock-making tools. By 1800, Terry had two apprentices, his shop could work on about twenty clocks at once, and he employed travelling salesmen to hawk his wares.

In 1807, his approach to mass-producing clocks caught the eye of a pair of merchants in Waterbury, who placed an order for four thousand clocks from Terry, this at a time when an order of even five hundred clocks in only three years seemed fantastical. Terry, seeing this as his chance to prove the worth of his technique, sold his old shop to an apprentice, bought a gristmill, and with two new partners busied himself fulfilling the contract. He spent the next two years converting his gristmill into a state-of-the-art facility, with water-powered saws, lathes, and planes, which could churn out identical, interchangeable clock parts that required no finishing work. Within a year of starting production, Terry's factory had fulfilled the contract, and ushered in an era when timekeeping was available to everyone, everywhere. Clocks which had sold for between $18 and $70 just a few years before were now going for $5.

For the first time, poor farmers could afford a timepiece. In 1814, Terry patented the thirty-hour Shelf Clock, a high quality piece that maintained acceptable accuracy and only had to be wound once a day. These clocks sold for around fifteen dollars, and were instantly popular. Travelling salesmen would buy a number in bulk and let farmers try the clocks for a month without payment, pioneering the thirty-day, no-money-down guarantee. These rural customers invariably fell in love with their clocks, and salesmen rarely had to take a clock away with them when they returned for payment. By 1820, Terry was making ten thousand clocks a year, and Connecticut was full of manufacturers copying his techniques.

In 1837, Chauncey Jerome, a longtime employee of Terry's, perfected a sheet brass clock that could be manufactured for only $6 and sold for as little as $10, only marginally more expensive than wooden clocks but many times more accurate. They instantly upset the clock market.

Eli Terry had helped to create what would be known as "the American system" of manufacturing. Over the next sixty years, the American watch industry would become so dominant that a Swiss watchmaker who took an unadjusted watch from the 1893 World's

Fair back to Switzerland and tested it against his country's best movements would see one of the cheapest, least complicated U.S. watches beat one of the best Swiss ones.

The Swiss watch, meanwhile, struggled to remain relevant. By the mid-nineteenth century, with the juggernaut of mass production bearing down on the cottage industries of France and Switzerland, even the venerable firm of Breguet et Fils had to find new avenues for business. In time, prices would fall to $1 for a standard pocket watch, which none of the Swiss manufacturers would be able to match until the twentieth century.

In the most rarefied circles, of course, there continued to be those chronophiles who appreciated fine mechanical watches. In 1902, a great "jewel" rush began, with manufacturers boasting sometimes over one hundred "jewels" (really rubies) that were arrayed all over the movement, even in positions that were non-functional. To an untrained buyer, after all, more jewels were better, and so watchmakers boasted of comically large numbers of jewels on the face of their over-engineered watches.

A collectors' arms race between two post-WWI financial titans yielded two extremely complicated watches. The first, the Packard Complication, was made by Patek Philippe for the automobile magnate James Ward Packard, a bespectacled watch lover who was in desperate, if seemingly friendly, competition with a banker in New York, Henry Graves. The Packard Complication, completed in 1927, was known as the most complex watch in the world and came with a star chart of the skies above Packard's Ohio home. In 1933, Graves commissioned a watch, also from Patek Philippe, with twenty-four complications, eclipsing Packard's record-breaking watch. The Graves would be unsurpassed for another half century, until Patek Philippe produced the Caliber 89, with thirty-three complications.

But such watches were the exception. The years following the creation of the Graves Complication were the Steel Age of Swiss watchmaking. The simple military-issue A-11 watches worn by American G.I.s in World War II popularized the wristwatch, and the large and complicated was replaced by the thin and delicate. Gold, once the standard material for most watches, gave way to stainless steel or chromed or electroplated metals. Switzerland led these decades with typical Alpine aplomb, maintaining the status quo without exploration or creativity.

The watch had become as romantic and well-constructed as

a weed trimmer. It was a tool, something that eased the burden of watching the clock at work or school, and it made an excellent coming-of-age or retirement present. The most prolific and best watch houses stayed in business by supplying military timepieces to armies, navies, and the burgeoning air forces of continental Europe and England. Panerai, which had made its name in 1935 when it created some of the first diving watches using Rolex movements and cases, added a patented crown-locking device during WWII and supplied frogmen with diving instruments, compasses, depth gauges, and watches, before shuttering in about 1950.

The little Swiss watchmaker had become an outdated fiction, perpetuated to convey quality and to goose sales. Why pay a faceless drone in a Hamilton factory in Illinois when you could tap the ingenuity of a gnomic watchmaker in the Jura mountains? Most watches bought in America were American-made and relatively cheap, so Swiss exporters like Omega and Rolex — supremely popular worldwide brands even in the 1950s and 1960s — had to offer an air of luxury and exclusivity to justify their price tags.

The original Apollo astronauts went into space with Omega Speedmasters on their wrists. These iconic watches were chosen because they were acceptably legible, with white hands and numerals on a black face, and they could be hand-wound — an important consideration because automatic watches' internal weights would be useless in weightless conditions. When Buzz Aldrin returned to earth, he complained mightily about the watches, saying they were unreadable and the buttons too small, but henceforth the Omega company would boast of its connection to spaceflight every five years or so on the anniversary of the Speedmaster's historic tumble through the stratosphere, attempting to position a humble device — akin to a protractor or slide rule — as a mythic tool of great men.

Then crisis arrived. On December 25, 1969, the Japanese watch company Seiko released the 35 SQ Astron, the world's first analog quartz watch. It had long been observed that a quartz crystal, exposed to an electric current, would vibrate at a constant and predictable rate, and that this property could be exploited to keep time. Quartz movements were more accurate than their mechanical counterparts and had the added advantage of being impervious to temperature changes. Quartz clocks had been made since the

1920s, but their bulk and delicacy limited them primarily to use as precision instruments in laboratories. It had taken Seiko more than ten years of R&D to bring its idea to market, but on the last Christmas of the 1960s, it did so.

The Astron's ticking seconds hand was a revelation for many — that kind of rhythmic movement was hard enough to engineer in mechanical watches — but the watch cost a daunting $1,250, about the same as a Toyota Corolla at the time. It was, however, the future. After a limited run of one hundred pieces, Seiko perfected the watch and began to sell improved models using integrated circuits. Prices dropped precipitously. Within seven years, Texas Instruments would debut the first quartz watch priced under $20.

The world flocked to quartz. These timepieces, so much simpler to make without the endless gears and cogs of mechanicals, could be stamped out in seconds, and thousands of them flooded the bars and clubs of the 1970s.

The old watch companies were dinosaurs, and Swiss watch sales dried up. The devastation wrought by quartz on the traditional mechanical watchmakers was similar to what would happen to cameras, as consumers abandoned their high-end Leica shooters and low-end Nikons, not to mention the rolls of film that fed a thousand sprockets when digital cameras were introduced.

Swiss watchmakers could have adapted. Around 1970, as the first mass-produced quartz watch movements began flowing into Switzerland, its artisans played an important role in reducing the size and complexity of the movements for placement into wristwatch cases. But whether due to a lack of foresight or a distaste for all things electronic, most Swiss manufacturers ignored the technology. They knew dials and gears, not transistors and batteries. The quartz peddlers soon left Europe for Japan, and stayed there.

The Swiss clung desperately to their past greatness, and an entire industry arose offering COSC-certified watches that had been tested extensively for accuracy over a long period of time. The COSC designation enabled some watchmakers, like Breitling, to charge more for their watches. But it did nothing to restore Switzerland as the center of watchmaking.

In 1972, a Swiss company released a watch that would eventually carve a path back to relevance for the industry. For years, watch luxury had meant gold; steel was the pedestrian metal reserved for low-end bar mitzvah gifts. But the porthole-shaped Royal Oak, from Audemars Piguet, was a luxury quartz steel watch for the polo set. Soon Breitling and Rolex followed suit, charging $8,000 and up for steel watches, which once would have been unthinkable. In the go-go 1980s, the trend took off, and Swiss watchmakers, along with mechanical watches, experienced a renaissance by embracing a new sense of mass luxury, adding odd colors and lots of shine to their designs.

Panerai, closed decades earlier, reformed in 1993 to capture those consumers nostalgic for military-grade gear, then reinvented itself again as a luxury watchmaker to ride the big watch boom of the late 1990s and 2000s, when huge, pie-plate-sized watches came into vogue. Most of the best known companies, including Breguet, followed the same pattern, emerging from years on life support to satiate a new breed of uber-rich, ultra-fashionable collector. After years spent adorning the wrists of pilots, scientists, and astronauts, watches suddenly colonized the fashion ghetto, and houses like Breguet shrewdly adapted, mastering the fine line between haute couture and haute technology.

But at the time of the Mayer museum's founding in Jerusalem, watchmaking as an art was still in a kind of dark age. David Lionel Salomons had willed the watches to his daughter, Vera, a stern, adventurous woman who trained as a nurse, got a divorce from her soldier husband, and spent much of her life travelling the globe, returning again and again to Jerusalem. The year her father died, she set about founding a home for the elderly there, along with housing for the blind and for immigrants.

After World War II, Vera turned her attention to fostering religious tolerance in the new state of Israel, and she began studying Islamic art and history and pursuing various eccentric projects. In one, she tried to buy the Wailing Wall for the Jews from a Muslim property trust for £100,000. In the course of her studies, she befriended a professor, Leon Arie Mayer, at the Hebrew University. The precise nature of their relationship isn't clear — it was rumored in Jerusalem that the two were lovers — but it was sufficiently close that Vera ultimately founded the L.A. Mayer Memorial Museum of Islamic Art. Moving between Israel, Switzerland, and Ireland in her final years, she died in 1969, at age eighty-one, never seeing the finished museum, which wouldn't open until

1974. The watches her father had left her, minus sixty-five pieces she had sold at Christie's in 1964, all went to the museum. Foremost among them was the Marie-Antoinette, which would rest there undisturbed until 1983.

Chapter 15

Geneva

The pre-holiday lights of modern Geneva in November fade into fog as you climb up the mountains into the towns that made this country's fortune. Sunlight is scarce and when it does appear it's bright and flat and comes in at a low angle over the city spires. Even in such weather, you can make it around the tip of the lake, through verdant, well-tended, and advertisement-free suburbs, and up into the mountains in forty minutes, a trip that would have taken Abraham-Louis Breguet days. The summers here are given over to the dairy farming that have made Swiss cheese and chocolate famous, but in the cold winter evenings the farmers, for centuries, stayed inside filing cogs and gears by candlelight, then selling them to merchants in the city.

Some of those selfsame farm families still live in the hills, and their children have abandoned the plow to join the watch industry. The skills generated by decades of piecework were passed down from grandparents to grandchildren, and the resulting concentration of watchmakers in this region is startling. While not everyone is a master, high in these mountains, everyone has brass, gold, and steel flowing in their veins. One watchmaker told me that in Switzerland a good student could either go into banking or watchmaking. There were no other jobs worth having.

The road into the mountains winds through switchbacks that open onto wide vistas of stone and pine and rich farmland. Grapevines scroll up the hills like veins of gold, while dark brown cows meander in the grass. Here, in the towns of the Vallée de Joux, is the world's greatest concentration of factories of the world's

146

leading watchmakers, including Patek Phillipe, Audemars Piguet, and Jaeger-LeCoultre. The Hotel des Horlogers, with its Salon de Chronographes dining room, is one of the few luxury hotels in the area and was renovated in 2008 by Audemars Piguet to supply the horologists of the Vallée and their well-heeled clients with a fine meal to go with their fine watches. The towns here are still quite small, but they are economic powerhouses. Like car lovers travelling to Germany to pick up their sports coupes fresh off the assembly line, rich watch fanatics make pilgrimages to their favorite ateliers to pick up their latest multi-thousand dollar purchases.

Next to a public park on the shore of Lac de Joux, there is a building — all stucco and bright, clean glass — that looks as if it should house a European tech start-up rather than the logistical arm of a luxury Swiss watch company. A giant, complicated watch above the front door announces that you have arrived at the corporate headquarters of Breguet.

A short drive onward, you come to the company's factory and training academy. The complex looks like an upscale office park. Inside, the lobby is empty and unremarkable, save for a 100x-scale replica of Breguet's No. 5 watch, and a comely, if curt, receptionist who opens the mail and guards the inner sanctum.

Through a set of security doors is a room far removed from the workshop of the company's founder, with its smudged gas lamps and lector reading the news of the day. Here, instead, you find something that resembles nothing so much as a microtechnology lab. The ziplock floor, plastic and seamless, is sealed against spills. The walls and work surfaces are spotless. No oil or grease mars the machines; even the heaviest presses and drills are hand-cleaned nightly. About two-hundred workers pad around in clean, white work smocks, white caps, and slip-on shoes. Every door is security-locked, and a collection of blue booties — for guests and inspectors popping in for a peek — sits by the entrance door to prevent the introduction of dirt and dust into the factory's clean rooms.

While many steps in the watchmaking process, such as braising metal, filing, and cutting gears and hands, are now automated, the machines are a mix of old and new. Some were made at the turn of the nineteenth century, and even many of the younger machines, excluding the brand new laser-guided milling machines and automated lamps and movement holders, date from the

1950s.

Many original *guilloche* engines are still in use today. One engineer in the 1860s found the older machines to be far superior, noting one to be "a singularly elegant piece of mechanism, and unlike earlier engraving machines." Once a watchmaker found a good tool, he rarely gave it up, as evidenced by the nineteenth-century equipment still used in Breguet's modern-day headquarters in the Jura mountains.

The factory has its share of huge machines and hissing presses, and is ugly in an industrial way, but the company has little problem attracting young people. They come from the surrounding farms, happy to spend three years in post-high school apprenticeships before they can take up a file or a screw. They are drawn by the beauty and prestige of the product, and the chance to work in the tradition of their parents and ancestors.

In a modern Breguet watch, the manufacturing steps are parceled out among between ten and twenty individual watchmakers, each of whom has one specific task. For some workers, the repetitive nature of the job is a kind of zen. One especially competent screw polisher, promoted to manager, asked to go back to her old job, which she found more meaningful. Although just a cog in the watchmaking machinery, she loved the small, precise part she played.

Every watch-in-progress makes its journey through the factory, from start to finish, on its own small plastic tray. To ferret out errors in the system, a detailed list of steps taken, by which watchmaker, is kept in computer files and in handwritten logs. Each watch is given a number — usually four or five digits — and this number follows the watch from stamping to final steps.

The watch movement begins with an *ebauche*. The blank factory, on the first floor, is staffed by experts who punch out blank after blank from sheets of brass or steel that come on long spools and are fed first into a cutter, then into a machine that pops tiny holes in each blank for the pinions and cams, and finally into a machine that presses out indentations for the wheels. The blanks are then washed and polished in a bath of nutshells or corn, washed again, and inspected for damage.

Every part of the watch, at every step of its creation, is measured and remeasured to ensure accuracy to within one micron and forestall timing issues further along in the process. Supervisors sit in a glassed-in area near the front of each workshop and examine the finished products every night before the watchmakers go home. Any problems are immediately called out, and the watch is either sent back down the manufacturing ladder or recycled completely. This time-consuming inspection process limits the company to making about forty thousand watches a year.

The factory's second floor is dedicated to the decoration of the larger pieces of the movement. As these parts are cut or stamped out of steel, gold, or brass, they are finely beveled, polished with a piece of wood covered in paper, and carefully engraved with a guilloché or burnishing engine. Burnishing engines delicately brush swirling dots (known as "pearlage") or parallel lines (known as Geneva Stripes) into the back of a nearly finished blank. Guilloché engines, as in Breguet's time, ornament the watch face with checkerboard patterns, long dashes, or odd rose-shaped spirals. They require an infallibly steady hand, and contemporary Breguet engravers use microscopes to see where they are touching the metal surface. Original guilloché machines are in short supply nowadays, and master watchmakers must comb swap meets and flea markets to find parts.

Meanwhile, downstairs, the movement proceeds to the assembly room, where each watchmaker, elbows resting in two designated spots on his bench, laboriously uses tweezers to place pieces smaller than a grain of sand into the nearly finished movement. He refers to a book, with a detailed diagram to ensure uniformity among the watches, as he places each piece and screws it down. Every room has a sticky entryway carpet made by 3M to catch dirt and stray pieces that fall to the ground during the course of the day, and apprentices dig through detritus to find other pieces that may have fallen.

When a movement is completed, it is tested using a machine that photographs the pallets and pallet wheel. If the pallets are touching the watch incorrectly, the watchmaker pulls it out of the machine and delicately pushes the pallets back into place — a job akin to checking the hinge on a locket, by eye, using only a rudimentary automated measuring device and tweezers. Modern techniques and materials have all but eradicated the traditional culprits in watchmaking error — friction and uneven gravity — but this late-stage scrutiny provides another safeguard for accuracy.

Finally, in the assembly room, the movements are fitted into cases, and buttons, dials, and hands are added. Most Breguet watches bear their serial numbers on their dials, and a separate station uses an inking machine to print the number onto the face manually. First, the printer tests the striking surface a few times by placing a plastic sheet over the dial and applying the ink. Once it's in the right place, the sheet is removed and a tiny number is printed on the dial. This is the watch's DNA, and when it is sold, the number, along with a customer's personal information, will be recorded in the Breguet library in Paris, taking its place alongside such past customers as Napoleon and Churchill.

The watchmakers then fire and apply the Breguet blued hands and close the case. A master watchmaker performs a final inspection, a strap is added, and the watch is shipped out in a hardwood box to a shop where it will wait until someone of means comes along and swoops it up. Each modern Breguet, in other words, goes through an accelerated version of the process used by Abraham-Louis at the turn of the nineteenth century.

Starting in 2006, as the rest of the factory went about this exacting work, a secret project was under way in a small workshop in the building's basement. There, a group of five dedicated watchmakers whose skills with metal far surpassed even the finest engravers and millwrights in the factory above were consumed with a single task. They were re-creating the Marie-Antoinette watch.

In the 1990s, luxury mechanical watches had come back into vogue in a big way. Rolex, once the only name that came to mind when one thought of high-end watches, was now joined by relative upstarts like Panerai, Omega, and Breitling, in addition to the more venerable firms dating back centuries. $14,000 for a single watch came to represent the low end. Watchmaking was back, and Breguet, founded in 1775, was newly resplendent and flush with cash. Switzerland became, once again, the watchmaking capital of the world. There was no such thing as a cheap Swiss watch. There were manufacturers who would buy Swiss parts and build the watches abroad — Russia and Hong Kong being two popular manufacturing points — and then send them back into the country for the final tweaking, enabling the watches to wear the "Swiss Made" moniker. One man, above all others, was at the center of this Swiss renaissance.

Born on February 19, 1928 in Beirut, Lebanon, to a well-to-do Lebanese-Greek Orthodox family, Nicolas Hayek began his career as a corporate consultant tasked with turning around two Swiss watch conglomerates, the Allgemeine Schweizerische Uhrenindustrie (ASUAG) and the Société Suisse pour l'Industrie Horlogère (SSIH). Both had been founded in the early 1930s and survived for decades. Between them they owned an array of major brands, including Omega and Tissot, as well as ETA SA Manufacture Horlogère Suisse, shortened to ETA, an ebauche factory founded in Neuchâtel in 1793. ETA's inexpensive, mass-produced Swiss movements had become industry standard, appearing in almost every watch made between the World Wars, and until quartz took over the industry, the company effectively controlled the watch market for six decades. By manufacturing mechanical and quartz watches, the company was able to limp through the crisis, but barely. ASUAG also owned Nivarox-FAR, the largest maker of hairsprings in the world. In short, these two companies were the embodiment of the Swiss watch market and were, when Hayek came along, failing.

In later years, Hayek had the face and girth of an unabashed hedonist, with a carefully trimmed beard under a mane of white hair. Prone to wearing four or more watches at a time (for a while he wore one for each brand), he looked like a rich uncle on holiday. His hands, large and meaty, belonged to a butcher and not a fine watchmaker.

But Hayek, who studied math and science and founded Hayek Engineering AG in 1979, was an extremely shrewd businessman. Charged with writing a report about the two conglomerates for the Japanese company Seiko, he instead recruited a group of investors, merged the nineteen smaller companies involved, and took ownership of the resulting corporation, which he named the Swatch Group. A cantankerous businessman, he quickly blew through the staid and stodgy Swiss watch business like a human tourbillon, insulting rivals and exhorting his employees – numbering 24,000 in 2009 – to greater heights. "One day a president of a Japanese company in America said to me: 'You cannot manufacture watches. Switzerland can make cheese but not watches. Why don't you sell Omega for four hundred million francs?'" he told the *Wall Street Journal.* "I told him 'Only after I'm dead.'"[119]

Hayek conceived of the new company as a manufacturer of "emotional products," so charged with romance that they became objects of desire and nostalgia. He saw in his products a projection of the Swiss heritage. Wrapped up in the tiny metal cases of his luxury brands like Omega and Tissot were centuries of Swiss tradition. In the bright faces and wild colors of his Swatch brand he saw the fun and rebirth of a reunited Europe. He viewed watches not as a mass-produced commodity but as heirlooms, signs of status, and a respect for tradition all rolled into something that could cost as little as $100 — in the case of a Swatch — or as much as $30 million.

When he created the Swatch group, high-end steel watches had begun to reconquer the luxury market, but the Swiss had lost most of the lower end, a calamity in an industry that made 60% of its money on entry-level consumers. "If you are an emotional consumer product, if you lose the lower market segment, you lose everything," Hayek told me. "Look what the British did. They decided that they didn't want to mass-produce cars, so in America you had General Motors, and the British kept Jaguar and Aston Martin, two high-end brands. Well, in the expensive market, you do not have a way to make money anymore. If you do not control the lower market segment, you do not control the overall market."

The lower end of the watch industry had come to be dominated by quartz models from Japan, with movements designed by an engineer from Texas Instruments. The Swiss, in Hayek's view, had chauvinistically rejected the American movements, to their own detriment. The Japanese, unburdened by snobbish tradition, welcomed the American-made movements and "took over the reputation of being the most accurate watches in the world, and in less than one and a half years, we had zero market share in the low end."

Hayek sought to reverse this trend. First, he and his team, including watchmakers Elmar Mock and Jacques Muller, created a simple quartz movement with 51 pieces instead of Japan's 151. The goal was to reduce the possibility of failure in a quartz watch. Because they were already so accurate, the only obvious way to improve them was to make them stronger and cheaper. Muller, wondering why no one on the beach wore a watch, realized that they were stodgy and, more important, too expensive.[120] The simple Swatch, with a quartz oscillator and a small actuator to move the hands, laser welded on a single circuit board, was his answer. The Swatch team would change the line once every six months, having the faces and cases designed by artists of the day (most famously, Keith Haring). The whimsical, low-end quartz watches gave Hayek an instant hit.

In 1982, when they launched the brand, they sold out the initial run of seventy thousand pieces in fifteen days. In 1983, the group sold one million watches, and by 1986 they had sold twelve million units. Collectors often bought two, one to wear and one to keep in its original package, and fans camped overnight outside of stores before new releases. Some rare Swatches, such as an oddly shaped fish-themed watch called the Andrew Logan Jellyfish, now sell for in excess of $20,000, not a bad return on an original $30 investment.

Although Swatches proved a fad, it was a lasting one, and their success sustained the Swatch Group's collection of older firms, including Breguet, through the quartz crisis. "I needed to keep my people in jobs at my ninety factories," Hayek explained later. "And to have work, you needed volume, and volume was only achievable with watches like Swatch."

Once he had stabilized the Swiss industry, Hayek turned his attention to his prestige brands. Although he knew little about Breguet prior to purchase ("It was just a name to me," he said), as his oldest and most prestigious brand it was the jewel in his crown. The company made only four thousand watches a year, posting an unimpressive annual profit of one million Swiss francs. The company hadn't had a hit in years.

When Hayek took over, Breguet's factories were in run-down buildings in Brassus and Le Sentier. After he purchased the company in 1999 from Bahraini investors for $175 million, he moved the headquarters to l'Abbaye, closer to the traditional heart of watchmaking, to simplify transportation of parts among different factories. Watchmakers were born, lived, and died in the Vallée de Joux, and there was a "Vallée mentality," as Hayek saw it, a method for doing one thing one way and never deviating from the path. It was his goal to shake things up, to create new movements, complications, cases, and watches that had never been seen before but still had a strong link to Breguet's earlier, best-known work. He mined the company's records for odd watches to reproduce in miniature, and the same Middle Eastern potentates who had once owned Breguet came knocking on Hayek's door, asking for new watches from the company.

At the new Breguet headquarters, which consisted mostly of offices where the marketing and design teams met and worked,

Hayek would roll through every few weeks like an itinerant preacher. When he was in the office, his door was never closed, and waves of supplicants arrived to pay homage, get his signature, or ask his sage advice on a watch face or business move.

Over the years, he assembled a substantial collection of original Breguet watches, including the Number 5, which had moon phase, power reserve, and large date indicators, and which Hayek had bought for $1.1 million. According to Hayek, in 2001 one of Breguet's rich customers, a sultan, called asking to buy the watch. Hayek demurred, saying it wasn't for sale. "Then he came back, he said, 'Okay then make me one,'" Hayek recalled. Two weeks later, the sultan thought better of it, called Hayek again, and upped his order to five. Ultimately, the Sultan ordered *ten* of the watches — five automatic and five manual.

Deconstructing the original No. 5, the Breguet team created a new movement small enough to fit inside a wristwatch case without sacrificing any of the complications. After making ten for the sultan, in 2002 the company offered the watch for sale in its catalog, dubbing it the Classique and pricing it at $32,000.

The success of the Number 5 wristwatch project led Hayek to dream bigger. When the Marie-Antoinette had disappeared in 1983, Hayek was distraught. Now, he felt confident that he could re-create the watch, which he knew would make a splash on the watch scene. He ordered it rebuilt and gave a small group of master watchmakers a large workshop and unlimited resources.

The project manager was known only by the one-name sobriquet Francois, lest rival factories try to poach him. He looked more like a starving artist than a watchmaker, but his skinny, nicotine-stained fingers could coax magic from steel and gold. He spent his days in the workshop and his weekends at the Genevan watch markets, buying parts that had become obsolete decades — if not centuries — before. For the Marie-Antoinette project, he saw to it that the entire team was unhindered by the rules and strictures imposed on the factory's other watchmakers.

The team began by doing research. Obviously, the original 160 wasn't available to take apart, and most of Breguet's firsthand notes had been lost in the French Revolution, but the team found a valuable resource in *The Art of Breguet*. Most helpfully, the book featured Daniels' close photographs of the Marie-Antoinette. The Daniels' book described Breguet's habits and the different techniques used by his watchmakers. Most important, Daniels had also made a detailed drawing of the Marie-Antoinette and taken close-up photographs of it.

The team examined other complex watches made by Breguet, including the Number 5 and the Duc de Praslin watch, at the Musée des Arts et Métiers in Paris. The Praslin had a perpetual calendar and a readout for the equation of time on multiple retrograde dials. Like the Marie-Antoinette, it was staid and understated, with a white face, Breguet numerals, and a playful back displaying a moon phase in a field of engraved clouds.

Using the photographs, drawings, and surviving Breguet watches, the watchmakers were able to divine the shape of some of the 160's parts, and the engineers were then able to match different parts to different complications. They had initially been stumped by a set of gears that seemed to be connected to the seconds hand, but after digging through other Breguet watches, the watchmakers discovered that the seconds hand was a dead-beat complication that made the seconds hand tick once per second like a modern quartz watch.

The watchmakers then scanned in the photographs and began building CAD/CAM models of the watch around the depicted movement. In this way, they were able to measure each piece individually and assess its depth inside the watch. Because each part had to fit with others with a minuscule degree of tolerance, the watchmakers had to geometrically divine the position of each of the 823 pieces. The re-creation of the Marie-Antoinette took two years to build and consisted of 823 minuscule parts.

Nicolas Hayek would unveil the watch at the prestigious 2008 Baselworld Expo in Switzerland. Experts valued the new watch, called the 1160, at over $11 million, briefly making it the most expensive watch in the world. It came in an inlaid wood box taken from a tree that had been felled by blight on the grounds of the Petit Trianon. The design on the top represented a scene from a painting by Louise Élisabeth Vigée Le Brun of a young Marie-Antoinette in blue, her hand holding a beautiful, rich white rose. A secret button on the side of the box unlatched the case, which opened with a pneumatic whisper to reveal the watch within, along with one of its white enameled faces.

Even before its public debut, however, the reconstructed 160 had been upstaged by a startling series of events. As his team was working on the re-creation, Hayek received an anonymous email from someone in France claiming to be in possession of the real,

No 160   Transport des Secours   f 8410

                                                          72

                                    14.10.812 Joly   59. 70
                                    14.10.812 Geilewiski   3.30
                                    26.12.812 Gedowitski   1
   36 grun or Fourrein 28   31.12.812 Weber   2.8.65   "
   steng[...] depointer   26.5.813   Kool   24
   Coté   6.10.813   Vincent   3
   Payait 28 1/2 jiner No:a F 139 f 1812   Savonin   7

                                    25.10.11   [...]   2
   fit or pictoplo f 6 f or f[...] 2.11.11   [...]   8
   [...] f 7 f or
   No [...] F 4.14 f 1813 17.12.11   27
                                    17.12.4   Savonin   2.2.85
   228 1/2 t No: U F 4.14 f 1813   31.12.11   Weber   "   6
                                    3.3.814   [...]   10
                                    29.4.814   Wattafrom   12
                                    29.4.814   Payen   3
                                    21.5.814   Vincent   13
                                    26.5.814   Savonin   16
                                    16.6.6   Skorzom   12
                                    28.6.4   Petit   2
                                    21.7.4   Vincent   3
                                    22.7.[...] Petit

                        Tot F 8 2193

Place of crime - Museum of Islam, 2 Palmach St., Jerusalem. Arrow A shows where the break-in was on the gate. Arrow B shows the place of water pressure. Arrow C shows the location of the improvised rope ladder.

"Pressure jack," a hydraulic jack.

Same as above.

Close up on the rope ladder.

The arrow points to the open always window broken into from which the burglars got into the museum.

Close up on the break in at the gate.

The window.

The arrow points to the place where the burglars removed the window air conditioner.

The arrow points to the wooden plate which served as a blockage to the window air conditioner.

לוח תצלומים

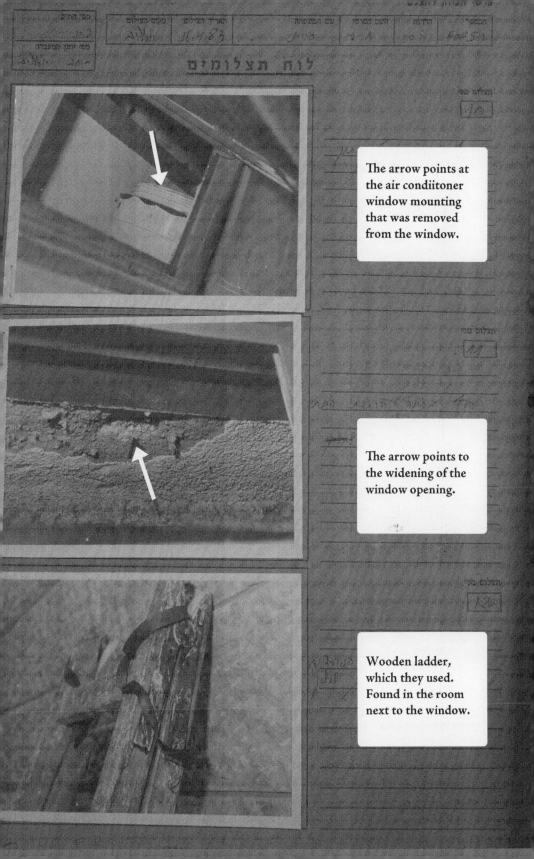

The arrow points at the air condiitoner window mounting that was removed from the window.

The arrow points to the widening of the window opening.

Wooden ladder, which they used. Found in the room next to the window.

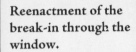

Reenactment of the break-in through the window.

Going in.

Coming out from the museum to the courtyard.

Arrow A points to where cigarette butts where found. Arrow B points to the place where an empty box of Time cigarettes was found. Arrow C points to the place where empty cola cans were found.

Cigarette butts.

Cigarette box that was found.

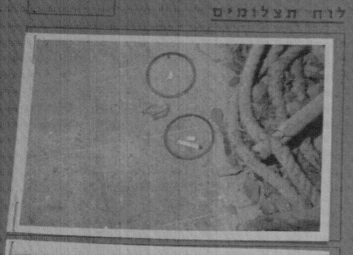

Same as above.

The arrow points to the place where the "mark" was found around the door frame.

The same.

The arrow points to an electric wire that started at the entrance to the museum and went all the way to the break-in window. Approx. 20 meters.

The arrow points to the electric wire next to the broken window.

The arrow points to the opening in the window which they broke into the museum.

Comforter blanket that was found on the floor next to the window.

Sack with packing boxes and foam that was found at the museum.

Break in tools wrapped in fabric that were found at the museum.

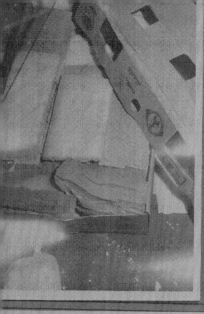

Close up of the same foam box

Close up of the break-in tools in the room of the museum.

The same break-in tools.

Close up of the break-in tools.

Display case where the watches were stolen from.

The same.

The same.

Keys that belonged to the watches (clocks) were found on the floor at the museum.

Bonn ce 14 Sept 1911

Monsieur.

Je n'est qu'au moment de mon départ de Bruxelles le 23 Juin que j'ai reçu Monsieur votre lettre du 13 may en réponse à la mienne des relativement à la monture de la feue Reine que j'aurois desire avoir et au mouvement que je voudrois faire faire et qui put entrer dans la boîte de montre que j'ai deja de vous. J'ai répondu a cette lettre ce mois 3 Juillet mais comme je crains que ma lettre vous soit pas parvenue je vous écris encore pour vous prier de me dire ou je dois vous adresser ma lettre et comment je pourrois vous faire parvenir ma Montre et convenir avec vous du mouvement a y faire. Veuilles bien Monsieur me donner votre reponse, a Dusseldorff chez J. S. Jonge banquier. Qui l'honneur d'etre Monsieur votre les humbles et les obeissant Serviteur

Mr Mrs Frères Muller Ngd   Le Cte de Fersen
à Fort S/m   general major au
1°   Service de la Suede

stolen Marie-Antoinette. As Hayek recalled later: "It said 'Mr. Hayek, I have the watch. I purchased it from the people who stole it, and I live near Jerusalem. I am ready to sell it to you, but I paid $120,000, and I want more money.'" The e-mailer informed Hayek that he would travel to Switzerland to close the deal.

Over the years, Hayek had fielded, and dismissed, many offers from people who claimed to have seen or owned the watch and requested a king's ransom in return. He was weary of false leads and skittish collectors who implied they had a connection to the missing masterpiece. He promptly informed the Swiss police about the latest offer.

"I did not want to have it," Hayek said later, "Because, look, it was a watch that had been stolen and it was probably in very bad shape. Now that I have rebuilt it, I have it. I have a much better one than that is perfect. What is the difference? If you have a woman that you love, whether she is 250 years old or 18 years old. Mine is 18 years old, and I let them have the one that was 250 years old."

Something about the mysterious e-mail left him with a hunch that the watch would soon resurface. Then, as he was playing a game of pool at his house one summer day in 2006, a report came on the radio. The Marie-Antoinette, it said, was back in Jerusalem.

Chapter 16

Tel Aviv

On August 16, 2006, after Zion Yakubov had met the mysterious pregnant lawyer and first held the Marie-Antoinette in his hands, the old jeweler made a call to Rachel Hasson at the Mayer Museum. Hasson and Yakubov had met two years before, when the art dealer brought a friend to see the items he had donated to the collection. Now, he explained the situation, told Hasson about the lawyer, and said, "Rachel, I just want to see if I saw your stuff." She invited him to the museum and they met in the library, a small, cool room that offered a respite from the day's oppressive heat.

Hasson had dealt with fakers before, and would normally have assumed that this was another one. But "sightings" of the collection were by now fairly uncommon. Hucksters had moved on to newer cons. So, she spoke briefly about the collection and then brought out the book *Watches & Clocks in the Sir David Salomons Collection*, the complete description of the collection written in 1980. Yakubov opened the book to a random page, thumbed through a few more, and pointed. On page 267, looking like a tin can with neat holes punched through it, was a gilt metal thermometer made by Thomas Jones in London, an odd eighteenth century instrument that had piqued Salomons' fancy when he bought it at the turn of the century.

"Yes," Yakubov said now. "I saw this in the lawyer's collection."

Hasson was breathless, "hysterical" almost, according to Eli Kahan, the museum chairman.

"Did you see the Queen?" she asked.

"I think so," the jeweler said, explaining that he hadn't seen enough to be sure. Why he chose such an unusual item to identify – a tiny thermometer that was not commonly known to be part of the Salomon's collection — remains open to conjecture, but to be too familiar with the stolen collection would have suggested complicity in the theft, something Yakubov couldn't afford.

He described three dirty, broken boxes full of a rat's nest of newspaper and patched with yellowing tape. The watches he saw were in good condition and mostly intact, although he did see a few broken pieces. But it was the prospect of reacquiring the Queen that stirred in Hasson the most excitement. As a young assistant curator she had seen it disappear in the night. Now, as mysteriously as it had gone, it might be back, stuck in a lawyer's office in torrid Tel Aviv.

It was settled: Yakubov would bow out of the deal and pressure the lawyer to approach the museum directly. All Rachel Hasson had to do was wait for the call.

It came on August 20, a Sunday. Efron-Gabai repeated her story: She was representing an overseas client who owned some items that had belonged to her deceased husband. They included clocks that had come from the L.A. Mayer Museum. Would Hasson be interested in meeting?

The museum now faced a major problem. In many art theft cases, the victimized institution does not actually want to see its former possession again. Once stolen, a piece of art or historical artifact becomes more valuable to its previous owner if it's never recovered. Why? Because once the insurance companies make their payout, the cash usually is plowed back into the museum. If the stolen items are later recovered, the cash must be returned to the insurance company, resulting in a dismal quarter – or quarters – especially for a non-profit. In short, theft, at least on a small scale, is good for a museum.

One auctioneer I talked to described a fascinating exchange with Cartier. The luxury jeweler had lost a few watches to theft some decades before and the watches were well-known enough to be noticed when they appeared on the open market. The auctioneer, making his normal rounds of watch shops in New York, stumbled upon these watches and called his contact at Cartier to report them.

"I know where they are," the auctioneer said and the Cart-

ier representative said they were missing and no longer existed.

The contact explained that Cartier had removed the watches
from its catalogs. They were no longer part of the official Cartier
collection, and so they no longer existed to Cartier's theft and fraud
department. Rather than go through the rigmarole of accepting
the relatively inexpensive watches back into the fold, they preferred
to simply sweep them under the rug. They could never be sold as
original ever again.

Rachel Hasson, at the Mayer Museum, was now in a similar situation. But this was on a different scale. The items in those
dirty boxes were the heart of the museum and chairman Eli Kahan
himself admitted that even the truncated collection currently on
display in the family gallery was a bigger draw than the Islamic art
that was the museum's focus.

Kahan is a quiet, reserved man with piercing blue eyes and a
retiree's easy demeanor. After retiring from the Foreign Trade Bank
in Jerusalem, he joined a number of philanthropic organizations
– his "babies," as he calls them – to spend his later years on something worthwhile. His role as chairman of the Mayer's board was
to maintain the museum's finances and to negotiate business on
behalf of the Swiss-based trust created by Vera Salomons to maintain the museum and two old age homes she built in Jerusalem.
The trust, run by a dour man named Albert Speer doled out the
money on Kahan's recommendation. His role, along with Hasson's,
was to address Vera Salomons' main complaint: that most Arabic
culture was seen down the barrel of a gun.

After consulting with the board, Kahan and Hasson decided
to meet with Efron-Gabai and see the boxes. On Monday, August
21, Hasson and Kahan drove from Jerusalem to Tel Aviv and
met with the lawyer at her offices. Hasson, in her diary, described
the loud-spoken former public defender as "sharp and shiny" and
quite intelligent. In the meeting, Efron-Gabai was all business, and
she chose her words carefully. She would not reveal the name or
whereabouts of her client, and she would not call the discussion a
ransom negotiation. She merely had some things she was returning to the museum in "good faith," she said, and when Hasson and
Kahan saw them she was sure they would understand the need for
secrecy.

She began by explaining that there were forty pieces in a bank
vault in Tel Aviv. Her client needed money, she said, and coyly not-

ed that the reward advertised for recovery of the watches was two million shekels ($550,000). No one is certain who suggested the final number, and Efron-Gabai refuses to comment on the case. All that anyone remembers is that someone suggested a large amount, and when the pair from the museum balked, the lawyer said that about 150,000 shekels ($35,000) might suffice.

Efron-Gabai asked the two to sign an agreement stipulating that her client — whom she called "Ms. England," because of her supposed nationality — was not liable for the theft of the watches and clocks. Hasson and Kahan signed the nondisclosure agreement and then excused themselves, saying they would discuss the matter on the trip back to the museum. Hasson wanted the clocks returned as quickly as possible, and Efron-Gabai, too, seemed to be in a hurry. When Hasson and Kahan were halfway back to Jerusalem, the lawyer called, asking them to complete the transaction immediately.

Kahan and Hasson demurred. They couldn't agree to anything without input from the board. A few phone calls later and the board was assembled, a group of older Israelis who had grown up with the museum.

Some members, including Spear in Switzerland, were outraged. "A man does not receive financial compensation when he returns property to its rightful owners," he railed. Kahan pleaded for understanding, arguing that the payment would be a gesture, not compensation. Instead of an outright sale, the money would be given as a donation of good will, and the watches would be returned. By phrasing the transaction in this way, Efron-Gabai, her anonymous client, and the museum would not have to report the return to the police, another stipulation in the contract.

The board also agreed to remain quiet about the exchange, at least until they could figure out a way to publicize the watches' return without admitting what they had done. To refuse to deal with thieves proffering booty was to risk driving them farther underground. But if it became known that the museum's leaders had negotiated with thieves, they would risk attracting other potential blackmailers.

After a brief back and forth that Kahan remembers as being amicable, the board decided to offer $30,000, and no more. If things got out of hand, they agreed, they would go to the police. The next day, Hasson and Kahan met with Efron-Gabai once more and presented the board-approved offer. The lawyer again stressed the importance of her client's privacy, and then she left the room. She returned, shortly, with a collection of boxes. One, a wine case, featured a line drawing of a cheery chef holding a bottle of cabernet sauvignon. This box was even more carelessly protected than the others. Efron-Gabai removed the pieces it held, each wrapped in crumbling paper like holiday dishes stored and forgotten.

In a few minutes, the contents of this box and the others were arrayed before Hasson. Whatever misgivings she and Kahan had felt when they first began these murky negotiations were put to rest. As Hasson peeled back the old newspaper from item after item, the breadth of the find revealed itself. There was Breguet's Sympathetique, with its small pocket watch and larger table clock, cunningly designed to maintain the identical time on both faces. Then came the famous "gun," the clockwork novelty by Jaquet Droz with a small watch in the stock and a bird that popped up to sing a tune when fired.

Many of the clocks and watches had suffered some damage, but it looked, from the way they were packed, as if they had never left the country. Hasson assumed that whoever "Ms. England" was, she had to know the provenance of these timepieces. Hasson and Kahan felt that they were close to uncovering the name of the thief, but the agreement they had signed barred them from going to the police.

When the lawyer brought out a small box marked in Hebrew, and opened it and tapped out its contents, Hasson, the matronly curator who twenty years before had awoken to an early morning phone call describing a burglary at her museum, began to cry. In the lawyer's hand was a gold and rock crystal watch, the Marie-Antoinette, intact and unharmed. The Queen was alive.

"I opened [the boxes to reveal the watches], and identified them from their numbers. Most were in good shape. Some were damaged," she said. "When I came to the Marie-Antoinette, I couldn't help crying, it was so moving and exciting to see it after so many years."[121]

Kahan remained calm through the negotiations, only later succumbing to shock when he and Hasson packed up the boxes and prepared to take them away.

Efron-Gabai asked again how much money would be paid in good will, and the pair offered the board-approved $30,000. Efron-Gabai allegedly refused. They then settled on $35,000, and Kahan wrote a check and handed it over. The mysterious Ms.

England would receive her tribute, and the museum curator and board chairman had gotten their treasure. "During all those years, when they were missing, I didn't pay any attention to the watches or the story," said Kahan. Now that they were back, he said "it was like a fairy tale."

As he realized what this collection meant for the museum – increased revenue, world prominence, a surge of popularity – as well as the historical value of the pieces in those disintegrating boxes, his mood changed from guardedly cautious to giddy. Fearing that he would crash his car on the way home, he and Hasson took a taxi back to the museum with the boxes in the trunk.

The clocks were theirs. After a slow and careful transfer of the boxes that probably, at least in spirit, mirrored the meticulous way the thief had originally removed the objects from the museum, the head of its security open the underground vault near the administrative office. Here, they kept the watches hidden from view, telling no one on the staff about their return. Even Boris Sankov, the museum's patient, long-haired, Russian resident watchmaker, was not told of their presence. Kahan scrawled on each box with a black Magic Marker, writing simply "Property of Eli Kahan. Do not touch."

Spear, a stickler for propriety, contacted the insurance agents he dealt with and explained the situation. The original insurance company that had paid out for the watches was gone, acquired and absorbed into a succession of conglomerates. Months of phone calls by Spear went nowhere. "No one remembered or cared," Spear says.

If the museum had had to pay back the entire amount, with interest, Speer calculated that it would be over $1.5 million. Instead, with a touch of shrewdness, Spear cited his own original documents and pointed out that the museum had received $700,000 for the loss of the collection. In the end, the insurance company agreed to "sell" the watches back to the museum for less than it paid for them: $400,000 for the forty found in Tel Aviv and $300,000 for any watches and clocks found elsewhere if they still existed. "We were very glad," Kahan recalls.

To try to hide something as monumental as a portion of the Salomons collection was iffy, and to hide it in the basement of the museum itself was folly. Although the small museum had a staff of only a few dozen people, it was inevitable that someone would eventually grow curious. A few weeks after taking possession of the watches, and after Hasson finally felt it safe to tell Sankov, she led the watchmaker to the collection. Sankov urged Hasson to go to the police, but she refused.

Sankov retrieved the watches and clocks from the vault, and he began restoring them, delighted to examine each piece after all these years. Inadvertently, his polishing rubbed away any fingerprints that might have provided the police with clues. A rumor slowly spread among the museum staff that Sankov was working on a new project, but somehow the news didn't leak outside the museum's thick, stone walls.

Sankov set about undoing the damage wrought by the thief, which for the most part was light or nonexistent. The only problems Sankov faced as he pried the cases open with his long, precise fingers, were the drying of the oil around the gears and the vagaries of temperature that knocked many of the movements out of whack.

There was some outright damage, however. One of the items — a golden automaton, about six inches tall, of an old woman on two canes—had been broken in half, and her head was missing, leading to the grim quip that she resembled Marie-Antoinette.

During this time, a rogue member of the museum board apparently tipped off the Jerusalem police, describing the situation and explaining the chain of events that led up to the return of the watches. Two police officers, Oded Shama and Oded Janiv, were assigned to the case, and although both were in their late thirties, they knew little about the original theft. Both had shaved heads, and both had a manner more jovial than inspectorial. In a city of constant change, there was little to interest the two detectives in this particular case, with its dusty old boxes, dead suspects, and closed insurance file. The Central Investigation Unit of Jerusalem, which normally investigated murders and major thefts, and which had conducted the original investigation into the Mayer Museum heist in 1983, was nominally on the case. But the contract signed with Efron-Gabai prohibited the museum from discussing it, so there was little to go on. No one who investigated the original break-in was still on the force. For months, the return of the watches was more a novelty to the two young detectives than anything else, exciting only for its brushes with intrigue and the unique nature of the theft. It was a cold case they didn't intend to pursue further.

Every day, Sankov, after working tirelessly on the watches, returned them to their cases in his workshop and shut it tight for the night. The museum began to contemplate a new exhibit of the collection, but no one knew quite how to break the story to the public. For a long while, the watches lay in their felt-lined boxes, invisible to all but a handful of people.

On the morning of November 11, 2007, more than a year after the collection came back to the museum, Danny Rubinstein, a well-known Israeli journalist, wrote a 790-word article in English in *Ha'aretz*, headlined "Priceless Clocks Stolen In Museum Heist Found 24 Years Later." Suddenly, the world learned that the denouement of one of the biggest unsolved thefts in Israeli and watchmaking history had nearly escaped it.

Rubinstein, a long-time journalist for *Ha'aretz* and now a college lecturer, is a blue-eyed older gentleman who grew up in Jerusalem's Nachlaot market district. For years, he took long walks through the city, sometimes alone, sometimes with friends, and he often visited Ohannes Markarian's shop in the Old City on Christian Quarter Road, a compressed stretch of pottery, clothing, and antiques merchants all vying for the attention of passers-by. He and Markarian spent hours talking about the theft, the watchmaker noting that instead of millions of shekels the museum should simply offer a free pass to the thief. Clearly, the old watchmaker said, the culprit wasn't interested in selling the pieces, so why not share them with the world, and he could visit them whenever he wanted?

Rubinstein spoke Arabic and often gave talks at the L.A. Mayer Museum, and he had been one of the first journalists to write about the break-in in 1983. He seemed to know everyone, or at least everyone knew him. He wears a ball cap to hide his face from the admirers who often approach him on the streets of the capital, regaling him with tales of old Jerusalem. He is the face of an older generation, one that still remembers the wars and the formation of the State of Israel.

One morning in November of 2007, Rubinstein was at a health clinic for a check-up when another old acquaintance, a retired police officer, came in.

"Danny," he said, "I remember you used to know Markarian. I assume you know his watches came back?"

Rubinstein was taken aback but quickly regained composure.

180

The retired policeman, realizing the reporter had not heard of the return of the watches, quickly recanted. "You can't print any of that," he said.

Using an old reporter's trick, Rubinstein smiled and said: "We already knew about it. What else can you tell me? We won't mention your name."

The story, what little of it there was, poured out, and Rubinstein began making calls.

Chapter 17

When Rubinstein's article on the recovery of the stolen watches appeared in *Ha'aretz* on November 11, 2007, the international press picked it up immediately. Hundreds of follow-up stories appeared, and watch bloggers and on-line watch forums were aflame with speculation. The tale was richly compelling: a heist, a watch worth an estimated $11 million, a mysterious widow, a taciturn lawyer. The same things that made the tale so hard for the police to follow gave it a frisson in the global media. It was an evocative detective story, suffused with intrigue. Where had the watches been all those years? Rubinstein closed his article on a note of conjecture, writing that "the identity of the thieves remains a mystery. However they are believed unlikely to have been inveterate watch collectors, but rather local operators, at least two in number."[122]

As calls from other reporters seeking comment came in to the Jerusalem Police, the embarrassed authorities realized they needed to dig further. The Central Investigation Unit, which normally investigated murders and major thefts, had conducted the original investigation in 1983. Now, the unit assigned the same two young detectives, Oded Shamah and Oded Janiv, to the case. Together with a team that included a muscular Russian investigator named Eddie Zharkov and two female detectives, the well-travelled Revital Zaraf and computer whiz Na'ama Mai, they began piecing together the puzzle. Their first stop was the L.A. Mayer Museum.

The group began by visiting Rachel Hasson and Eli Khan in the library. They went over the negotiations and the return of the watches. The museum staff knew almost nothing, and Hasson said very little, citing her promise to keep mum about the lawyer and her mysterious client. Janiv found Hasson's reticence frustrating. "She had none of the details of the widow," Janiv said later. "She also refused to talk to the press and would not talk to the police because that was also in the agreement."

But Yakubov, the watchmaker, produced a document found on one of the boxes, and it led the detectives to the warehouse where Efron-Gabai had stored the items. At the warehouse, in central Israel, the police found bills of lading from a woman in Los Angeles, Nili Shamrat.

Entering Shamrat's name into a police computer, Detective Mai came up with nothing. Then she performed a similar Google search. In seconds, a story by reporter Dalia Karpel appeared: "Eagle's Wings Cut," published on May 26, 2004. There in black and white, a snapshot showed a skinny man with a dark buzz cut lying in a hospital bed after being shot by the Israeli police in the 1970s. His name, according to the article, was Na'aman Diller. Arrayed around the image were four other pictures taken after this man committed a series of ingenious robberies between 1967 and the early 1980s, when he disappeared. Next to the photos was a paragraph of text:

Diller's 59-year-old wife, Nili Shamrat – who also flew in from the United States – tearfully eulogized him. Supported by a childhood friend, she spoke softly, "My darling, so gentle, noble and talented. You have returned to your roots."[123]

"Bingo," Mai shouted, running down the hall to her partners to show them the printout.

According to town lore, one summer morning in 1957 a North American T-6 Harvard, one of the smaller training planes in the Israeli Air Force, buzzed low and fast over the eucalyptus trees and under the low power lines of Kibbutz Ein HaHoresh, a small community about sixty kilometers north of Jerusalem. The plane, painted bright yellow and, by its markings, based at the IAF training school at Petach Tikva, "went on to skim the fish ponds at Kibbutz Maabarot, coming in so low that it knocked a farmer off his tractor." The pilot then pulled up, waggled his wings, and disappeared into the horizon and into infamy.

The pilot's name was Na'aman Diller, and his family had been early members of Ein HaHoresh, literally the "Plowman's Spring," a small settlement founded in 1931 and home to some five hundred idealistic and taciturn settlers. The town motto was a verse about flight and acceptance:

Our best years behind us
We did not chase winds in a dream
No dream more beautiful than our actions

Although Ein HaHoresh had many brave sons and daughters in the Israeli military, it was Na'man Diller who took the motto to heart and took to the air at an early age. Now, he was about to be grounded.

As the plane flew overhead, one resident, Giora Furman, then twenty-two and a flight school instructor on vacation, approached Aaron Shavit, the commander of the nearby IAF flight school and inquired as to the name of the "falcon" who buzzed his village. "He promised to find out," Furman would recall years later. "The next day he kicked Diller out of the course."

Recklessness and repentance were the two constants in Diller's life. His widow, Shamrat, would later describe him as kind and friendly, outgoing but quiet in large groups, the heart of any gathering. Look at pictures of him and you're drawn to his deeply lined face, the pat of curly hair that he sometimes shaved to a military buzz, and his large blue eyes. He was whippet-thin, even as a child, and had the studied, careful demeanor of an athlete at rest. He exhibited flashes of sobering intelligence, and at the same time his manner marked him as a man of the earth, a *kibbutznick*, someone who would make his parents proud.

"In some ways," said Shamrat. "It separated him from so many other people, but [he] was very quick to understand things. In Hebrew, there is an expression that says somebody has golden hands, meaning that he can do everything. He was very, very technically and mechanically oriented."

In 1957, Na'aman was to be one of Ein HaHoresh's wind chasers, protecting the hard-won homeland from the massing forces at her borders. Israel then was a wild and rugged place. That January, four Israeli POWs were traded for an astonishing 5,850 Egyptian prisoners, including a number of military generals. In March, another four soldiers were kidnapped in Petra, and the small planes of the IAF ran reconnaissance along the borders, hoping to avoid further losses. The Israeli government tasked the nascent IAF, flying used WWII planes and jets sourced from friendly Western nations, with protecting troops on the ground, and the soldiers were always in trouble. To be a Kibbutzim was an honor in itself, and to be a Kibbutzim military man was the highest honor a young man could bestow on his proud parents.

Na'aman had been born on January 7, 1939, to an idealistic young Polish woman, Ernestine Friedman, nicknamed Arne. She was a psychologist from Jaroslaw, Poland, a small town west of Wroclaw, home to one of the few Jewish synagogues remaining on the San River. When she landed in Israel, near Eilat, in 1935, she barely spoke Hebrew. She was assigned to teach kindergarten, but when the children asked her the name of a flower or bug she couldn't answer. Instead, she would promise to look it up and return with the answer in the morning. "There was a stage when I stopped going for walks in the garden with the children so they wouldn't ask so many questions," she said.[124]

She was overbearing, opinionated, and dedicated to the Zionist cause. Her husband, Na'aman's father, was Zvi Diller, a taciturn man who fell in love with Arne "because she worked hard." Like Na'aman, he was tall and skinny with dark hair. He was the quiet to Arne's storm, accepting and stoic in the face of his wife's outbursts.

The boy, born at the brand new Beilinson Hospital in Petach Tikva, was healthy and seemingly happy. But in his first few years he would lose much of the hale good health and hearty strength associated with his father and mother. Arne worked in the kibbutz kindergarten until a wave of typhus spread through Israel and Palestine, leaving her weak and bedridden. Out of work for months as she recovered, she reported back to the kindergarten only to be told she now had to toil in the fields with her husband. Refusing to work under the sun, she left Zvi and their young son and moved to Tel Aviv. Na'aman was one year old.

Two years later she returned, chastened by her inability to find a permanent job in Tel Aviv. Ein HaHoresh now needed teachers, and they gave her a position at the school again. But after being away so long, she now felt herself an outsider and not "accepted" by the Kibbutz.

Trouble started almost immediately. The kindergarten had two rooms separated by a thin wall. Arne taught one group, while her son sat in another. When she spoke louder than a near-whisper, Na'aman would cry for her. Having her own class to teach, she could do nothing. The boy's constant mewling caused a rift with the other teachers, who felt that he was weak and spoiled.

The other children noticed it as well and began to pick on him. Absalom Artzi, a classmate, uncharitably recalled him as being a scrawny coward. "He was a weakling and kids are mean to weaklings. He was alone and had no one to protect him," he said. As an older child, Na'aman came to love reading; he would recall that his "kingdom was in books."

Even his mother had trouble loving him. In a 1971 psychologist's interview, she said Na'aman was "unwanted." By then, his escapades could have hardened her opinion of her son, but from the beginning something had pushed him from her. Perhaps, she said, he reminded her of the isolation of the kibbutz, or perhaps it was because he was a "good boy but not a good kid," as she characterized him in an interview. As a result, the psychologists believed, he always had something to prove.

Na'aman went to jail for a year thanks to his 1957 airplane joyride. His mother, visiting him in the military brig, found him disconsolate: he missed flying. "It was the most wonderful thing I ever felt," he said. "Up and down. I was quick as a bird and as canny as a reptile." He was discharged from active duty but remained in the Army reserves.

Na'aman returned to the kibbutz and lived quietly with his parents. But his fall from the IAF had changed him. He seemed haunted, now, and he kept his eyes open for an opportunity to leave. He knew he needed money.

One Saturday in July, 1959, a neighbor caught Na'aman riffling through a strongbox that held donations designated for Ein HaHoresh's soldiers. The rest of the kibbutz was at a funeral for another soldier killed in a plane crash, and Na'aman had exploited their grief to enrich himself. After a unanimous vote, the kibbutz leaders expelled him from the settlement. The kibbutz lifestyle was all about trust, and for a son of the group to betray it to such a degree was almost unthinkable. One member remembered that the kibbutzim "almost lynched him on the spot."

In Israel, kibbutzim were close to national heroes. They consisted of small, dedicated groups, usually no more than two hundred members, living in relative isolation on Israel's windswept plains and burning deserts. They were self-sufficient. Although now known for farming, they were the source of most of Israel's early industrial efforts. Kibbutzim were Israel's builders.

Na'aman's misbehavior wasn't entirely unexpected. According to one contemporary, Yitzchak Baram, "Na'aman stole all the time. We called it petty theft. When he was in the army he had a girlfriend in Beit Lid and he would steal cars from the kibbutz to go visit her." But innocent joyriding was a long way from wholesale larceny.

Thrust out into the world for the first time, Diller's plan was simple: to find wealth, no matter the price. Assessing him psychologically in 1967, Dr. Dov Alexandrovich would find that he had a "mental disorder that affects the thought process. Here is a person who shows early signs of schizophrenia." Diller's lawyer requested this psychological investigation, during his second arraignment for breaking and entering, in order to enter a plea of innocence due to insanity. But no one in Diller's life remembers him taking any psychotropic drugs or exhibiting signs of mental illness—suggesting it might have been a dodge to avoid prosecution.

This much was sure: Na'aman "felt inferior," and he thought that money possessed an "omnipotent power" that could repair his life.

In 1957, exiled from the kibbutz in disgrace, he vowed to change his life and moved in with an aunt in Tel Aviv. He was an intelligent young man with an IQ of about 130, which put him in the top 3 percent nationally.

By 1960 he was working at Bank Leumi, Israel's storied banking group, and going to school for accounting. Outwardly, he became a normal, well-adjusted young man headed for great things. He was, he said, looking for "a way to get ahead in life." He spent time working at an insurance company and a Ministry of Education archive, trying to "prove his worth" by making more money. But the money never arrived, and by 1967 he was making other plans for his future. He had quit his job and was secretly being sent money by his mother. He still lived with his Aunt Hila and her husband Aryeh Reznik, a minor Israeli sculptor, in an apartment on Emanuel Avenue. He kept to himself.

Tel Aviv in the 1960s was awash with change. New immigrants were arriving by the boat- and planeload and with them new methods for bilking the next wave. Gangsters from Russia were rolling through town, ensuring that smuggling and antiquities theft was rampant. It was the era of the suave cat burglar. Sean Connery's James Bond was the most popular film character of the era, and his exploits in *You Only Live Twice* were breaking box-office records at the Hod Theatre in Tel Aviv. Albeit with a slightly criminal twist, it was on this image that many of Israel's aspiring criminals modeled their wardrobes and methods. Na'aman was among them.

Putting his military training to use, Na'aman had collected a number of plans and diagrams of buildings around Tel Aviv in his "operations log." For years, he studied security systems and tested the fence and window bars at various landmarks. Even without professional experience, he began to understand the mindset of security professionals.

Diller became interested – some would say obsessed – with health. He began losing his hair, and he blamed his diet. Becoming a vegan, he grew even thinner and became obsessed with cleanliness, showering at least twice a day. It was also during this time that he fell in love with a young woman named Nili Shamrat, whom Diller's mother described as a "flower girl." "I met Na'aman at a party and it was love at first sight," Shamrat said years later. "The relationship was very, very vibrant and very strong. Na'aman actually was a very romantic person." Shamrat had long, wavy hair and was Diller's physical opposite. Whereas Na'aman, the former soldier, was all angles and corners, Nili was skinny yet vivacious, a picture of health and intellect. She knew nothing of Na'aman's past, and he kept it that way for years. She lived in Israel for a few years longer, but by 1980 had moved to the United States and out of Na'aman's life. During these years, he lived the life of an ascetic, eating little, and planning.

On October 8, 1967, a small story appeared on the ITIM news wire describing a foiled break-in in a northern suburb of Tel Aviv on Keren Kayemet Boulevard. The morning before, a neighbor had heard noises coming from number 47, a Halva'a Behisachon Bank branch with a vault in the basement. A window in back led to an empty field. Arriving there at around 8 a.m., Sergeant Eliezer Merhavi and Constable Ronnie Chandler found the grate over the window broken. They pulled it back, and Nadler, the smaller of the two, climbed through.

Inside, the bank was dark and quiet. Chandler moved quickly

and silently to the vault, where he found a surprising sight: a man-sized hole cut straight through six inches of steel. Nadler moved through the hole, his gun drawn, and received a face full of tear gas.

Blind and staggering, Chandler fell forward onto the man inside the room. He began to grapple him with him and, although he could barely see anything, Chandler, a "champion featherweight boxer," began throwing tight punches at the burglar's face. The burglar pulled a pistol from his jacket and fired once. At the sound of the report, Merhavi ran down the hall to help his partner just as the burglar was coming out of the vault.

In the fight that followed, Merhavi pulled his gun and shot the burglar in the foot. The man lay wounded and blinded from residual tear gas, as the policemen called for back-up and rounded up the thief's gear—canvas sacks full of hammers, chisels, lock picks, and, more importantly, the loot he had just taken from the bank vault. In his wallet, they found a license for a late model Opel hatchback in the name of Na'aman Diller, age 28, late of Ein HaHoresh. In his car, parked a few blocks away, they found the contents of fifty safety deposit boxes, including $8,000 in cash and diamonds and jewelry worth a little over one hundred thousand dollars.

Diller was transported to Ichilov Hospital, the first (but not last) time that he was driven away from a burglary site in an ambulance. The papers lapped up the story, dubbing him the "Kibbutznik burglar."

Diller's preparations for the robbery had begun five months earlier, when he started digging a shallow ditch from a small shack along nearby Be'er Tuvya street, a tiny circular road accessible only though a copse of trees. He ran the ditch through an empty courtyard, digging slowly and carefully and even leaving hazard barriers up when he went home at night. He wore postal service overalls as he dug and told anyone who inquired that he was "testing some wires."

Into this ditch, over the next few weeks, he began laying a 164-foot length of iron pipe and two wires in sections. The pipe stopped at the barred rear window of the bank. Diller worked slowly, steadily, and with great precision. His goal was to become part of the scenery, a normal worker with a normal job to do. Then, at the end of May, the army called Diller up to fight in the Six

Days War, and he had to set his project aside, half-finished. For the next two months, he bristled under military order and discipline, itching to return to his work.

By July, he was out of uniform and back in his ditch. He had hidden the pipe under a load of dirt and capped the ends before he left. The plants in the courtyard had, by now, grown over most of the work site. He resumed his slow, methodical labor, appearing to all the world to be a lone member of a road crew forced by his higher ups to perform the unglamorous job of ditch digging. Finally, by October, he had crossed the field, leaving a small length of pipe and cable sticking out of the ground.

He left for about a week, then returned on Wednesday, October 4, the eve of Rosh Hashanah. He was driving a stolen Ford Taunus Transit van, a globular-looking, German-made work van that was commonly seen cruising around Europe and Israel retrofitted as an ice cream truck in the late 1960s. He parked the van near the field and again went away. He returned on Friday the 6th at 11 o'clock in the morning.

Jerusalem was quiet. Diller would have most of Friday and all of Saturday to work unobstructed, and he knew no one would be at the bank until Monday. He had the neighborhood to himself.

Having cased the bank for months, Diller knew that the rear alarm was primitive and easy to shut off. He removed the grate from the back window, opened it, and climbed inside. He slowly brought in his tools, laying them out like a painter preparing his work area. Then he went back out the window, replaced the grate, and by noon was home, showered, and resting for his return in the evening.

At eleven that night, he returned in his small Opel. He pulled a small canister of oxygen from the van – he had six in total – and connected it to the pipe. He then connected a battery to the leads and walked back to the window. He was carrying a canister of acetylene and a home-made oxy-acetylene torch. The battery wires would power his lighter and lamps. The oxygen flowed from the van to the back room through the buried pipe, ensuring he would not have to lug a set of extremely conspicuous canisters across the garden.

The vault was protected by a six-inch thick steel door. He set about cutting through the metal a layer at a time, inching his way closer to the inside. Hours later, he had made a hole big enough to step through without trouble.

Finally, he was inside. He quickly cut through three bank safes and pulled open fifty safe deposit boxes. He left with a bag full of loot, and later on Saturday morning he returned for more. By this time he had been working for forty-eight hours straight and he was exhausted. Faced with another set of safes, Diller began pounding at the locks with reckless abandon, assuming that everyone would be asleep. A neighbor, awoken by the banging, called the police.

After months of careful planning and a six-month operation, Diller was foiled by his own impatience. When the tear gas cleared, police were convinced there had been multiple thieves, and that they had escaped. They served Diller with a search warrant at his bedside in Tel Aviv's Ichilov Hospital and broke down the door to his small apartment. There, they realized the truth: Diller had acted alone. A library of books on welding and safecracking littered his sparsely furnished home. They found two live hand grenades taken from the Army reserve armory and foreign currency. They also found his operations log detailing the entire plan.

As Diller lay handcuffed to a bed, he began to speak with a lawyer and a psychologist. The plan was to plead insanity, so Diller explained himself and his actions. The psychologist, Dr. Dov Alexanderovitz, interviewed him extensively and found that Diller was able to "maintain some kind of connection to reality. At the same time, because of his disorder, he is forced to give up on many areas of his life, including his sex life." Instead, Diller explained, he gained a sort of pleasure from theft.

"It's something like the thrill of a man at a beautiful woman when he knows she could be his," he said. "You're tense, concentrated on an object you want to carry. You do not even need the thing you stole, you need only the excitement."

When word of his arrest trickled back to Ein HaHoresh, the kibbutz was outraged. They struck Diller's name from the kibbutz registry, and argued over whether the kibbutz would help Arne Diller pay her son's legal fees. In November, Na'aman's mother took a one-year leave of absence in order to support her son as he stood trial in Tel Aviv. The psychiatric evaluation swayed the jury and slowly the punishment was whittled down to a few years in prison before being passed along to the judge.

Around this time, Diller's family changed their name to Lidor (a loose anagram) to disassociate themselves from the *shanda* of their black sheep. Na'aman also soon changed his last name to Lidor, and when the family later changed it back, he did too. Ultimately, this maneuver would allow him to keep and carry two passports, a useful tool for a cat burglar.

In March of 1968 he was sentenced to four years in prison for the bank theft and disappeared behind bars. By all indications, he was a model prisoner, taciturn and obedient, and in February of 1971, he was released early for good behavior. He returned to Tel Aviv to live with his mother, and that same month was diagnosed with skin cancer.

On July 17, 1971, another tiny item crossed the Itim wires. "Rubin paintings stolen from son," the piece read. A dozen paintings had been taken from the home of Davi Rubin, son of Reuven Rubin, the famous Israeli painter whose early landscape work has been compared to Cezanne's. His home at 14 Rehov Bialik had been ransacked over a weekend, and the neighbors had heard nothing. Rubin, who had been out of town, returned to find many of his father's famous oils, including *Flute Player and Landscape with Olive trees*, gone. Also stolen were two Picasso etchings and a dove-shaped diamond pin that Reuven had made for his wife on their fortieth anniversary. Reuven Rubin, his son recalled, "never recovered and returned to the way he was before the burglary." He grew sick with worry and died three years later.

This theft seemed almost magical. The locked doors had not been forced or picked, and the house, except for the damage caused by the theft, held no clues. One morning after the burglary, however, David Rubin noticed one of the bars on a high window was askew. He dragged a chair to the window and tapped it. It moved and he found that it had been cut and wrapped in colored tape and smoothed over with dark putty. The police knew this to be a classic Diller move – he had admitted trying this trick, and it seemed Diller's specialty was the difficult entrance and the easy-going exit.

The police followed Diller for a few weeks, until on August 16 they spotted him in a stolen van with the wrong license plates. They stopped him, searched his home and van, and came up with a few of the Rubins' etchings but none of the paintings nor the pin. While admitting that he had stolen the paintings, he refused to return them, saying that "he didn't think it was necessary to have

192

mercy on the wealthy Rubin, who had bank accounts in Switzerland." The police also discovered that he had participated in or performed twenty-three robberies in the six months since his release from prison.

Diller's exploits became tabloid fodder, and in the scribbler's imagination he became a Robin Hood, a postmodern "aristocratic burglar" and a "modern poet-philosopher" according to one writer, Uri Keisari. Diller's ascetic attributes and careful planning were reminiscent of a warrior monk's training, and many found it hard to hate a man who thumbed his nose at the bourgeois Israeli upper crust. In fact, the Kibbutznik burglar, said Keisari, was a victim "of bacteria from a disease that is spreading throughout the country. It is the disease of the quantity which is ruining the quality. The fenceless kibbutz is one of our last remaining fortresses. How long will these ideological monasteries last?"

The official report on the theft was long and broad. The police accused Diller – now Lidor – of stealing license plates, breaking into a ministry office to steal and forge ID cards, stealing fur and jewelry from apartments in Tel Aviv and even forging checks using a faked stamp. All told, he had stolen nearly of half a million dollars in property, although his exact proceeds were not known. He stored his plunder in various abandoned vans under tarps around town, a set of mobile safety deposit boxes that kept the goods away from his home and mother. Photographs taken from a stand of trees show him walking away from one of his vans, his face firm but with a slight crease of a smile on his lips.

During his trial, the defense brought in psychologists who claimed that Diller had a narcissistic and schizoid personality, albeit "one with very rich internal content and significant creative bonds, with the sensitivity of an artist." In 1972, a judge sent him back to prison and required psychological evaluations throughout. He began to see Dr. Ephraim Lehman, an Israeli psychologist who later moved to Germany and with whom Diller prepared his own lawyer-less appeal. His motion was dismissed by a judge who found that Diller's "ambition for superiority causes him to try to impose his will on society, and he does not accept its authority and laws."

Diller spent four more years in prison before again being released for good behavior. But this time, Nili Shamrat had grown tired of waiting and had left him, eventually marrying in the United States. He wrote that he missed her dearly: "One who I loved and planned on marrying, who continued to write beautiful letters to me during my second long incarceration, is gone and we could not turn the wheel backward when I was released." He told his parents he wanted to study vegan medicine, a controversial branch of medicine that avoided all animal products and focused on herbs and plants.

In the fall of 1977, Diller used his forgery skills to make a fake German passport. He made his own stamps from rubber blocks and wood and matched the inks, the typefaces, and photographic styles of other passports he had purchased or stolen. Using his phony passport, he travelled to Holland where, contrary to his stated intention to study medicine, he robbed an Amsterdam jewelry store. The Amsterdam police, being rather more proactive than their Israeli colleagues, grabbed him immediately and found a van nearby full of oxygen tanks. Although the Dutch authorities were at first confused by his passport, after running his fingerprints through Interpol they found that they had caught the notorious Diller. In fluid, slightly accented English and some Dutch, Diller explained that in a few short months he had completed eleven robberies and stolen four cars. He received another three years in prison.

This cycle of contrition and sin continued unabated. He met a woman named Julia Vilda who was a Dutch Christian missionary—until then. ("When she met Diller," Oded Janiv said later, "she was not a nun anymore.") She had been assigned to his prison to bring prisoners to Jesus. Instead, Diller brought her to him. When he got out in 1980, he lived with her as she tried to help him continue his studies in vegan medicine. That same year, he stole a car near a group of police officers and in the ensuing chase he hit a tree and was knocked out cold and injured. The Dutch authorities, tired of the Israeli's antics, sent him back to Jerusalem.

Julia came with him, wheeling Diller down the gangway and into the bustle of Tel Aviv, where they took an apartment in Yad Eliyahu. He thrashed around looking for a job, and finally settled on burning out the window grate of a bathroom in a local bank branch with an oxygen torch and trying to break into a heavily guarded ATM. He was arrested again, and he received one year.

Diller was forty-two and exhausted. His lawyer, Tzvi Lydski, called him a "lonely dog with a broken foot," and the formerly proud man was described as sitting with his "head bowed and his face unshaven" in court.[125] "I am burdened by my defeat, my failures and my handicap," he said. "I am far from a saint, but I try to reach the level of a repentant person."

Apparently this play-acting worked, for he was soon released. He seemed to disappear for a while, visiting Holland and France, and he continued his diet and exercise regimens. In Tel Aviv, he lived at 20 Sokolov Street, a block of modern apartments on a quiet tree-lined street. His mother had bought him a flat there in the early 1980s. One relative recalls seeing him on a bus during this period, wearing a wig and with a new nose that had apparently "shrunk."

It seemed his cycle had been broken. After all of the bad blood, he appeared to become closer to his mother Arne, and by the 1990s he was able to rekindle his relationship with Nili Shamrat, calling her daily to wake her up at her home in California. She had divorced her first husband and now lived alone in an apartment in Tarzana, where she worked as a teacher and guidance counselor. Nili began to visit him every summer, spending months at his apartment on Sokolov Street or travelling with him through Europe. He seemed a changed person, no longer under the sway of his old impulses. He was neither rich nor penniless. He always seemed to be buying or selling something, a practice that Shamrat assumed was the source of his money.

By 2003, Diller's cancer had returned. He spent months in a Tel Aviv hospice, where he was visited by his mother and by Shamrat. On April 15, 2003, Na'aman and Nili were married by the Jerusalem Rabbinate. It was, coincidentally or not, the twentieth anniversary of the L.A. Mayer theft. Shamrat returned to the U.S. shortly after the wedding. She would not return for a little more than a year.

On April 13, 2004, Diller didn't call Nili to wish her good morning. By the 15th, she was worried, and she called Arne. One of his nephews, Arne told her, had found him at 20 Sokolov on the floor, "wallowing in his own excrement," and he was sent to the hospice at Tel Hashomer. Shamrat arrived in Jerusalem in time to see him lapse into unconsciousness. The cancer had spread a fiery path through his body and he died on the morning of April 20, 2004, his new bride and his mother by his side. His mother buried him at the cemetery at Ein Hahoresh, the community that had ousted him so many years before. He was sixty-five.

Chapter 18

What happened next is a point of contention between Israeli detectives and Nili Shamrat. Shamrat, who at the time was a tenth-grade adviser at the Shal Havet Jewish Day School in Los Angeles, claims not to remember what was said in the trying months between her wedding to Diller and his death.

I began speaking to Shamrat in 2009, when a close relation put me in contact with her. We spoke primarily over the phone, and it was clear she was still very much in love with the man once called the "Kibbutznik burglar." It was strange – to speak about a Diller that many didn't know while the facts of the case began to pile up and meld into a mélange of fact and fiction. The press painted a picture of a narcissistic international playboy, while Shamrat told of a man who made delicious fruit sorbet and delightful vegan meals.

"Na'aman was a very, very unique person," she said one afternoon, wistfully recalling his ability to fix things around the house. She called it his "golden hand." She had a slight accent and her voice grew soft with her reminiscences.

"He did things that were definitely a crime, but he was really very positive in so many instances, so many other ways," she said.

According to the police, Diller took her to the L.A. Mayer museum shortly after their wedding, and showed her how he had accomplished the break-in. She was dumbstruck that her husband, the man she had known for almost three decades, had pulled off a final robbery before settling into the leisurely pace of middle age. She said he showed her a number of boxes at his home and at his Aunt Hilda's empty apartment and explained that they came from

the museum. These were the boxes that Shamrat gave to Ephron-Gabai to return to the museum, and these were the boxes that
contained the Marie-Antoinette.

"I came to her and I said I had inherited things that my husband stole," said Shamrat. "Before he died he told me that he stole
them from that museum and that I wanted to return them to the
museum. And I only had one condition: anonymity."

She chose the lawyer based on a friend's recommendation
in Tel Aviv, and thought this would be the best and most legally
prudent way to return the watches. She says she does not remember who first mentioned the possibility of a reward, but as far as
she recalls it was mutually agreed upon that Ephron-Gabai would
mention but not press the point. "I don't care what happens," she
told the lawyer, "these things have to be returned to the museum."

I asked her why she didn't just leave the items on the door-
step of the museum. Why didn't she just ship them anonymously?
She replied that she had no experience with this sort of thing
and that she knew that these things need to be returned post-
haste.

"I think the main reason was that I thought, really thought,
that if any issue is like that, you go to a lawyer," she said. "Not
having a lot of experience with lawyers in Israel, or hardly any I
thought that the most common thing to do was to go to a lawyer
who will take care of it."

"You know I could have left it and then nothing would have
happened, but for me something that was stolen needs to be returned."

She wanted to do the right thing.

After the return of the watches, the police approached the
Lidor/Diller family. They learned details about his previous crimes
in other countries and information on Shamrat herself. The family
told them about his lover, Julia, in Holland, and also revealed that
Na'aman had owned a number of safety deposit boxes in Switzerland, the Netherlands, and France before his death. They said he
received about 1,800 euros a month from a bank account in Paris,
his main source of income, but the family, suspicious of its black
sheep, believed he had more. By January 2008, the Israeli police
had organized cross-jurisdictional investigations in Holland and
Paris, where they hoped to find the last missing pieces from the

L.A. Mayer collection.

The Jerusalem police also released a general statement requesting that no Israeli journalist write about the case and asking police to remain quiet when talking to reporters. But on October 29, 2010, ignoring the gag rule, Danny Rubinstein published another article in *Calcalist Magazine,* entitled "Na'aman Diller Is The Man Behind Israel's Biggest Robbery." In it, Nili Shamrat made her first statement, saying that she was "very uncomfortable" talking about it. "The museum received the clocks back. Na'aman is a forgotten story. The important thing is the collection was returned, and people can see it and everyone is happy."[126] However, the police had already tracked down most of the other watches and were beginning to plan a case against Shamrat with the help of the L.A. police department.

Revital Zaraf was the first to find a new cache of watches. In May 2008, she had travelled to the Netherlands, where she had trouble adjusting to the cold. The warehouse on the outskirts of the Hague felt like a freezer to the tan, dark-haired detective. She had come with a member of the Dutch police, carrying a slip of paper with the name of a man who more than two decades earlier had rented one of the storage spaces. As they walked the vast room, threading through a labyrinth of boxes, the Dutch officer consulted a list of renters, zeroing in on one locker in particular. It belonged to Julia, who lived nearby, and earlier, Zaraf had gone to see her.

The interview was fairly quick. Julia hadn't spoken to Diller in years, and she was sad to hear of his passing. She explained that he had asked her to hold a few items for him until his return. As time went by, and he never resurfaced, she forgot about him.

What they found inside the locker was disappointing: just boxes full of papers. But Zaraf also found the number of a safe deposit box in the city, and soon she and the Dutch detective were there with a search warrant. Inside a metal box, in smaller, cardboard medicine boxes nestled in yellowed newspaper, they found six watches. Revital recognized them as having been among those stolen from the Mayer museum. Scattered at the bottom of the box, she found fake passport stamps and photographs of a skinny man with hollow cheeks and large aviator-style glasses. They were of Diller, taken during his most active criminal period.

In L.A., another case was building. In December 2007, Israeli National Police were routed to the California Department of

Insurance (CDI) Fraud Division, and a CDI detective travelled to Israel, where he went over the details of the case before returning to Los Angeles to prepare for a formal investigation by California police.

A few days later, detective Oded Janiv flew to Los Angeles. At 6 a.m. on a warm May morning, Janiv arrived with CDI detectives and an L.A.P.D. SWAT team at the Tarzana home of Nili Shamrat. Warning Janiv that Shamrat might be armed (a concept that amused the Israeli detectives to no end), the Los Angeles police told him to stand back while one of the Americans knocked on the door.

Shamrat opened it. She was a thin woman with curly brown hair and a runner's thin physique. She took care of herself, eating small portions of mostly vegetarian food, and had been inspired by Diller to stay in shape. The U.S. detectives, on seeing this charming Californian, lowered their guns. They went inside.

The cops sat down with Shamrat. She was worried.

As she started to answer questions in accented English, another woman, her sister, came to the room, and in hushed Hebrew asked what was wrong. "This is probably about Na'aman," Shamrat answered in Hebrew, unaware that there was an Israeli detective present.

The house was small and cozy. A few pieces of Judaica hung from the walls. But, next to the commonplace, the investigators found three rare eighteenth-century oil paintings and an antique Latin manuscript stolen from the L.A. Mayer Museum, as well as some small labels from the original exhibit explaining the items in English and Hebrew. Shamrat denied any knowledge that the goods were stolen, and the police eventually left, but the next day she called to admit that she was the widow of Na'aman Diller. She told the police she had no more treasures. They believed her. But her effort to escape her husband's sins was for naught. Insurance Commissioner Steve Poizner of the California Department of Insurance charged her with acceptance of stolen property.

On March 2, 2010, almost two years later, she received five years of probation and three hundred hours of community service for her complicity in the theft. She lost her job at the school and has not really worked since. She felt terrible and she wishes things had gone differently. But she never wished she hadn't met the love of her young life, the quiet, skinny, strong man with golden hands, her Na'aman.

For the Israelis there were still a few loose ends to tie up, including determining the location of the remaining watches. It seemed to the Israeli detectives that most of the watches were intact and safe. Oded Sarna picked up another fifty watches out of a safety deposit box in Paris under Diller's name and received a plaque from the Paris Antiquities Authority for returning the Breguet masterpieces to their rightful home.

Then the trail went cold. Diller's real skill was burglary, and he was a horrible fence. He had almost been caught in the late 1980s trying to sell the watches, a mistake he never made again. Travelling on a fake passport, he took a train to Geneva, apparently to sell some of the stolen Breguets. At the Swiss border, customs officials checked his papers and pulled him off of the train. In his bag they found six watches but did not think to identify them further and instead sent him back into France, forcing him to sell his watches on the spot to buy a return ticket. Detective Janiv believed the watches were still in Swiss custody or floating around in someone's collection.

In the end, 96 of the 106 watches reappeared, including the Marie-Antoinette. The L.A. Mayer exhibit reopened on July 21, 2009, with only 55 of the 96 remaining clocks on display. The rest are kept under lock and key in Boris Sankov's workshop. The rest are stored inside a massive vault built into the foundation of the little museum.

Inside L.A. Mayer, the bustle of Jerusalem falls away. The new space is quiet and cool, and guards lounge in their chairs as school groups and scholars pay admission and stroll in to look at the trove of Islamic art in the heart of the Jewish state. Some only come for the watches. After all, a good watch was not just a collection of gears, but a symbol of permanence amid life's flux.

The Marie-Antoinette was the ultimate expression of that thought. The woman who inspired it, the man who loved her, and the maestro who kept the beat were all long gone. All that remained was this golden distillation of time, romance, and obsession.

Now that watch hangs in a clear case, protected from theft by a state-of-the-art security system. Sankov hadn't dared to wind it. It was too fragile and precious, although he did say that it still ran. Outside, Israel and the Middle East were roiled by conflict. Switzerland, France, and the rest of the world were wracked by a banking crisis. Here, in a bulletproof glass case, amid a constellation of tiny spotlights, suspended by arcs of crimson velvet and a golden chain, just as Marie-Antoinette would have carried it in the halls of Versailles had she been allowed to live out her days in peace, was a gold watch that had lived through everything this world could throw at it and thrive, a testament to the skill and endless dedication of one man to the art of watchmaking.

The watch is viewable from all angles, and it looks surprisingly small in this windowless room, a crown jewel surrounded by the rest of the Salomons collection. The real Marie-Antoinette is just as striking as Swatch's re-creation. It looks battle-scarred. Its golden case appears scratched by an unschooled polisher's rag, and its cogs and wheels and spindles, minimally cleaned by Sankov, are dark and discolored, yet the edges still shine in places. Sankov found Diller to have treated the watches clumsily, but much of the damage was minor and easily repaired. Apparently because Diller's efforts to sell off minor jewels and gold from the timepieces often failed, he had stopped disassembling them and instead simply became their steward. He, like so many held in the thrall of Marie-Antoinette and her namesake watch, was beset by the majesty of a beautiful thing.

Every night, the room is closed behind a foot-thick steel safe door, and it is under constant surveillance. The Queen, long sought-after and a symbol of so much lost, was finally found and was not be likely to go missing again.

Chapter 19

Las Vegas
In June of 2014, I flew from New York City to Las Vegas to the heart of modern horology. The JCK Show in Las Vegas — its name an abbreviation of *Jewelers' Circular Keystone,* a

magazine founded in 1875 – is the premiere American watch and jewelry show and a place for the established jewelers to converge en masse to stock up for the season. Worldwide, JCK is second only to BaselWorld in Basel, Switzerland, an event that plays host to watchmaking's glitterati for almost two weeks every March.

At JCK, watches are seen more as fashion items than as works of engineering or experimentation. But a small minority of watchmakers are still creating watches the way Breguet did in his atelier. I checked into the Paris hotel, with its outsized model Eiffel Tower outside and French-themed *casino*, and walked the strip to the imposing Venetian hotel, where under lavish chandeliers and applied moldings that would rival Versailles in opulence if not quality, I entered the world of *haute horlogerie*, Las Vegas style.

Like any convention, the show is split up among multiple rooms, and each manufacturer or dealer has a booth. There are giveaways – towels, candies, or notebooks are popular – and the higher-end brands escape the rabble by hiring $10,000-a-night suites in the hotel's upper floors, accessible only by appointment and armed escort.

Watchmaking in the modern age lives in a halfway place between art and commerce. The old piecework of the Swiss has been replaced by whirring robot arms on an assembly line, and Nicolas Hayek's "pyramidal base" of watches consists of watches that cost a few dollars to make and sell for a king's ransom. The mark-up for the jeweler, one manufacturer told me, is thirty to fifty percent. This means a watch a jeweler buys for $250 can sell for $500 or more in the store. Imagine this writ larger on some of the more opulent pieces, and a price of $100,000 in the jeweler's window means a price of $50,000 wholesale.

This goes a long way toward explaining why most watches are "expensive." Watchmakers want to distribute their wares to shops – called "doors" in the business. While many manufacturers like Seiko and Citizen want more and more doors, including many department and discount stores, higher-end makers try to reduce the number of doors to which they sell. This creates scarcity, and when the watchmaker markets his wares on the pages of glossy magazines – when Cindy Crawford or another actor or starlet is seen wearing a Chanel J12 white ceramic watch (about $9,000 retail) – the dearth of product ensures the distributor can maintain his markup while the watchmaker makes a sale.

Take Stephen Hallock, former president of MB&F North America. This boyish entrepreneur wears custom shirts, handsome tailored jackets, and the latest jeans of the season. He keeps fit and trim, his beard raffishly unkempt and his hair soft and tousled. MB&F – which stands for Maximilian Büsser & Friends – is a small company that calls on the talents of a number of master watchmakers, Büsser included, to create what Hallock calls horological machines. These watches are not your grandfather's Rolex. Starting at about $200,000, they are masterpieces of design and horology, incorporating odd, rare materials with a disregard for watchmaking's traditional forms. See, for example, the MB&F HM3 Frog. It looks like a stylized cyber-frog, with two bulbous crystals displaying the time and a rotor – shaped like a battle-ax – twirling over the "thoroughbred" movement in a window shaped like a jolly mouth. The effect is at once whimsical and alien and as far from a watch as anyone has ever seen.

Hallock is a techie who fell into a love of watches, and his movement in the circles of Silicon Valley allows him access to such luminaries as Andy Rubin, Vice President of Engineering at Google. Like a modern-day Breguet and Gide, Büsser pushes the state of horological art while Hallock sells the resulting timepieces to the rich and powerful.

Hallock's main thrust, however, is to limit the availability of his watches. By offering the MB&F line in a few spots around the globe – New York, Tokyo, Beijing, Paris – he ensures a scarcity that begets desire. "I'm closing doors," he said. "Not opening them."

Even watchmakers like Büsser are living in a world far removed from Breguet's. Culturally, mechanical watches reached their heyday after World War II, and their prestige had petered out by 1980. Instead of selling clocks that tell time, Büsser and his ilk sell clocks that fulfill desire.

The question, then, is who has donned the patrimony of Breguet and the great watchmakers. Is it Seiko, with its massive Japanese factory and dedication to high-speed automation? Or is it men like Büsser and Francois-Paul Journe, founder of F.P. Journe and a proponent of Breguet's passionate style? In the end, which watch won? The Marie-Antoinette, the apex of a man's efforts in horology, or the *souscription*, the apex of a man's efforts to make horology accessible to the masses?

There is no real answer. The watch industry is booming, and

for every million "fashion watches" sold there are a dozen collector's pieces, items of such complexity and beauty that they cost hundreds of thousands of dollars and are seen by only a few people in their lifetimes.

In 2007, I drove from New York City to Lancaster, Pennsylvania, for a weekend of unsurpassed watch geekery. I was headed to the National Association of Watch and Clock Collectors' semi-annual Mid-Eastern Regional meeting. Watch collecting can be a solitary hobby, a gradual, painstaking effort by a dedicated fan who, out of shame or fear of misunderstanding, hides his consuming passion from the world. The members of the NAWCC are not these timid men. They are vocal, exuberant, and obsessed with a dying art.

Lancaster is watch country. The foothills of the Alleghenies begin about thirty miles north of this old mill town, and twenty miles south the Susquehanna River rolls down to Havre de Grace and out into the sea. The same features that made this land rich during its smoky, steelmaking days — the proximity of ore, transportation, and cheap labor — have made it an American analog of the Jura Mountains of Switzerland.

The area is home to three great institutions, a triangle forming the last bastion of watchmaking in America. The NAWCC headquarters, in Lancaster proper, offers watchmaking classes and houses a museum and library where a full-time staff still works to spread a seemingly obsolete craft. To the west, in Mount Joy, is RGM, a small factory turning out some of the most beautiful watches in America. To the north is Rolex's Lititz Watch Technicum, one of the preeminent watchmaking schools in the New World.

By the late 1980s, watchmakers competent to rebuild the classic watches gracing the wrists of potentates and starlets were scarce. The industry, now worth almost $2 billion in the United States, needs four thousand new watchmakers to replace the older ones who are retiring. Watchmaking, with its fixation on the physical over the digital, is not an obvious career choice for the young. In 2002, Rolex bankrolled the founding of the Lititz school, in a building designed by the architect Michael Graves, to ensure that there would continue to be people trained to build and service the company's watches.

In a twenty-year span, beginning in the early 1950s, American watch companies fell one after another. The Waltham Watch Company in Massachusetts shuttered in 1957 and was followed in 1964 by Elgin National Watch Company in Illinois. Elgin had once been the maker of half of the pocket watches in the world, and was immortalized by Robert Johnson in 1936 when he sang "Walkin' Blues": "She's got Elgin movements/from her head down to her toes." Gruen, originally based in Ohio, closed in 1977.

Everyone, from doughboys to beatniks, working girls to ladies who lunch, had worn watches made by these companies; they were formidable economic forces in the world market. Bomb timers, gun sights, and avionic readouts came out of their factories in wartime, and their watches were purchased by the millions. Today, they survive mainly as the detritus of decades past at the bottom of old coffee cans and in forgotten corners of long-closed drawers. They have art deco designs, thin, square cases, and faces that are almost illegible by modern standards. They turn up on eBay by the thousands, with tarnished cases and seized movements and bargain prices. Collectors at the regional level revel in such cultural flotsam, penning long, esoteric articles in the monthly *Watch & Clock Bulletin* (a recent issue was dedicated to "The Longcase Painted Dial in Liverpool") and meeting regularly to go over their favorite finds and discuss restoration techniques.

This year's regional was held at the convention center in nearby York. The average attendee at these events is over fifty and trending toward retirement, and many regionals are advertised as vacation packages. They are a way for snowbirds to put their RVs to good use, periodically stopping as they drive south for the winter to pick up vintage clock parts or refresh old friendships. The regionals are held in places like Chattanooga, Houston, and even Dearborn, Michigan, but the Mid-Eastern regional — and the national meeting that is also held here — is among the largest in the country, popular with the mostly male clock and watch collectors of a certain age and stripe, who are inexorably drawn to this picturesque and wallet-friendly spot in the Alleghenies.

In the convention center, on eight rows of tables running the length of the room, watches and clocks are arrayed in a mishmash that seems more flea market than formal gathering. Visitors hop from table to table asking after odd and discontinued watches, parts, and bands. If you have an old watch, these are the folks to take it to, but the dealers' familiarity with the classics tends to breed contempt, and they look upon lower-end "common" watches, the kind grandfathers across the country once wore, the way a gathering of geologists might appraise driveway gravel.

Every collector has a story about his first clock, or most expensive watch, or craziest garage-sale find. First clocks are often the most expensive, because many beginning collectors are lured in by false promises, only to find themselves stuck with an oversized case clock probably made with millions of others in a factory that has long since gone out of business. Garage-sale finds are the hobby's grails: A dedicated collector stops at an old shop or stoop sale, idly brushes through a box of timeworn jewelry, and suddenly sees, flashing out from the jumble of paste and cheap bracelets, a watch face that is instantly recognizable. He buys it for a pittance, and a legend is born.

In December 1983, a Chicago man named Chuck Maddox walked into a pawnshop before heading out Christmas shopping with his family. There, in the jewelry case, he noticed a huge watch called the Omega Speedmaster Professional Mark II. The earlier Omega Speedmaster Professional was familiar to aficionados as the moon watch, but Maddox, who at the time worked in heavy construction, knew little of that history, and purchased the watch for $115. He wore it, unserviced, for sixteen years before researching its provenance, an act akin to hanging an unknown, original Picasso in the bathroom for a decade. The watch is worth $2,000 today. When Maddox had the watch repaired and restored to its original luster and beauty in 1999, he became hooked on watches and, until his death in May 2008, was a formidable, well-known figure on the watch circuit.

I didn't buy anything at the regional, but most of the collectors were selling case clocks and older wristwatches at bargain prices. A roomful of knowledgeable watch people tends to drive prices down considerably. There isn't talk of the latest fashion trends here. You're more likely to hear about the Lemania 5100 movement or the Zenith El Primero, two early chronograph wristwatch movements, or the vagaries of fish oil in the guts of old case clocks. The most experienced collectors are looking for prime, new-condition, old-stock watches, the ones locked in a dealer's case and never removed, watches still in their original boxes with their original papers. Let the rest of the world rumble through boxes and boxes of broken Hamiltons and shattered Tissots. To a collector, finding a classic 1950s Speedmaster or Rolex is like stumbling on an intact, mummified bog man in the heath.

Telling time has been the pastime of great men for eons, from the wash of a gnomon across the dust on an early sundial to the whispering of the Praetorian guards in Caesar's ear. Whether watches are being examined by a retired Navy man in a *USS Missouri* ball cap in the heart of Pennsylvania Dutch country or riding on the wrists of presidents and prime ministers, they are a resolute bridge between our past and our future.

A few decades ago, regionals were the only way for collectors to paw through each other's cases, looking for that elusive piece. Now, blogs and auction Web sites allow watch fans to share their daily timepiece choices in posts like "TGIF! What are you wearing today?," quickly followed by camera phone pictures of wrists wearing almost every known watch — from hundred-thousand-dollar timepieces to popular Seiko divers that barely brush the $100 mark.

Younger enthusiasts progress along a predictable arc. There's the first acquisition. Then they discover like minds on sites such as the Poor Man's Watch Forum and ABlogtoWatch, edited by a former lawyer turned watch fanatic. Then there's the growth spurt, fueled by the sense that one's collection isn't complete until every space in one's specially designed watch box is filled. While, in my collecting heyday, I must have owned sixty watches, a female friend owns hundreds and hundreds of quartz novelty watches from the '80s and '90s.

Breguet would almost certainly have relished this thriving democracy of watch aficionados, the spiritual heirs of his souscription dream.

Watch fans tend to congregate around large cities in America. The top watch-owning cities are, in order, New York, Boston, Detroit, Buffalo, and San Francisco. Sleepy towns in the South like Memphis and Nashville wear the fewest watches. Perhaps those areas run at a different pace than the rest of the world — as a New Yorker, I like to think so — but throughout the country there are still millions of people wearing millions of watches.

At the same time, as more Americans, and even some Europeans, rely on cellphones and computers and car dashboards for the time, watch wearing has declined dramatically. Only one in ten teenagers wears a watch every day, and watch sales have fallen as much as 17% year over year since 2000. When people do wear watches, they are increasingly sports models designed to time workouts. Watchmaking remains a $15 billion industry, but it is buoyed by the higher average prices paid by die-hards who must have the latest Rolex or Omega.

That market, too, has its collectors. At the height of the dot-com boom, cyberpunk novelist William Gibson became slowly addicted to eBay and spent hours trawling the myriad watches offered there, eventually taking to buying multi-thousand-dollar timepieces. Eric Singer, drummer for the band KISS, wears a vintage TAG Heuer Monaco race chronograph and a unique Rolex diver that, instead of rubber, uses an odd lead seal to ensure waterfastness. Marc Andreesen, creator of the Mosaic Web browser, wears an oversized Jaeger-LeCoultre with a world-time register, and Bernie Madoff, the disgraced Ponzi schemer, amassed a collection of some forty classics, including a number of Rolexes from the 1940s. One, a Monoblocco "prisoner watch," had originally been offered for sale — with payment expected after the war — to British POWs who'd had their watches confiscated by the Germans. After Madoff's arrest, the collection sold at auction for $4 million.

Watch companies often team up with stars of stage, sport, and screen to flog their product to the public. After Omega purchased the rights to become James Bond's watch of choice, the company's sales shot up almost forty percent. TAG Heuer uses Eric Clapton. Rolex uses Tiger Woods. Raymond Weil uses Charlize Theron, or did until she showed up at an event wearing a Christian Dior watch; Weil subsequently sued her for ten million British pounds — about $15 million — for breaching her endorsement contract.

Watchmaking these days is 49 percent manufacturing and 51 percent marketing. The Swatch Group's portfolio includes watches at every price point, from $100 plastic watches to $1 million monstrosities. A few million watches are sold every year, and the industry has quadrupled since the 1980s. In 2007, Swiss watchmakers grossed 13.7 billion Swiss francs, or about $11 billion (compared with $50 billion for the entire luxury apparel industry).

There is little interaction among the various strata of the modern market. On the low end, makers like Timex and Fossil sell three-handed quartz watches with no complications. Companies like Seiko and Citizen, which during the quartz crisis sold affordable watches with "features" like data banks, calculators, and musical alarms, have gone upscale, Seiko with its Seiko Grand watches and Citizen and Casio with their higher-end "wrist computers," with features including barometers, altimeters, and world time readouts. In 2008, the range in quality between $10 and $100 was slim: Most watches at these prices are mass-produced and use movements spit out by a machine in seconds.

One step up, the $500-$8,000 market encompasses a whole gamut of possible complications and features, but one thing is certain: Each watch almost certainly uses an ETA mechanical or quartz movement. Since Nicolas Hayek took over ETA and formed the Swatch Group in 1983, ETA has regained its dominance in mid-tier movements. Most watchmakers purchase a base ETA movement and then add complications to it, often burnishing and decorating it by hand. Manufacturers can order watches with multiple features, including GMT hand, date and day registers, and hacking seconds — a method for stopping the seconds hand when the crown is pulled out. Omega, Breitling, and Movado all use ETA movements in even their most expensive watches. The outside of two of these watches can be completely different but the heart of all of them beats the same.

Before the quartz juggernaut, watch lines took a year or so to modify and even longer to push into production. Now, with a highly regimented and skilled crew, watchmakers can add refinements to movements almost overnight. Many watchmakers and sellers find that collectors will buy essentially the same watch for essentially the same price — even if they own the earlier model — whenever an internal change is implemented. When Rolex began using silicon in some if its movements, passionate collectors sold or shelved their old models and picked up the new ones — the equivalent of a Lexus owner selling or garaging his car because the company added a different trunk release button in the 2009 model.

Finally, high-end manufacturers like Breguet and Jaeger-Le-Coultre pride themselves on small batch productions of watches made entirely by hand. Breguet, which makes about forty thousand watches per year, stands out for its high prices and marketing focus on its most complex and complicated watches. Recently, the company has been promoting the Reveil du Tsar, a piece based on a watch made in 1813 for Czar Alexander of Russia. Despite its $40,000 price tag, Breguet heavily advertises the watch in the national and international press as a mainstream option for the rich connoisseur. Breguet, like such companies as Prada and Aston Martin, is betting that someone, somewhere, with a lot of disposable income, will make an exorbitant impulse purchase or at least be intrigued enough by the brand to buy one of the company's lower-end offerings. Either way, it's a win.

Large profits have allowed Breguet, and more broadly the Swatch Group, to become a patron of the arts and sciences and to open watchmaking schools in the United States and abroad. They also allowed the company to set about rebuilding Breguet's masterpiece from fumes, a process that took considerably less time, and considerably more money, than it took to build the original.

But all the fine timepieces in the world can't match the feeling of elation and awe I feel that the Marie-Antoinette, Breguet's masterpiece, still exists. It is, in short, the watch that defined watchmaking, a compact horological library, and an expression of love and devotion as amazing as the Taj Mahal. The long river of its tragic story, its disappearance and acrimonious reappearance, the fates of its owners, and the wild tales that surround it have turned this watch from a mere collection of cogs into something more, something eternal and timeless, something sublime.

And so it ticks forever, alone in beauty and desired by all who see it. It was a gift to a queen that became a gift to the world and now it is back home, safe and sound.

Acknowledgments

First and foremost I'd like to thank my little ones, Guthrie, Milla, and Kasper, for sticking by me for these many months as I, not unlike Breguet, retired to my attic workshop for days at a time. This, like all my work, is for them.

I'd also like to thank my fellow and former bloggers on TechCrunch; Doug Aamoth, Matt Burns, Devin Coldewey, Nicholas Deleon, Dave Freeman, Greg Kumparak, Jordan Crook, Natasha Lomas, Darrell Etherington, Alexia Tsotsis, Matthew Panzarino, and Peter Ha. I'd also like to thank Michael Arrington, Heather Harde, and the rest of the original TechCrunch crew. Your patience and support was unparalleled.

Thanks to Marc Bascou of the Louvre Museum and Noemie

Wuger of Breguet for their input and help tracking down sources and books. I'd also like to thank Breguet's U.S. representative Amy Chia for getting the ball rolling. Special thanks go to the late Swatch Group CEO Nicholas Hayek, one of the most outspoken — and funniest — watch company heads in history. It is a distinct honor to have met him.

I also have to thank Emmanuel Breguet, family historian, for the unprecedented access he gave me to the records and letters of his ancestor along with insight into his excellent book, *Breguet Watchmakers Since 1775*.

Special thanks to my friend Ariel Adams who kept me updated on modern horology while I had my nose stuck in ancient clockwork. My buddy Victor Marks was also integral in getting this book into proper shape.

Also thanks to Jonas Nordin and my friends in Helsinki and Sweden for their assistance in Baltic history. Thanks also to Kathy Chaney, Salomons Site Librarian, at Canterbury Christ Church University. Also thanks to Philip Poniz of Patrizzi & Co. for his further insight into the history of watches and watchmaking.

Special thanks to Berkeley Beyers, my quiet, able factchecker, whose assistance in research in my scorching hot attic in the New York summer will not be forgotten. Also thanks to Ezra Butler for assistance in some of the translation.

Thanks also to Nili Shamrat for agreeing to speak to me candidly about the love of her life.

Very special thanks to the team at Uvda who were instrumental in supplying me with the chronology of the theft and subsequent investigations. This great group — Nadav Zeevi, Chaim Rivlin, Barak Sher, along with Ran Golan at Keshet TV — helped me put the final pieces of the puzzle together after months of research. I'd also like to thank Igal Sarna in Tel Aviv who gave me a cultural understanding of the theft in the Israeli context. Roi Carthy, Ezra Butler, and Yael Beeri were also instrumental in helping me understand Tel Aviv. Danny Rubinstein told me the whole story as he knew it and told it well.

Other folks who helped along the way include the two Odeds, Oded Janiv and Oded Shamah, the investigators who patiently walked me through the loss and recovery of the L.A. Mayer collection. Also thanks to Rachel Hasson and Ali Kahan. Mrs. Hasson

212

was such a good host that she made me feel welcome even when she was on vacation.

Thanks to the team at ZolaBooks who made this version of the book a reality. As always Bryce Durbin was instrumental in making this book with me.

I'd also like to mention a few important figures in my writing life, Theresa DeFrancis, Tony Earley, Kathy Kane, Fred Brock, Scott McKenzie, Charlie White, and Stephen Solomon, all of who affected me in ways they probably aren't aware. My love of watches was inspired by my father, Robert Biggs, who gave me the Seamaster he bought in Germany in 1969 and which has since brought me luck.

Special thanks to Sophie, Sacha, and Gille in Paris for their hospitality. Also a tip of the chip and profound thanks to Allen Kurzweil.

I'd also like to thank my amazing agent Larry Weissman who, a few years ago, was intrigued by one of my ideas and then hounded me through a proposal boot camp so grueling that I've come out a changed writer. He is a valued ally and a wonderful friend. I am also grateful for the work his lovely wife Sascha Alper put into this project throughout. I'd also like to thank Benjamin Wallace whose amazing book and later, whose guidance, taught me how to write a compelling narrative about an object of desire.

Budapest 2015

Bibliography

Doing time: The incredible watch collection of disgraced financier Bernard Madoff goes under the hammer. *Daily Mail*, 15, November, 2009.

Sir David Lionel Salomons (1851 – 1925). [Web page].
Available from: http://www.canterbury.ac.uk/salomons-museum/tree/d-lionel-salomons.asp
[accessed June 18, 2010]

"The Lives of Three French Working Men." New Monthly Magazine, 1867. p. 335.

. "The Paris Exhibition". Fraser's magazine for town and country, 1867. **76**.

." Nautical magazine and journal of the Royal Naval Reserve." Chronometers and Their Makers In England and France, 1858. p. 136.

Edward Daniel Bryce — Tank Corps. [Web page].
Available from: http://1914-1918.invisionzone.com/forums/lofiversion/index.php/t40747.html
[accessed June 25, 2010]

. Watch for Swatch! Engineer Jacques Muller Has Found a Way to Make a Quality Swiss Cheapo. *People*, 1984 (3).

. "Rose Engine." English mechanic and world of science, 1889 (1259), p. 220.

Marine chronometer no. 2741 by Breguet et Fils. [Web Page].
Available from: http://www.britishmuseum.org/explore/

highlights/highlight_objects/pe_mla/m/marine_chronometer_
no_2741_by.aspx
[accessed June 3, 2010]

Williams, Helen Maria, *Letters Written in France*. Broadview
Press.

Abraham, Davidovich, *Advanced issues in criminology theo-
ries*.

Andress, D., 2006. *The Terror: the merciless war for freedom in
revolutionary France* /. 1st American ed. New York: Farrar, Straus,
and Giroux.

BEAWES, W., 1752. *Lex mercatoria rediviva: or, The merchant's directory. Being a compleat guide to all men in business, etc.*
LondonTheAuthor,1752.

BURNELL, G. R., 1862. *The Annual Retrospect of Engineering and Architecture; a record of progress in the sciences of civil, military, and naval construction. Edited by G. R. Burnell. vol. 1.* London,1862.

Backmann, R., 2010. *A wall in Palestine.* 1st U.S. ed. New
York: Picador.

Barton, H. A., 1986. *Scandinavia in the Revolutionary era, 1760-1815.* Minneapolis: University Of Minnesota
Press.

Barton, H. A. & Fersen, H. A. v., 1975. *Count Hans Axel von
Fersen: aristocrat in an age of revolution* /. Boston: Twayne Publish-
ers.

Beauchesne, A. d., Louis, Louis, Dupanloup, F. & John Boyd
Thacher Collection (Library of Congress), 1871. *Louis XVII, sa
vie, son agonie, sa mort: captivité de la famille royale au Temple* /. 8.
éd., ed. Paris: Henri Plon.

Bennet, John, 1858. Watchwork versus Slopwork. *English-
woman's journal, Volume 1,* p. 282.

Benvenuti, F. F. & John Boyd Thacher Collection (Library of Congress), 1880. *Episodes of the French Revolution from 1789 to 1795: (with an appendix embodying the principal events in France from 1789 to the present time) : examined from a political and philosophical point of view /*. London: Simpkin, Marshall and Co.

Bombelles,, 1982. *Journal*. Geneve: Librairie Droz SA.

Booth, M. L., 1860. *New and complete clock and watchmakers' manual ...* New York: J. Wiley, p. 42.

Breguet, Emmanuel, 1997. *Breguet, Watchmakers Since 1775, the Life and Legacy of Abraham-Louis Breguet* . Paris: Alain de Gourcuff éditeur, p. 22.

Britten, F. J., 1896. *watch & clock makers' handbook, dictionary and guide*. 9th ed. London: Spon.

Britten, F. J. (. J., 1894. *Former clock & watchmakers and their work: including an account of the development of horological instruments from the earliest mechanism, with portraits of masters of the art ; a directory of over five thousand names, and some examples of modern construction*. London: E. & F.N. Spon.

Bruton, E., 1989. *History of clocks and watches*. New York: Crescent Books.

Burlingame, R., 1966. *Dictator clock: 5,000 years of telling time*. New York: Macmillan.

Cadbury, D., Louis & Louis, 2002. *The lost king of France: a true story of revolution, revenge, and DNA /*. 1st ed. New York: St. Martin's Press.

Cadbury, D., Louis & Louis, 2002. *The lost king of France: a true story of revolution, revenge, and DNA /*. 1st ed. New York: St. Martin's Press.

Campan & Marie A., 1823. *Mémoires sur la vie privée de*

Marie-Antoinette, reine de France et de Navarre: suivis de souvenirs et anecdotes historiques sur les règnes de Louis XIV, de Louis XV et de Louis XVI. Bruxelles: A. Wahlen et compe.

Carrera, R., 1977. *Les heures de l'amour: [montres et automates érotiques] = Hours of love = Die Stunden der Liebe /.* Lausanne: Scriptar.

Chapuis, A. & Jaquet, E., 1956. *The history of the self-winding watch, 1770-1931.* English ed. (revised) Neuchatel: Éditions du Griffon.

Cipolla, C. M. (. M., 19771978. *Clocks and culture, 1300-1700.* New York: Norton.

Clerizo, Michael, 2010. Nicolas Hayek: Time Bandit. *Wall Street Journal,* June 10.

Coryn, M. S., Marie A. & Fersen, H. A. v., 1938. *Marie-Antoinette and Axel de Fersen.* London: T. Butterworth ltd.

Court, Andy and Michael Rotem, 1988. Clashing cops bungle recovery of treasures. *Jerusalem Post,* .

Cuss, T. P. C., 1952. *The story of watches. [With illustrations.].* London.

Daniels, G. & Breguet, A. L., 1975. *The art of Breguet.* London: Sotheby Parke Bernet, p. 5.

Daniels, G., Salomons, D., Markarian, O., Yad L. A. Me'ir, makhon le-omanut ha-Islam & Yad L.A. Me'ir, makhon le-omanut ha-Islam., 1980. *Watches & clocks in the Sir David Salomons collection: including scientific instruments, boxes, and automata /.* London: Published in association with the L.A. Mayer Memorial Institute for Islamic Art by Sotheby Publications.

Daniels, George, 2006. *All In Good Time: Reflections of a Watchmaker.* 2006 ed. Isle of Man.

Davidson, I., Voltaire & Voltaire, 2004. *Voltaire in exile: the last years /*. 1st American ed. New York: Grove Press.

Dean, Macabee, 1980. Phoenix launches campaign to protect homes from burglars. *Jerusalem Post*, 06/08.

Dubois, Pierre , 1849. *Histoire de l'horlogerie depuis son origine jusqu'à nos jours.* Paris: ADMINISTRATION DU MOYEN AGE ET LA RENAISSANCE, p. 392.

Dumas, A., 1850. *watchmaker.* London: Henry Lea.

Durant, W., 1963. *The age of Louis XIV: history of European civilization...1648-1715.* Simon & Schuster.

Durant, W. & Durant, A., 1967. *story of civilization, part 9 : The age of Voltaire.* New York: Simon & Schuster.

Durant, W., Napoleon, Durant, A. & Rouben Mamoulian Collection (Library of Congress), 1975. *The age of Napoleon: a history of European civilization from 1789 to 1815 /.* New York: Simon and Schuster.

Edey, W., 1967. *French clocks.* New York: Walker, p. 19.

Ekirch, A. R., 2005. *At day's close: night in times past /.* 1st ed. New York: Norton, p. 67.

Elisabeth, Angoulême, M. T. C., Wormeley, K. P. & Cléry, 1902. *The life and letters of Madame Élisabeth de France.* [Versailles ed.] Boston: Hardy, Pratt & co.

Erickson, Carolly, 1991. *To the Scaffold.* St. Martin's Griffin.

Falk, D., 2008. *In search of time: the science of a curious dimension.* 1st U.S. ed. New York: Thomas Dunne Books, St. Martin's Press.

Farr, E., Marie A. & Fersen, H. A. v., 1995. *Marie-Antoinette and Count Axel Fersen: the untold love story /.* London: P. Owen, p.

40.

Fersen, H. A. v., 1902. *Diary and correspondence of Count Axel Fersen, grand-marshal of Sweden: relating to the court of France;*. [Versailles ed.]. Boston: Hardy, Pratt & co., p. 5.

Fersen, H. A. v., Marie A. & Söderhjelm, A., 1930. *Fersen et Marie-Antoinette*. Paris: Éditions Kra.

Foucaud, E. & Frost, J., 1848. *The book of illustrious mechanics of Europe and America*. Aberdeen: T&T Clark.

Fraser, A. & Louis, 2006. *Love and Louis XIV: the women in the life of the Sun king /*. 1st U.S. ed. New York: Nan A. Talese/ Doubleday.

Fraser, Antonia, 2001. *Marie-Antoinette*. Anchor Books.

Frey, L. & Frey, M., 2004. *The French Revolution*. Westport, Conn.: Greenwood Press.

Gardiner, B. M. C., 1902. *The French revolution 1789-1795*. 11th impression. ed. London: Longmans, Green, and co.

Gaulot, P., Marie A., Fersen, H. A. v. & Hoey, F. C., 1894. *A friend of the Queen (Marie Antionette—Count de Fersen) from the French of Paul Gaulot*. London: W. Heinemann.

Gelardi, J. P., 2008. *In triumph's wake: royal mothers, tragic daughters, and the price they paid for glory /*. 1st ed. New York: St. Martin's Press.

Godley, Eveline, 1905. Art, Drama, and Music. *Annual register*, p. 101.

Gordon, G. F. C., 1925. *Clockmaking Past and Present*. London: Crosby Lockwood and son.

Greaves, R. L., Zaller, R. & Roberts, J. T., 1992. *Civilizations of the West: the human adventure*. NewYork,NY: HarperCollins.

Haggard, A., Louis & Marie A., 1909. *Louis XVI and Marie-Antoinette*. London: Hutchinson & co.

Hardman, John, 1993. *Louis XVI*. Yale University Press.

Harrold, M. C. & Bulletin of the National Association of Watch and Clock Collectors, Inc., 1981. *American watchmaking: a technical history of the American watch industry, 1850-1930 /*. S.l.: M.C. Harrold.

Heidenstam, O. G. v., Marie A., Fersen, H. A. v., Barnave, A., Whale, W. S. & Jackson, E., 1926. *The letters of Marie-Antoinette, Fersen, and Barnave*. London: John Lane.

Heilbron, J. L., 2003. *The Oxford companion to the history of modern science*. Oxford: Oxford University Press.

Heller, Jeffery, 1982. Burglary rate slow, but insolved crimes up. *Jerusalem Post*, 06/05.

Hering, D. W. & James Arthur Foundation., 1932. *The lure of the clock: an account of the James Arthur collection of clocks and watches at New York university,*. New York city: The New York university press.

Herman, E., 2006. *Sex with the queen: 900 years of vile kings, virile lovers, and passionate politics /*. 1st ed. New York: W. Morrow.

Hibbert, C., 1980. *The days of the French Revolution*. 1st U.S. ed. New York: Morrow.

Hirshberg, J., 1996. *Music in the Jewish Community of Palestine 1880-1948: A Social History (Clarendon Paperbacks)*. New Ed ed. Clarendon Press.

Hobsbawm, E. J., 1996. *The age of revolution 1789-1848*. 1st Vintage Books ed. New York: Vintage Books.

Howe, H., 1847. *Memoirs of the most eminent American mechanics: also, lives of distinguished European mechanics; together with a collection of anecdotes, descriptions, &c. &c., relating to the mechanic arts.* New York: Harper & brothers.

Imbert d. S., Marie A. & Martin, E. G., 1891. *Marie-Antoinette at the Tuileries, 1789-1791.* New York: C. Scribner's sons.

Itim, 1967. Suspect remanded in ingenious bid on bank. *Jerusalem Post,* 10/10.

Itim, 1981. Bank thief Diller jailed until verdict. *Jerusalem Post,* 26/4.

Itim, 1982. Police break ring of fences, recover millions. *Jerusalem Post,* 05/01.

Itim Wire, 1967. Burglary of bank foiled. *Jerusalem Post,* 08/10.

Jones, C., 2005. *Paris: biography of a city /.* 1st American ed. New York: Viking.

Karpel, Dalia, 2004. נשר קצוץ כנפיים. *Ha'aretz,* 25/05. p. http://www.haaretz.co.il/hasite/pages/ShArt.jhtml?itemNo=431926&sw=%E7%E9%F0%E5%EA.

Kirsta, Alix, 2009. Marie-Antoinette : the queen, her watch and the master burglar. *The Telegraph,* 24/04.

Kurzweil, Allen, 2002. *Grand Complication.* Hyperion Books.

Landes, D. S., 1983. *Revolution in time: clocks and the making of the modern world /.* Cambridge, Mass.: Belknap Press of Harvard University Press, p. 265-266.

Le R. L. E., Saint-Simon, L. d. R. & Fitou, J., 2001. *Saint-Simon and the court of Louis XIV.* Chicago: University of Chicago

Press.

Lenotre, G., Marie A. & Stawell, R., 1906. *The flight of Marie-Antoinette*. London: W. Heinemann.

Leroux, Marcus, 2008. Madoff casts shadow over Rolex as chief executive Patrick Heiniger quits. *Sunday Times,* 20, December.

Lever, E. & Marie-Antoinette, 1991. *Marie-Antoinette*. Paris: Fayard.

Levy, J., 2002. *Really useful: the origins of everyday things /*. Buffalo, NY: Firefly Books.

Lewis, W. H., 19571953. *The splendid century: life in the France of Louis XIV*. Garden City, N.Y.: Doubleday.

Loomis, S., Marie A., Louis & Fersen, H. A. v., 1972. *The fatal friendship: Marie-Antoinette, Count Fersen & the flight to Varennes*. London: Davis-Poynter Ltd.

Macey, S. L. & Macey, S. L., 1994. *Encyclopedia of time*. New York: Garland Pub.

Margolin, Wendy, 2002. Ohannes Markarian, master craftsman. *Jerusalem Post,* 3/29. p. 6.

Marie A., Marie A. & Bernier, O., 1985. *Secrets of Marie-Antoinette*. 1st ed. Garden City, N.Y.: Doubleday.

Milham, W. I., 1947. *Time and timekeepers: including the history, construction, care, and accuracy of clocks and watches*. New York: Macmillan.

Mokhtefi, E., 2002. *Paris: an illustrated history*. New York: Hippocrene.

Morgan, T., 19681967. *Epitaph for kings*. New York: Putnam.

Morris, G. & Morris, G., 1971. *A diary of the French Revolution*. Freeport, N.Y.: Books for Libraries Press.

Morris, M. C. O., 1874. *The prisoners of the temple: or discrowned and crowned*. London: Burns and Oates.

Mossiker, F., 1961. *The Queen's necklace*. New York: Simon and Schuster.

Nagel, S., Angoulême, M. C. & Marie A., 2008. *Marie-Thérèse, child of terror: the fate of Marie-Antoinette's daughter /*. 1st U.S. ed. New York: Bloomsbury.

Nicolet, Jean-Claude , *THE TOURBILLON*. [Essay].
Available from: http://www.europastar.com/watch-knowledge/1004082417-the-tourbillon.html
[accessed June 16, 2010]

O'Brian, Patrick, 1970. *master and commander—the far side of the world*. William Collins Sons & Co.

Parton, J., 1881. *Life of Voltaire*. London.

Pendergast, S. & Pendergast, T., 2002. *Bowling, beatniks, and bell-bottoms: pop culture of twentieth-century America /*. Detroit: U X L.

Pernoud, G. & Flaissier, S., 19611960. *The French Revolution*. [1st American ed.] New York: Putnam.

Perugini, M. E., 1918. *The art of ballet*. London: Martin Secker.

Price, M., Louis, Marie A. & Breteuil, L. L. T., 2003. *The road from Versailles: Louis XVI, Marie-Antoinette, and the fall of the French monarchy /*. 1st U.S. ed. New York: St. Martin's Press.

Rabinowitz, Malka, 1978. Jerusalem's Home for Islamic Art. *Jerusalem Post*, 10, 4. p. B1.

Reverend S. Baring Gould, M.A., 1886. The Locksmith Gamain. *The Gentleman's Magazine, Volume CCLX*, January to June. p. 364.

Robb, G., 2007. *The discovery of France: a historical geography from the Revolution to the First World War /*. 1st American ed. New York: Norton.

Robert Rosenberg, 1983. Taking Time. *Jerusalem Post*, 29/04.

Rosenberg, Robert, 1983. Stolen signs ay be clue in heist. *Jerusalem Post*, 19/04.

Rosenberg, Robert, 1983. Museums check security following theft. *Jerusalem Post*, 24/04.

Rubinstein, Danny, 2007. Hickory, dickory, dock: stolen museum loot found. *Haaretz*, 11/11.

Rubinstein, Danny, 2008. Naaman Diller is the man behind Israel's biggest robbery. *Calcalist*, 29/10.

Saint-Amand, I. d., 1892. *Marie-Antoinette and The Downfall of Royalty*. [S.l.]: Hutchinson.

Sale, Jonathan , 1996. LIKE A HORSELESS CARRIAGE. *The Independent*, 28 April . p. http://www.independent.co.uk/arts-entertainment/like-a-horseless-carriage-1307255.html.

Salomons, D., 1891. *Electric light installations and management of accumulators: a practical handbook*. 6th ed rev and enlarged. London: Whittaker and Co.

Salomons, David Lionel , 1921. *Breguet: 1747-1823*. London, p. 46.

Saunier, C., Tripplin, J. J. S. & Rigg, E. S., 1945. *The watchmaker's hand-book, intended as a workshop companion for those engaged in watchmaking and the allied mechanical arts.* London: Technical Press.

Scurr, R. & Robespierre, M., 2006. *Fatal purity: Robespierre and the French Revolution /.* 1st ed. New York: Metropolitan Books.

Selby, I. d. L., 1994. *Wrist watches: the collector's guide to selecting, acquiring, and enjoying new and vintage wrist watches /.* Philadelphia: Courage Books.

Seward, D. & Marie A., 1981. *Marie-Antoinette.* New York: St. Martin's Press.⊠
Skjöldebrand, A. F. & Schück, H., 19031904. *Excellensen grefve A. F. Skjöldebrands memoarer utg.* Stockholm: H. Geber.

Smythe, L. C., Marie A. & Mercy d. F., 1902. *The guardian of Marie-Antoinette: letters from the Comte de Mercy-Argenteau, Austrian ambassador to the court of Versailles, to Marie Thérèse, empress of Austria, 1770-1780,.* New York: Dodd, Mead and company.

Sobel, D. & Harrison, J., 1995. *Longitude: the true story of a lone genius who solved the greatest scientific problem of his time /.* New York: Walker.

Spawforth, A. & Château de Versailles (Versailles, France), 2008. *Versailles: a biography of a palace /.* 1st ed. New York: St. Martin's Press.

Temple, R. & Temple, C., 1870. *Invention and discovery [from The Temple anecdotes].* Lond.

Thomson, D., 1984. *Renaissance Paris: architecture and growth, 1475-1600 /.* Berkeley: University of California Press.

Tocqueville, Alexis de , 1856. *The Old Regime and the Revolution .* New York: Harper & Brothers.

Trolle-Wachtmeister, Hans Gabriel , 1889. *Anteckningar och minnen*. Sweden.

Tysilio & Roberts, P., 1811. *The chronicle of the kings of Britain: tr. from the Welsh copy attributed to Tysilio, and illustr. with copious notes; to which are added, original dissertations. By P. Roberts.* London: E. Williams, p. 308.

Washington, G., 183940. *The writings of George Washington: being his correspondence, addresses, messages, and other papers, official and private.* Boston: Ferdinand Andrews.

Weber, C. & Marie A., 2006. *Queen of fashion: what Marie-Antoinette wore to the Revolution /.* 1st ed. New York: H. Holt.

Webster, N. H., Louis & Marie A., 1938. *Louis XVI and Marie-Antoinette during the revolution.* New York: G. P. Putnam's sons.

Weigert, Gideon, 1974. Arabs learn about Islamic culture. *Jerusalem Post*, 24/6. p. B1.

Weitz, Gidi, 2008. מגנדי ועד גומדי: משפט הפשע החשוב ביותר בהיסטוריה הישראלית נפתח מחדש. *Ha'aretz*, 05/12.

Wilford, J. N., 1982. *The mapmakers.* 1st Vintage Books ed. New York: Vintage Books.

Withrow, W.H., 1983. Protestant Memories of Neuchatel and Morat. *Methodist Magazine,* .

Wood, E. J., 1866. *Curiosities of clocks and watches, from the earliest times.* London: R. Bentley, p. 140.

Youde, Kate, 2010. Father time: Why George Daniels is the world's best horologist. *The Independent*, 5/9.

Younghusband, H. A. M. & Marie A., 1912. *Marie-Antoinette, her early youth (1770-1774).* London: Macmillan.

Yudelman, Michal, 1983. Five held for $3m. museum heist.

Jerusalem Post, 7/02.

Zweig, S., Marie A., Paul, E. & Paul, C., 1933. *Marie-Antoinette, the portrait of an average woman.* New York: The Viking press, p. 85.

1. At this point, recollections conflict. The unnamed client apparently requested no money, but Efron-Gabai reminded her that in a past a multimillion dollar reward had been offered by various parties – no one ever expected the items to be returned, so the incentive was more of a symbolic sum. If not the reward, then perhaps a small payment as an act of goodwill from the museum? After all, the client had not stolen anything and she was essentially doing a good deed. Whether the client asked for a reward or not is still unclear.

2. Jones, C. Paris: Biography of a City. New York: Viking,. p.63 2005

3. Howe, H.,. Memoirs of the most eminent American mechanics: also, lives of distinguished European mechanics; together with a collection of anecdotes, descriptions, &c. &c., relating to the mechanic arts. New York: Harper & Brothers. p. 384

4. "Nautical magazine and journal of the Royal Naval Reserve." <u>Chronometers and Their Makers In England and France</u> 27 (1858): 136. 1847.

5. Washington, G.,. The writings of George Washington: Being His Correspondence, Addresses, Messages, And Other Papers, Official and Private. Boston: Ferdinand Andrews. p 449. 1835.

6. Morris, G. A Diary of the French Revolution. Freeport, N.Y.: Books for Libraries Press. p. 35. 1971.

7. Loomis, p. 14

8. Loomis, p. 14

9. Barton, p. 2.

10. Morgan, T. Epitaph for Kings. New York: Putnam, . p.

120. 1968

11. Erickson, p. 144

12. Barton, p. 21

13. Loomis, p. 61

14. Gaulot, P., Marie A., Fersen, H. A. v. & F. C. Hoey, A friend of the Queen (Marie Antionette—Count de Fersen) from the French of Paul Gaulot. London: W. Heinemann, p. 10. 1894

15. Farr p. 39

16. Loomis, p 7

17. Perugini, M. E. The art of ballet. London: Martin Secker, 1918. P 171

18. Seward, D. & Marie A. Marie-Antoinette. New York: St. Martin's Press. p. 28. 1981

19. Seward, p. 35.

20. Younghusband, H. A. M. & Marie A., Marie-Antoinette, her early youth (1770-1774). London: Macmillan. p. 126. 1912.

21. Reverend S. Baring Gould, M.A., 1886. The Locksmith Gamain. The Gentleman's Magazine, Volume CCLX, January to June. p. 365

22. Lever, E. & Marie-Antoinette, 1991. Marie-Antoinette. Paris: Fayard. p. 123

23. Comtess de Boigne, Memoires (1907), p. 32.

24. Loomis, p. 81. These words are unusually candid for Fersen and can be read in any number of ways, although the most common understanding is that Fersen's goal here was to remain true

to Marie-Antoinette. Loomis writes that these lines can be taken in many contexts but that "there are many people who believe that this woman was Marie-Antoinette." Cleaving with the traditional understanding of their relationship we can say, without a doubt, that Fersen and Marie-Antoinette were close friends and he acted, in many ways, as her honest and trustworthy chevalier. Thoughts differ as to the actual nature of the relationships and, in the context of this book I take the path of least resistance: that Fersen and the Queen had a very real relationship that, if not sexual, was certainly amorous.

25. The Breguet archives detailing this era (known as First Era records, the Second Era coming with the addition of Gide to the organization, and the third coming in the early 1800s when Breguet was part of the watchmaking establishment) were destroyed so only a few salient facts remain: The 160 was commission by an "officer of the Queen's Guard" and Axel Fersen was in Paris during this period, probably in 1783. As we shall see, it is easy to connect the dots and surmise that Fersen was the mysterious officer. We can assume the order came in the form of a letter from the New World if we take this line of reasoning.

We do know that Axel Fersen was in Paris in June, 1783, and returned to Sweden in September. Two questions remain: did he visit Breguet at his shop and would he be able to pay for the watch? He owned a number of Breguet pieces and so the opportunity to place the commission could have happened while having another piece repaired. As for the second question, we know that Breguet, much to his business-partner's chagrin, was free with credit and Fersen was far from a dissipated noble.

There is also some belief that the captain of the queen's guard, Monsieur de la Croizette, ordered the watch for Marie-Antoinette on behalf of an admirer or, slightly more likely, the king himself. The commission would have come just before the Affair of the Necklace in 1784, the swindle that convinced Boehmer and Bassenge to send a 2,000,000 livres necklace, sight unseen, in the care of the Cardinal de Rohan. Rohan was conned by a Jeanne de la Motte and the necklace ended up sold for its jewels in England and the Queen disgraced. If the watch was commissioned by the king, the expectation would have been that Breguet would have stopped work immediately after the Affair of the Necklace. Instead, he soldiered on, pointing to an outside actor who, up until a time, maintained contact with the watchmaker and convinced him to continue the job even long after its intended was dead.

The final, least romantic, theory is that the watch "became" the Marie-Antoinette later on in its life, adopting a royal moniker as a marketing ploy to snag wistful royalists. While Breguet was an excellent marketer, he was far from mercenary.

In the end, the story of Fersen makes the most sense in the context of the day and is, in the end, the most heartbreaking.

26. Salomons, p. 34

27. Farr, p. 95

28. Wood, E. J. [. o. c. Curiosities of clocks and watches, from the earliest times.. London: R. Bentley, 1866.. p. 3.

29. Milham, p 55.

30. Ekirch, A. R. At Day's Close: Night In Times Past. New York: Norton, 2005. 2005. p. 67

31. Milham, W. I. Time And Timekeepers: Including the History, Construction, Care, and Accuracy Of Clocks and Watches. NewYork: Macmillan, 1947. p. 1

32. Wood, E. J., Curiosities Of Clocks and Watches, From The Earliest Times.. London: R. Bentley, 1866. 1866. Print.

33. Landes, p. 248

34. Landes, p. 259

35. Landes, p. 240

36. Landes, p. 263

37. Herries, 30 August 1857. Accounts and Papers 23: Trade of Various Countries: Switzerland. <u>Parliamentary Papers 1857-58 vol. 55</u>
<u>Papers, 1857-8, vol. 55,</u> p. 49.

38. Salomons, p 9.

39. Levy, J. Really Useful: The Origins Of Everyday Things /. Buffalo, NY: Firefly Books, 2002. p.101.

40. Landes, p. 264

41. Landes, p. 236

42. Landes, p. 262

43. Withrow, W.H. "Protestant Memories of Neuchâtel and Morat." <u>Methodist Magazine</u> 37 (1983) p. 17.

44. Foucaud, E. & Frost, J. <u>The book of illustrious mechanics of Europe and America.,</u> Aberdeen: T&T Clark, 1848. Print. p. 70.

45. Landes, p. 253

46. Breguet's early apprenticeship records have been destroyed although it is believed he worked with Lépine, Berthoud, and a even John Arnold in England. In fact, some Breguet watches bear such a striking resemblance to watches made by these manufacturers that it is clear that they were "master" projects built to exacting standards and designed as a final exam of sorts in order to pass to the next level in the guild.

47. Salomons, p 12

48. Foucaud, p. 71

49. Britten, F. J. Watch & Clock Makers' Handbook, Dictionary and Guide., 9th ed., London: Spon, 1896. P.39.

50. Breguet, p. 24

51. Booth, M. L. New and Complete Clock and Watchmakers' Manual .... New York: J. Wiley, 1860. 1860. p.42.

52. Breguet p. 33

53. Hardman, John. Louis XVI. Yale University Press, 1993... P 33

54. Breguet, p. 35

55. Dubois, Pierre , 1849. <u>Histoire de l'horlogerie depuis son origine jusqu'à nos jours</u>. Paris: ADMINISTRATION DU MOYEN AGE ET LA RENAISSANCE, p. 392.

56. Salomons, p. 11.

57. Salomons, p.11

58. Coryn, M. S., Marie A. & Fersen, H. A. v. Marie-Antoinette and Axel de Fersen. London: T. Butterworth ltd., 1938. Print. p. 106

59. Noted in Coryn: "This almanac is still preserved by the descendants of Fersen at the Chateau of Lovstad in Sweden"

60. Loomis, p. 83

61. Herman, E., 2006. Sex With the Queen: 900 Years Of Vile Kings, Virile Lovers, and Passionate Politics /. 1st ed. New York: W. Morrow. p.303

62. A number of conflicting reports on the theft have clouded the true chronology of events and the death of many of the major players has further confounded efforts to reconstruct the thief's trail. However, this information – taken from police reports and interviews – is surmised to be the closest approximation of the theft available.

63. Weigert, Gideon. "Arabs learn about Islamic culture." Jerusalem Post 24/6 1974: B1. Print.

64. As Emmauel Breguet notes in an unpublished essay, Abraham-Louis was not "introduced" to the court but noticed, a far more important point of pride for a young watchmaker. In these years – around 1780 until 1786 – royals like Madame Elisabeth, the king's sister as well as Prince Joseph of Monaco owned Breguet watches. Breguet's existing ledgers feature a number of famous names and the king would be loath to travel to Paris to see a man about a watch. Hence we have this bit of horological lore.

65. Saunier, C., Tripplin, J. J. S. & Rigg, E. S. The Watchmaker's Hand-Book, Intended As A Workshop Companion For Those Engaged In Watchmaking And The Allied Mechanical Arts.. London: Technical Press, 1945. P.133.

66. Macey, S. L. & Macey, S. L. Encyclopedia of time. New York: Garland Pub., 1994. P.231.

67. Temple, R. & Temple, C. Invention and discovery [from The Temple anecdotes]. Lond.,1870. Print. p. 102.

68. Dubois, p. 61.

69. Ibid 72

70. Salomons, p 72

71. Dubois, p. 32

72. Salomons, p. 13

73. Foucaud, p. 71

74. Breguet, p. 67

75. Breguet, p. 62

76. Again, we surmise his proximity to the Quai would have brought him here on occasion.

77. Williams, Helen Maria. <u>Letters Written in France.</u> Broadview Press. p 253

78. Saint-Amand, I. d. <u>Marie-Antoinette and The Downfall of Royalty.</u> [S.l.]: Hutchinson, 1892. p. 248.

79. Ibid.

80. Imbert d. S., Marie A. & Martin, E. G. Marie-Antoinette at the Tuileries, 1789-1791. New York: C. Scribner's sons, 1891. Print. p. 2

81. Imbert p. 1

82. Farr p.148

83. Farr, p.145.

84. Barton, p. 112

85. Haggard, A., Louis & Marie A., 1909. <u>Louis XVI and Marie-Antoinette.</u> London: Hutchinson & co. p. 458

86. Margolin, Wendy. "Ohannes Markarian, master craftsman." Jerusalem Post 3/29 2002: 6. Print.

87. Rosenberg

88. Rosenberg

89. ibid.

90. Barton, 117

91. Loomis, p. 107

92. Lenotre, G., Marie A. & Stawell, R. The flight of Marie-Antoinette. London: W. Heinemann, 1906. Print. p

93. Elisabeth, Angoulême, M. T. C., Wormeley, K. P. & Cléry, 1902. The Life And Letters Of Madame Élisabeth De France. [Versailles ed.] Boston: Hardy, Pratt & co. p 219

94. Barton, p. 147

95. Barton, p.148

96. Beauchesne, A. d., Louis, Louis, Dupanloup, F. & John Boyd Thacher Collection (Library of Congress), 1871. Louis XVII, sa vie, son agonie, sa mort: captivité de la famille royale au Temple /. 8. éd., ed. Paris: Henri Plon. p.327
Chapter 13

97. Youde, Kate. "Father time: Why George Daniels is the world's best horologist." The Independent 5/9 2010. Print.

98. Daniels, George. All In Good Time: Reflections of a Watchmaker. 2006 ed. Isle of Man2006. P. 63.

99. Daniels, p.64.

100. Kurzweil, Allen. Grand Complication. Hyperion Books, 2002. p. 161.

101. Barton, p. 351

102. Skjöldebrand, A. F. Memoarer p. 102

103. Barton, p.367

104. Barton, p. 370

105. Greaves, R. L., Zaller, R. & Roberts, J. T. Civilizations of the West: the human adventure. NewYork,NY: HarperCollins, 1992. P.664

106. "The Paris Exhibition." Fraser's magazine for town and

country 76 (1867).

107. Heraud, John A. "A Critical Introduction to Fourier's Theory." Monthly Magazine 6 (1841): 261.

108. Marine chronometer no. 2741 by Breguet et Fils. [Web Page].
Available from: http://www.britishmuseum.org/explore/highlights/highlight_objects/pe_mla/m/marine_chronometer_no_2741_by.aspx
[accessed June 3, 2010]

109. Heilbron, J. L., 2003. The Oxford companion to the history of modern science. Oxford: Oxford University Press.p. 8

110. Breguet, p 284

111. "The Lives of Three French Working Men." New Monthly Magazine 140 (1867): 335. Print.

112. Godley, Eveline. "Art, Drama, and Music." Annual register (1905): 101. Print.

113. Sir David Lionel Salomons (1851 – 1925). 2009. Webpage. June 18, 2010.

114. ibid. p.3

115. Salomons, p.4

116. Loomis p 109

118. "Rose Engine." English mechanic and world of science 49.1259 (1889): 220. Print.

119. Clerizo, Michael, 2010. Nicolas Hayek: Time Bandit. Wall Street Journal, June 10.

120. 1984. Watch for Swatch! Engineer Jacques Muller

237

Has Found a Way to Make a Quality Swiss Cheapo. People, 22 (3).

121. Kirsta, Alix. "Marie-Antoinette : The Queen, Her Watch And The Master Burglar." The Telegraph 24/04 2009. Print.

122. Rubinstein, Danny. "Hickory, Dickory, Dock: Stolen Museum Loot Found." Haaretz 11/11 2007. Print.

123. Karpel, Dalia, 2004. נשר קצוץ כנפיים. Ha'aretz, 25/05. p. http://www.haaretz.co.il/hasite/pages/ShArt.jhtml?item-No=431926&sw=%E7%E9%F0%E5%EA.

124. Most of these quotes are taken from Dalia Karpel's excellent biography of Diller. His immediate family would not speak to me for this book.

125. Itim, 1981. Bank thief Diller jailed until verdict. Jerusalem Post, 26/4.

126. Rubinstein, Danny. "Naaman Diller Is The Man Behind Israel's Biggest Robbery." Calcalist 29/10 2008.

Made in the USA
Lexington, KY
30 June 2015